The
New Teacher
Book

Finding Purpose, Balance, and Hope
During Your First Years in the Classroom

Second Edition

Edited by Terry Burant, Linda Christensen,
Kelley Dawson Salas, and Stephanie Walters

A Rethinking Schools Publication

The New Teacher Book
Finding Purpose, Balance, and Hope During Your First Years in the Classroom,
Second Edition
Edited by Terry Burant, Linda Christensen, Kelley Dawson Salas, and Stephanie
Walters

A Rethinking Schools Publication

Rethinking Schools Ltd. is a nonprofit educational publisher of books, booklets, and a
quarterly journal on school reform, with a focus on issues of equity and social justice.
To request additional copies of this book or a catalog of other publications, or to
subscribe to the quarterly journal *Rethinking Schools*, contact:

Rethinking Schools
1001 East Keefe Avenue
Milwaukee, WI 53212 USA
www.rethinkingschools.org

The New Teacher Book
Finding Purpose, Balance, and Hope During Your First Years in the Classroom,
Second Edition
© 2010, Rethinking Schools, Ltd.

Graphic Design: Kate Hawley
Cover Photograph: Barbara J. Miner

Library of Congress Cataloging-in-Publication Data

The new teacher book : finding purpose, balance, and hope during your first
years in the classroom / edited by Terry Burant ... [et al.]. -- 2nd ed.
    p. cm.
  Includes index.
  ISBN 978-0-942961-47-8
1. First year teachers. 2. First year teachers--In-service
training--Handbooks, manuals, etc. 3. Effective teaching. 4. Teaching. I.
Burant, Terry, 1958-
  LB2844.1.N4N476 2010
  371.1--dc22
                        2010035979

This is what we are about:

We plant seeds that one day will grow.

We water seeds already planted, knowing that they hold future promise.

We lay foundations that will need further development.

We provide yeast that produces effects beyond our capabilities.

We cannot do everything
and there is a sense of liberation in realizing that.

This enables us to do something,
and do it very well.

It may be incomplete, but it is a beginning, a step along the way ...

We may never see the end results,
but that is the difference between the master builder and the worker.

We are workers, not master builders, ministers, not messiahs.

We are prophets of a future not our own.

— from a prayer written by Bishop Ken Untener
for the anniversary of the martyrdom of
Archbishop Oscar Romero

Contents

**Chapter 4: Discipline: Rescuing the Remains of the Day
When Class Doesn't Go as Planned**

Chapter 5: Making Change in the World Beyond the Classroom

Acknowledgements

The *New Teacher Book* started in our classrooms, became animated when we talked with colleagues, and got hammered out during our work with *Rethinking Schools*. This edition came to life in conversations at coffee shops and between marathon Rethinking Schools meetings.

We'd like to thank the previous editors, Rita Tenorio and Dale Weiss for their work and ideas that still run through the pages of this book, and our previous book editor, Leon Lynn, for his imaginative work and logistical support. We'd also like to thank *Rethinking Schools* editors Wayne Au, Bill Bigelow, Stan Karp, David Levine, Larry Miller, Bob Peterson, Jody Sokolower, Melissa Bollow Tempel, Rita Tenorio, and Kathy Williams who helped conceptualize this book, and who continually pushed us to make it clear, concise, and useful to new teachers. Mike Trokan spearheaded the marketing and distribution efforts needed to put this book into teachers' hands. Tegan Dowling anchored our Milwaukee office. Kate Hawley brought an artist's eye to the design of the book. And finally, we'd like to acknowledge the work of Jacqueline Lalley, production editor, who helped bring the pieces of this book together in a unified package.

We also thank the many talented, dedicated, and idealistic people who continue to enter the teaching profession. We dedicate this book to you.

Terry Burant
Linda Christensen
Kelley Dawson Salas
Stephanie Walters

Introduction
Why We Wrote This Book

When the editors of *Rethinking Schools* first conceived of this book, we thought back to our days as new teachers. We hoped to create the book we needed in those sometimes exhilarating, sometimes lonely, often hard first days of our teaching careers.

This book is meant as a conversation among colleagues. We hope a conversation that helps you keep your vision and values intact as you struggle in institutions that may or may not be those citadels of idealism where you imagined yourself teaching.

We wrote this book because it's important for the profession that new teachers with social justice ideals stay in the classroom. Our communities need teachers who see the beauty and intelligence of every student who walks through their doors and who are willing to keep trying to reach those who have already been told they aren't worthy. Our students need teachers who value students' home language and who know how to build academic strength from those roots. We need teachers who learn how to develop curriculum that ties students' lives, history, and academic disciplines together to demonstrate their expertise when top-down curriculum mandates explode across a district. Our school districts need teachers who can advocate against the dumbing-down of curriculum, against testing mania, and against turning our classrooms over to corporate-created curriculum. Our country needs teachers who understand the connections between race, class, and tracking. How else do we make a lasting change?

We wrote this book because we want you to hold on to those impulses that brought you to teaching: a deep caring for students, the opportunity to be the one who sparks student growth and change, as well as the desire to be involved in work that matters. We need teachers who want to work in a place where human connections matter more than profit.

We wrote this book because we have had days—many days—where our teaching aspirations did not meet the reality of the chaos we encountered. We have experienced those late afternoons crying-alone-in-the-classroom kind of days when a lesson bombed or we felt like our students hosted a party in the room and we were the uninvited guests. We wrote this book hoping it might offer solace and comfort on those long days when you wonder if you are cut out to be a teacher after all.

We also wrote this book because we understand the connection between what happens behind the classroom door and what happens outside of it. A key skill for new teachers is to see ourselves as defenders of public schools—looking for allies among parents, community groups, other unions, everyone who has a stake in fighting privatization and corporate rule. Given the full court press against public schools, we need to remind *all* teachers to not be so classroom-focused that we don't pay attention to the larger political context that is shaping our lives in the classroom. The other reason to open the classroom door and peer outside is that new teachers' survival often depends on connecting with other teachers for support and assistance for social, political, and pedagogical reasons. Isolated new teachers are bound to burn out.

There is a huge difference between having lots of book knowledge about a given area—literature, history, math, science—and knowing how to translate that knowledge into lessons that help struggling students learn. All teachers—new and veteran—need skills to develop curriculum that celebrates the delightful aspects of our students' lives. And we need strategies that tie the tragedy of some students' lives and the tragedy that the world delivers—hurricanes, poverty, famine, war. We need to discover ways to weave these into our curriculum. That takes time.

Rethinking Schools editors have assembled numerous books that focus on creating social justice curriculum: from *Rethinking Columbus* to *Rethinking Mathematics* to *Rethinking Globalization* to *Teaching for Joy and Justice.* We hope you will look to them for curricular help. In those books, we celebrate the lessons and units and strategies that worked for our students, that created days when we walked out of the building celebrating the joy of teaching.

And what we know from our years in the classroom is that we only get good at it when we do it year after year. So we wrote this book to tell you that you will get better as the years move on if you continue to study your classroom, hone your craft, read professional literature, and keep up with world news. Teaching is an art. Keep practicing.

—The Editors

Undivided Attention

A grand piano wrapped in quilted pads by movers,
tied up with canvas straps—like classical music's
birthday gift to the insane—
is gently nudged without its legs
out an eighth-floor window on 62nd Street.

It dangles in April air from the neck of the mover's crane,
Chopin-shiny black lacquer squares
and dirty white crisscross patterns hanging like the second-to-last
note of a concerto played on the edge of the seat,
the edge of tears, the edge of eight stories up going over, and
I'm trying to teach math in the building across the street.

Who can teach when there are such lessons to be learned?
All the greatest common factors are delivered by
long-necked cranes and flatbed trucks
or come through everything, even air.
Like snow.

See, snow falls for the first time every year, and every year
my students rush to the window
as if snow were more interesting than math,
which, of course, it is.

So please.

Let me teach like a Steinway,
spinning slowly in April air,
so almost-falling, so hinderingly
dangling from the neck of movers' crane.
So on the edge of losing everything.

Let me teach like the first snow, falling.

—Taylor Mali

Chapter 1

Getting Off to a Good Start

Time to Learn

by Kelley Dawson Salas

My alarm had not yet gone off, but I was wide awake. My stomach was in knots and I knew I would not be able to eat breakfast. I longed to turn over, go back to sleep, wait for the alarm, hit snooze.

But there was no way. It was September, a school day, a few weeks into my first year of teaching.

I was teaching 3rd grade at a bilingual school on Milwaukee's south side. Those who had hired me and placed

Bob Gale

me in a fast-track alternative teacher certification program had been eager to get me into the classroom. But on mornings like this, I felt I'd been misled, that I'd been tricked into taking this job without enough training, and with no real idea of what to expect. I was spending six hours a day in my classroom and nearly another six hours planning, rehearsing, and worrying. Even sleep became an extension of my job, as I searched my dreams for the perfect combination of compassion, creativity, and classroom control.

Needless to say, I hadn't found the magic formula, either in my classroom or in my dreams. I worried that my teaching career was going to be short-lived.

I dragged myself out of bed and called a friend. My worries poured forth: I'm no good at this. It's too hard for me to learn the things I need to learn. There are so many jobs that would be easier and pay better. Finally, I asked the question: Should I just walk away from this whole thing?

My friend's advice proved wise. The job of a first-year teacher is hard enough, he said. Don't add to your difficulties by beating up on yourself. Let up a little so you have the time and the space to become a good teacher.

I took the advice. I stopped thinking I would conquer the teaching profession in my first few months on the job. Yet my fears persisted. The kind of teacher I wanted to become was fairly clear in my mind. But it seemed to have nothing to do with the reality I experienced every day. I wondered how I could ever get there.

Ideals vs. Reality

I knew I wanted to build a classroom community in which students felt safe, both emotionally and physically. I wanted each student to be able to bring his or her cultural background and experiences into the classroom and to feel important and valued. I hoped to create an atmosphere of respect and cooperation. I wanted students to "behave themselves" without feeling threatened or burdened by punishments. I was also committed to high academic expectations and helping each student learn and progress. I wanted to infuse an anti-racist, social justice perspective into my classroom and I hoped to share my own background as a political activist with my students. I wanted to encourage my students to think critically and to learn to take action to create a more just world.

I was teaching in a two-way bilingual classroom, where both English-dominant and Spanish-dominant students came together and instruction took place in both languages. I knew it was going to be a challenge to meet my students' diverse cultural and academic needs, especially in reading and language proficiency. I also knew that as an Anglo teacher in a classroom of Latino and African American students, I would have to examine my actions and interactions through a critical lens. I would have to listen to parents and to other teachers, especially parents and teachers of color.

Those were the ideals and beliefs that had led me to become a teacher. Once I actually started teaching, however, reality soon set in. I struggled with discipline, organization, and curriculum. I felt disillusioned when my students seemed more comfortable with an authoritarian style rather than one that emphasized self-discipline. I found little support for teaching about social justice and anti-racism. Administrators, colleagues, and classmates in my certification program were willing to listen to my ideas, but they did not respond as enthusiastically as I had hoped. No one seemed eager to collaborate, or to offer ideas to help me improve my teaching.

Faced with trying to do and learn everything at the same time, I sought advice from as many people as I could.

VOICES
FROM THE CLASSROOM

"It's useful for new teachers to reflect on the difference between being a 'good person' and being a 'good teacher.' It is important to be nurturing and supportive of your students, but it's also important to challenge them to work hard and to help them assume responsibility for making their own schooling successful. If you're able to maintain a little critical distance to reflect on situations and not internalize or personalize everything, it will help smooth out the emotional ups and downs, which can get pretty intense."

—Stan Karp

I heard different messages and it was hard to know whom to listen to. For example, some educators told me that I needed to use borderline-authoritarian classroom management techniques. Once I was "experienced," they said, I could vary them. My teaching style reflected my ambivalence about that advice. Some days, I tried to understand why certain students were misbehaving. I talked with students, showed compassion, called home, held conferences. But at other times I became tired of this and allowed myself to follow a veteran teacher's well-intentioned but flawed advice: "With this group, you'll just have to act like a drill sergeant."

I felt that part of the discipline puzzle would be solved if I could just offer my students good, engaging lessons. And yet I was overwhelmed by the task of choosing the content I wanted to teach. Again, the advice I received and expectations laid out for me were traditional: Follow the curriculum. I was sent to inservices on the basal, a program called Power Writing, and our district's new math series. I could see some value in each, but I also saw gaping holes. The social studies curriculum, in particular, seemed worlds away from what I wanted to teach. The textbook was almost impenetrable and seemed totally disconnected from the lives of my students. But I was using it because I wasn't sure what else to do.

The assessment program was equally circumscribed. Our district requires lots of standardized testing and test preparation. School administrators handed me a stack of Target Teach materials in October and told me to administer four practice reading tests before the actual reading test in March. They expected me to tabulate the results of each practice test and reteach the specific testing skills that my students lacked.

VOICES
FROM THE CLASSROOM

"Being a teacher is not an occupation that exists within you only when you are on location. Being a teacher permeates every fiber of your being all of the time. It is something that never leaves you."

—Kathy Williams

Subtle Steps Forward

I spent the fall sorting through the various expectations and figuring out where and how they related to my own goals. As first semester ended, I had made little progress in teaching social justice issues. But I had experimented with creating a positive classroom community and an organized, disciplined environment. I had also begun to pick and choose useful pieces from my school's reading, writing, and math curricula.

One example was my evolving reading program. Like many teachers, I had little access to multiple copies of books outside of our basals. In the beginning of the year, I followed the advice of administrators and my mentor in my certification program: I used my teacher's guide faithfully and trudged through the basal story by story. But by mid-semester I scrapped this plan and picked selected stories. I also dropped many of the suggested lessons and invented my own. Instead of dutifully teaching "The Three Little Hawaiian Pigs," which felt like a superficial attempt to put a multicultural spin on a traditional tale, I chose to teach more true-to-life stories such as *Halmoni and the Picnic,* a children's book by Sook Nyul Choi about a Korean immigrant girl and her grandmother, and *Chicken Sunday*, Patricia Polacco's story built around intergenerational, cross-cultural friendships. I helped students compare the cultural backgrounds of the characters in *Chicken Sunday*, and discussed why Halmoni might feel shy about having her classmates meet her grandmother.

It was not exactly where I wanted to be, but it was a subtle step in the right direction.

In January I decided to take a further step away from the "traditional" follow-the-book advice offered to new teachers: I didn't want to wait to teach about issues of racism and social justice. Perhaps this was the first time that I felt I had enough of the basics in place to spend significant time working on my own curriculum. Or perhaps I realized that the time would never be "just right."

Justice and Civil Rights

In preparation for our school's African American history program in February, I taught a unit on the Civil Rights Movement, drawing ideas from a *Rethinking Schools* article by Kate Lyman. As we began I was floored to learn that my 3rd graders had very little understanding of the concept of "rights." Our studies centered around the Montgomery, Ala., bus boycott and the integration of the schools in Little Rock, Ark. We discussed racism, discrimination, justice, rights, mass movements, and freedom. Students wrote and performed a play about the bus boycott. They researched famous people of color who had fought for change. For the first time, I felt I was attempting the kind of teaching I wanted to do.

I was also acutely aware of my unit's limitations. It focused on the changes brought about by the Civil Rights Movement, but downplayed the racism and injustice that continue today. Our studies highlighted the achievements of a few well-known leaders, but somewhat underplayed the important contributions made by thousands of other participants. And despite my fledgling awareness of different theories of multicultural/anti-racist education, I did not manage to include activities that helped students themselves become activists in identifying and fighting the racism that existed in their own community.

Despite these weaknesses, I learned a lot teaching that unit. One important lesson: Teaching about something real and important is more effective in creating an orderly, disciplined classroom environment than acting like a drill sergeant.

Just as I was beginning this unit, my mentor said she wanted me to work on discipline. She insisted that I needed to be firmer and more consistent with my students. "You aren't going to like doing it," she told me, "but you have to do it."

I agreed with my mentor that my discipline had been inconsistent. But I felt this was partly because I had not been teaching the quality of lessons my students deserved. During the Civil Rights Movement unit, I was able to offer lessons that I believed were worth their time. I also felt fewer qualms about consistently applying our classroom rules; rule enforcement stopped being a series of punishments for bored students and instead became a prerequisite to accomplishing serious and relevant learning.

Standardized Tests

The moment was sweet, but it didn't last long. By March, the 3rd-grade reading test was upon us. My teaching was derailed for three weeks as I coaxed, prodded, and bribed my students through their first experience with a standardized test. Going into the testing, I thought my students were well prepared. But nonetheless the testing process was grueling.

I felt very official as I followed my test administrator's script: "You may now begin the test." Immediately, two students began to cry. I made a beeline for one of them and our teaching assistant headed for the other. After 15 minutes of sweet-talking, trips to the drinking fountain, and pats on the back, all of the students were working on the test.

I walked around, looking over students' shoulders and trying to maintain a positive outward appearance. Inside, I worried. I was not overly concerned about how students would do on the test, but wondered how this stressful experience would affect the confidence of several students who didn't have a lot of self-esteem to lose. Even though I prefaced the test-taking with weeks of "this doesn't really tell people anything about who you are," some students felt great pressure to succeed.

I didn't receive the results of the reading test until almost the last week of school. The principal presented them to my partner teacher and me with a comment of congratulations—our students had done well. I fought the urge to be proud, forcing myself to remember that the test was not a particularly accurate or useful measure of students' reading skills (or of my teaching skills). I smiled, thanked my principal, filed the result sheet away, and went on with my day. My students and I had gone through a lot and the final chapter felt anticlimactic.

There was no letup after the 3rd-grade reading test. Evenings and weekends, I still struggled to find the energy to attend classes and complete my certification program. Before I knew it, I was staying up late to finish my last round of report cards. I had made it through my first year.

Lessons from My First Year

What did I accomplish during that whirlwind of a first year? Looking back, I can see that my uncertainty at the beginning of the year and the conservative advice I received made for a slow start. It took time to pull together a group of people whose advice I accepted and trusted, to sort through the demands of my school and district, and to feel confident enough to assert my own vision. It took some experimenting to see that discipline is not a question of bossing students but of providing interesting, challenging material and helping them meet the challenge.

It seems ironic to me now that I spent so much time fretting over such things. I know I have to provide an organized, disciplined classroom environment, and administer state-mandated standardized tests. But I do not have to act like a boss, follow a prescribed "teacher-proof" curriculum, or agree to excessive test prep activities. As a professional I have the authority to do what I think is most beneficial to my students.

During that first year I caught glimpses of myself doing the kind of teaching I wanted, but it wasn't much to show for a whole year. I reminded myself of the advice that had served me well all year: Don't get too down on yourself; maintain high expectations but take time and space to develop your skills.

I learned that it was easy to become isolated in my classroom and that it takes extra energy to connect with other educators. Equally important, I learned that without such outside help, it's difficult to grow.

Part of the confidence I needed to take even small steps in advancing my vision came from conversations with colleagues. Although I continued to feel overwhelmed by the traditional nature of my professional training, I pulled together a loose cadre of teacher friends and co-workers and talked with them regularly. In particular, teacher friends that I had long known through political activism offered encouragement and support.

Pulling together a supportive group of colleagues during one's first year of teaching can seem like just one more burden, but I found it worth the extra effort. There was no one place where I found support. As part of my alternative certification, I attended class twice a week with new teachers going through the same experience I was. I collaborated with colleagues at school. I attended events held by education activist groups such as Rethinking Schools. It has made a difference.

I often still feel the way I did on that September morning during my first month of teaching: dissatisfied and worried that I am not making enough progress. While keeping a critical eye on my own practice, I have also begun to think more critically about teacher education programs. Even though I am now certified, I still need ongoing professional training. Like many new and veteran teachers, I need help with effective teaching methods, curriculum, classroom organization, and discipline. Like all teachers, I need help examining my biases, developing culturally competent practices, and being a teacher that works against racism and classism in our schools instead of reinforcing them.

I often feel that these responsibilities fall squarely on my own shoulders and that there is little support from the educational system. This, I think, is what leads so many new teachers to drop out.

Whenever I feel overwhelmed by the lack of support,

VOICES
FROM THE CLASSROOM

"Forgive yourself for making mistakes: Your first year of teaching will undoubtedly be full of them. Don't be harsher on yourself than you would be on your most trying student."

—Dale Weiss

I fight the urge to leave teaching. Instead, I try to speak up about what teachers need to succeed.

As I struggle toward my vision of good teaching, I remind myself of what I have accomplished so far. I am less isolated and have close ties with other progressive teachers. I am more confident about developing curriculum and a teaching style that reflect my politics. I still need time and guidance, but some of the conditions are in place for me to someday become the teacher I want to be.

I have a long way to go. But I'm on my way.

References

Chicken Sunday, by Patricia Polacco (New York: Puffin, 1998).

"From Snarling Dogs to Bloody Sunday," by Kate Lyman, in *Rethinking Schools*, Vol. 14, No. 1.

Halmoni and the Picnic, by Sook Nyul Choi (Boston: Houghton Mifflin, 1993).

Should I try to be a friend to my students?

Q/A

This is a complicated question. The short answer is no. They've got friends; you've got friends. True friendship requires equality, and in many respects you and your students are not equals. You are a leader, you are a guide, you are a mentor, you are an evaluator.

I've seen new teachers so desperate to be liked by their students that they cannot maintain discipline in the classroom, are not academically rigorous, and end up doing a great disservice to students. However, the "don't smile until Christmas" advice is also misplaced.

At its core, teaching is about relationships, and unless you have a solid, respectful, supportive relationship with your students, you won't be able to teach effectively and students won't be able to learn effectively.

Also, frankly, if you're not having fun teaching, then you won't last as a teacher. You need to create activities in which you and the students are having a good time. You need to create activities in which you are able to appreciate the best qualities of the students. This is for them, but it's also for you. But working to build a playful, joyful, respectful, hardworking classroom is different from being the students' "friend."

—Bill Bigelow

How I Survived
My First Year

by Bill Bigelow

It was a Friday afternoon and the end of my sixth-period
freshman social studies class. As two of my students
walked out the door, I overheard one say to the other:
"Do you know what this class reminds me of? A local TV
commercial."

It was a crushing comment. I knew exactly what she
meant. It was my first year as a teacher. And as hard as I
was working, the class still felt ragged, amateurish—well-
intended, but sloppy. Her metaphor, invoking the image of
a salesman trying too hard, was perfect.

As the last student filed out, the best I could do was
remember the words of Lee Hays of the Weavers: "Like

Randall Enos

kidney stones and the Nixon presidency, this too will pass."

Thirty years later, there are still days when my class feels a bit like a local TV ad. But I continue to experiment, continue to study my own classroom practice. And looking back, I think I learned some things that first year that might be useful to pass on.

The first couple of years in the classroom establish what could be called a teacher's "professional trajectory." Most of us come out of college full of theory and hope. But then our lofty aims often bump up against the conservative cultures of our new schools, and students who often have been hardened by life and public schooling.

How we respond to this clash of idealism vs. cynicism begins to create patterns that help define the teachers we'll become.

Which is not to say that the mistakes we make early on are repeated over and over throughout our careers. I probably did more things wrong than right my first year, and I'd like to think that I've grown since then.

Show Them Your Humanity

The most useful piece of advice in the infancy of my career came from Tom McKenna, my cooperating teacher during my student teaching at Grant High School. It wasn't spoken advice, but he demonstrated it countless times in his classroom demeanor: Show the students that you love and respect them; play with them; joke with them; let them see your humanity. Good lesson plans are essential, yes, but ultimately students respond to the teacher as a human being.

Easier said than done, to be sure. Some days I would start out full of love and humor, but the students' surliness would defeat me by period's end. However, on better days, days when I had designed lessons that channeled rather than suppressed their fitful energy, or when I found some way to coax them to share their real stories—and thus I could share mine—I glimpsed the classroom life that was meant to be. We stopped being boss and workers, guard and inmates. The pictures of Molly, Tony, Tara, Tonya, Scott, Ken, Dee, et al. that I carry in my head are from those days.

—Bill Bigelow

Perhaps the best we can do is to ensure that early in our teaching lives we create mechanisms of self-reflection that allow us to grow, and allow us to continually rethink our curricula and classroom approaches. Nurturing these critical mechanisms may be vital if we're to maintain our hope in increasingly trying times.

My First Job

Year number one was not easy, as can be gathered from the incident described above. Typical of the circumstances of most first-year teachers, principals did not line up to compete for my services. I began on the substitute list, and was lucky to land that spot. I know there are people who enjoy subbing: no papers to correct, no lesson plans to fret over, frequent changes of scenery, and so forth. But I hated it. I didn't know the kids' names; they often began in let's-terrorize-the-sub mode; teachers invariably left awful lesson plans ("Review chapter 20 and have them study for the test") but resented it if I didn't follow them to the letter; and I rarely had an opportunity to practice my craft: teaching.

Finally, in late October I did get a job—at Grant High School in Portland, Ore., where I had completed my student teaching. It was a school with a diverse student body, about 30 percent African American, with its European American students drawn from both working-class and "up on the ridge" neighborhoods. I had two preps: U.S. history and something called "freshman social studies" (and baseball coaching in the spring).

As I was to learn, I'd been hired to teach "overflow" classes, classes that had been formed because Grant's enrollment was much higher than expected. Teachers chose the "surplus" students they would donate to these new classes. Then the administration hired a sub to babysit while they sought permission from higher-ups to offer a contract to a regular teacher. In the meantime, the kids had driven two subs to quit. I was hired during the tenure of sub number three. My position was officially designated "temporary." In other words, I would automatically lose my job at the end of the year—unless another teacher fell ill, retired, died, quit, or had a baby.

My first meeting with the administrative team of principal, vice principal, and curriculum specialist was perfunctory. I was told that "freshman social studies" meant one semester of career education, one semester of world geography, and no, they weren't sure which came first. Nor did they know which, or even if, textbooks were used. But I could pick up my two-ream allotment of ditto paper from the department chair.

They gave me a key to Room 10 and sent me to review my "work station," as the principal, an ex-Navy man, called it. Room 10 was a runt: a tiny basement classroom crammed with 1950s-style student desks and a loud, hulking heating unit in the rear. But it was mine. It turned out students had been issued textbooks—for U.S. history, something like *God Bless America: We're Number One,* and for world geography, the cleverly titled *World Geography.*

Don't Be the Lone Ranger

Before the students came the questions: Should I use these textbooks? How do I grade? What kind of "discipline" policy should I have? How should I arrange the classroom? What do I teach on the first day?

My answers to these and other typical new-teacher questions are less important than the process of answering them. And this is perhaps the most valuable lesson I drew from that first year: Don't be the Lone Ranger. In September I had organized a study/support group with several teachers, some brand new, others with a few years of experience. We were united by a broad vision of creating lively and thoughtful classrooms where we provoked students to question the roots of social problems and encouraged them to believe that they could make a difference in the world. This group became my haven, offering comfort in times of stress—which was most of the time—and concrete advice to vexing questions.

(I don't mean to suggest that these support groups are only for the inexperienced. I've been in a study/action group, Portland Area Rethinking Schools, for many years, and this group and a subgroup aimed at sharing curriculum on global justice issues continue to offer essential support. They remind me that I'm not alone and they offer practical advice.)

We met weekly and usually divided our time between discussion of issues in education—tracking, discipline, teacher union politics, school funding, etc.—and specific classroom problems we encountered. Sometimes we brainstormed ideas for particular units people were developing: for example, Native American history or the U.S. Constitution. It was also to this group that I brought complaints of rowdy classes and recalcitrant students, practical concerns about leading discussions or structuring a major project, and questions of how curricularly adventurous I could be without incurring the wrath of an administrator.

I'm a bit embarrassed to admit it, but I was glad that the group was composed mostly of teachers from other schools. Because of the huge gulf between my classroom ideals and my day-to-day practice, I felt somewhat ashamed and was reluctant to share my stumbles and doubts with more experienced colleagues in the building.

There were only eight of us in the group but we taught in four different districts; two were Title I teachers and three worked in alternative programs. The diversity of work situations yanked me out of the isolation of my classroom cubicle and forced me to see a bigger educational picture. Sheryl Hirshon's frequent despair with her Title I classes in a rural Oregon community may have been of a different sort than my frequent despair at urban Grant High School. But each of us could learn from how the other analyzed and confronted our difficult situations. (Sheryl ended up leaving teaching, moved to Nicaragua,

VOICES
FROM THE CLASSROOM

"I think new teachers need a combination of the practical and the visionary. For survival purposes it's important to find people to share your experiences and struggles as you go through them. It's also important to find someone who can orient you to your school's strengths, weaknesses, and possibilities."

—Stan Karp

taught for years in literacy programs there, and wrote the wonderful book about the 1979 literacy crusade, *And Also Teach Them to Read*.)

Occasionally our meetings turned into aimless whining sessions. But other times, a simple comment could remind us of our ideals and keep us on the path. I remember in a weak moment confessing that I was going to start relying on the textbook: I was just too tired, scrambling to create my own curriculum from scratch, retyping excerpts from assorted books in the days before we teachers were allowed access to a copy machine, and when personal computers were still a thing of the future.

My friend Peter Thacker, sympathetic yet disapproving, simply asked: "Bill, do you really want to do that?"

OK, it bordered on a guilt trip. But that's all it took for me to remember that in fact I really didn't want to do that. The group was simultaneously collective conscience and inspiration.

Moving Beyond the Textbooks

Not all textbooks are so wretched, although as I recall mine were pretty awful. But as a beginning teacher I needed to see myself as a producer, not merely a consumer, of curriculum. It's hard work to translate the world into engaging lesson plans, but unless we're content to subordinate our classrooms to the priorities of the corporations that produce textbooks and other canned curricula, that's exactly what we have to do every day.

It's not that textbooks are a vast wasteland of corporate propaganda with no value whatsoever. I've borrowed lots of good ideas from textbook study guides. But they can easily narrow, distort, and misdirect our efforts.

To offer just one example: In *Lies My Teacher Told Me*, James Loewen's valuable critique of contemporary U.S. history textbooks, he demonstrates that all major texts downplay or totally ignore the history of the struggle against racism in the United States. Especially as a beginning teacher, if I had relied on textbooks to shape the outlines of my U.S.

history curriculum, I would have neglected crucial areas of inquiry—and may never have realized it.

In addition to the support group, my planning book was another confidant of sorts. In it I would describe the activities I intended to do each week. Then I would record in some detail what actually happened. This was especially useful the following summer, when I could sit on the porch and leisurely flip through the book looking for patterns in students' responses to various lessons and teaching methods.

When I read back through that planning book today, I'm reminded of how helpless I often felt. From Nov. 28, 1978, for example: "Things seem to be getting much rowdier in both my freshman classes. And I'm not sure exactly what to do." I wrote frequently about their "groans." But having the journal to look back on after that first year also allowed me to search out the causes of the rowdiness and groans. I saw that my failure to engage them was more pronounced when I tried to pound them with information. My observations after a lecture on the roots of the Civil War were blunt, and a trifle pathetic: "People were very bored. I guess I should find another way to present it—even though it's interesting to me."

What's obvious to me now was not so obvious at the time: When students experience social dynamics from the inside—with role plays, stories, improvisations—they aren't so rowdy and they aren't so bored. There's a direct relationship between curriculum and "classroom management" that isn't always explicitly acknowledged in teaching-methods courses prospective teachers take.

The following year, I designed a simulation to get at the prewar sectional conflicts, and wrote a role play that

VOICES
FROM THE CLASSROOM

"A teacher I worked with told me, 'One night at about 7 p.m. I was still working on a curriculum unit for Sarah, Plain and Tall, *and I realized that all over the city other teachers were probably also developing lessons for the same book. It just didn't make sense.' And it doesn't. Establish a community of people who develop curriculum together. The work not only goes faster, but it's usually better because you have someone to talk through your ideas with."*

—Linda Christensen

showed students firsthand why Lincoln's election led to Southern secession. The role play also prompted students to think critically about the "Lincoln freed the slaves" myth. The point is simply that it was vital that I had some mechanisms to be self-reflective that first year.

(A wonderful book that helped me develop a more student-friendly, hands-on curriculum was *Changing Learning, Changing Lives*, by Barbara Gates, Susan Klaw, and Adria Steinberg. Sadly, the book is long out of print, but you can often find a used copy through bookstores or internet-based book-finding services.)

Feeling Like a Jilted Lover

The principal made his one and only appearance in my classroom on March 15. Actually, he didn't come in, but knocked on the door and waited in the hallway. When I answered he handed me my official termination notice.

It was expected. I'd known I wouldn't be back because I was a temporary. But still there had been that slight hope. I guess by contract or law March 15 was the final date to notify teachers if they wouldn't be returning. I had about three months to let my unemployment sink in.

When that June date finally came, I packed my little white Toyota with the files, books, posters, and other knickknacks I'd accumulated throughout the year. I stood looking at the bare walls, my tiny oak desk, and Hulk the heater. And I left.

My tears didn't start until I was in the safety of my living room.

Tom McKenna, my cooperating teacher when I was a student teacher, had said that at the end of the year he always felt like a jilted lover. "Wait, there was more I wanted to say to you," he would think as the students filed out for the last time. And: "I always cared more about this than you did."

Sitting there on my couch, I now knew exactly what he meant. When it's over, you're left with the should-have-dones, the sense of missed opportunities, and the finality of it all. The end-of-the-year cry has become one of my worklife rituals: "There was more we had to say to each other."

The school district had made it clear that I was not guaranteed a job the following September. Thanks to this official non-guarantee I was able to collect unemployment that summer—in spite of the state functionary who told me with a sneer: "Unemployment benefits are not vacation pay for teachers, ya know."

But job or no job, benefits or no benefits, I'd made it. I'd finished my hardest year.

I would like to be able to say that the kids pulled me through. I always found that image of "young, idealistic superteacher and students vs. hostile world" very appealing. And some years the kids did pull me through. But that first year, the more significant survival strategy was my reliance on a network of colleagues who shared a vision of the kind of classroom life, and the kind of world, we wanted to build.

That first year, we pulled each other through.

References
And Also Teach Them to Read, by Sheryl Hirshon (Westport, CT: Lawrence Hill & Co., 1984).

Changing Learning, Changing Lives, by Barbara Gates, Susan Klaw, and Adria Steinberg (New York: The Feminist Press, 1979).

Lies My Teacher Told Me, by James Loewen (New York: Touchstone, 2007).

Q/A What should I wear to school?

This is one of the most common questions beginning teachers wonder about, male or female, even though it might not be a question they'd feel comfortable asking in a teacher education course or a new teacher seminar. Although a Rethinking Schools book is no substitute for a fashion magazine, questions about dressing for school warrant careful thought by new and veteran teachers alike.

Beyond personal taste, comfort, and clothing that functions well within the time constraints of teaching, the fashion choices teachers make send messages about respect, expertise, and commitment to teaching and to the community in which your school is situated. Although not necessarily obvious, dressing well may be even more important to your success as a teacher in a school with students from lower-income families, students of color, and students from varied cultural backgrounds.

For example, several years ago, I conducted several studies at a large urban high school where a majority of the students were Latino/a. Researching the daily life of a 9th-grade English class over the course of a semester in this school, I was most struck by the level of respect the students showed for both the subject and the teacher, a young white man who wore a different necktie each day to school. When I asked him about his style, he told me that he definitely noticed a difference in his students' behavior and participation when he switched from jeans and polo shirts to shirts and ties. In interviews with me, his students kept referring to the respect they felt from their teacher and the importance of the content he taught in his class. Although it wasn't all about the tie, without clothing that signified that attention had been paid to his presentation, his students might have easily seen him, he thought, as one more teacher who didn't care enough about his job or his students to dress like a professional. Later, as I devoted more attention to a line of research about teacher fashion, the teachers of color I interviewed were nearly unanimous in their commitment to dressing well each day to express their respect for their students and their students' families.

Dressing well can also be a boost to your confidence as a new teacher. One of my internal mantras is "Dress better than you feel" and on days when I don't really feel like getting out of bed to go to school, I follow this advice. Invariably, I feel better about what I am doing by the time I leave my apartment; and, if, for example, my bus driver tells me that I look nice that day, or if my fashion-forward students notice and comment on my cute shoes, that confidence, shallow as this might sound, can grow and feed itself all day long.

Oddly enough, getting dressed for school is now a sizable part of my daily pleasure. I find it comforting to have high-quality fabrics against my skin when my world gets a little hectic as a teacher. And there are many days when a quick glance down at my favorite pair of sky blue cowboy boots gives me a boost of joy when I am sitting at the computer entering grades or in the storeroom mixing chemicals. As much as I dress for my job, I also dress for myself. And, that habit shows in my confidence and contributes to the whole effort of bringing my best self to school each day.

—Terry Burant

It really is true that clothes make the man (or woman). How we dress does matter—to our colleagues, and our supervisors; to our students (no matter how young) and to their parents, and we shouldn't take it lightly.

It is critical to take cues from your fellow teachers. At my first school, teachers rarely wore jeans and gym shoes were most definitely taboo. I took my dress code cues from my friends and was careful not to break the unwritten wardrobe rules. But at my next school I found myself terribly overdressed—teachers wore jeans regularly. I had to decide if a wardrobe adjustment was in order.

Skirts and heels? Not always an option because practicality is key. As a 2nd-grade teacher heels definitely were not going to be a part of my daily uniform and often skirts missed the mark, too. Sitting on the floor did not always jibe with my penchant for donning skirts, but I learned to work them into my teacher wardrobe because I love to wear them. And how we feel in our clothes is so important. If we like the way we look in our clothes that is going to show to the people we work with everyday. When my kids said, "You look nice today, Ms. Walters," it put a smile on my face, helped me through the day, and made me think about what I'd wear the next.

—Stephanie Walters

Q/A What are some tips for putting together a new teacher look that respects your students and gives you confidence?

Rather than encouraging you to make an appointment with a private shopping consultant, what follows are some ideas for consideration when putting together a new teacher wardrobe as well as some practical advice for making your teacher fashion statement work for you in your busy life.

First, if you've lived the last few years in Uggs, flip-flops, college sweatshirts, and jeans, or if you are entering teaching from another profession with a different fashion vibe, it is worth your time to stand back and develop a thoughtful plan for your new look as a teacher. Pay attention as well to the norms and culture in your building and notice what your administrators and other teachers are wearing to school. This doesn't mean that you need to dress the way they do; however, it is useful to take a close look around to see the range of fashion choices.

Second, consider whether your favorite outfits are appropriate for a job where you are in the company of children or teenagers. Check with your contract and with the guidelines established by your employer. Although there might not be statements in your contract against low-cut tops, pierced stomachs showing when you teach, or hair or beard length, students will pay close attention to your dress and they may unduly focus on your appearance rather than your curriculum if you are too outrageous or if you dress like you are about to mow a lawn rather than teach a class. If students are counting the number of days you wore the same pair of pants, are staring at your dirty toenails sticking out of worn sandals, or trying to figure out how you can actually walk in your sky-high stilettos, they aren't focusing on fractions, poetry, or chemical reactions.

Next, analyze your typical schedule and plan your clothing to match the demands of the day. For example, on Tuesdays this year, on reverse schedules at my high school, I spent the first five periods moving from room to room on three separate floors of the building; Tuesdays were not my days for heels! And, in teaching high school chemistry, I always pay attention to whether I have labs scheduled or not since I often find myself running around the room on lab days and I want to make sure I have comfortable shoes that are up for the task. I also don't want to wreck my favorite sweaters with chemicals so I have a few lab outfits that work for me (along with a lab coat that also adds a certain aura of authority too).

It is so important to dress for success. Yes, I know it is cliché, but it is also true. Clothes with rips, stains, and wrinkles scream, "I don't care about how I look!" It's also not a good idea to dress like your students! How much respect will students have for you if you are wearing the same basketball jersey to school as they are? It is important to set yourself apart from your students and clothing helps you to accomplish that.

—Terry Burant

Teaching for Social Justice

by Herbert Kohl

I t is a sad statement on the moral sensibility of our schools and society that one has to advocate for teaching for social justice. As one of my elementary school students once told me, "You know, Mr. Kohl, you can get arrested for stirring up justice."

One problem is that many people—children as well as adults—do not believe that justice is worth fighting for. One cannot assume an idea or cause will be embraced merely because it is just, fair, or compassionate. Contemporary

Rob Dunlavey

35

society values self-interest and personal gain over compassion and the communal good.

So what are social justice teachers—those who care about nurturing all children and who are enraged at the prospect of students dying young, going hungry, or living meaningless and despairing lives—to do? How can they go against the grain and use their classrooms to work in the service of their students?

My suggestions are both pedagogical and personal.

First, don't teach against your conscience. Don't align yourself with texts, people, or rules that hurt children. Resist them as creatively and effectively as you can, whether through humor or by developing alternative curricula. Try to survive, but don't make your survival in a particular job the overriding determinant of what you will or won't do. Don't become isolated or alone in your efforts; reach out to other teachers, community leaders, church people, and parents who feel as you do. Find a school where you can do your work and then stand up for the quality of your work. Don't quit in the face of opposition; make people work hard if they intend to fire or reprimand you for teaching equity and justice.

Second, hone your craft as a teacher. When I first began teaching, I jumped into struggles for social justice. During one of my efforts a community person asked: "So, what's going on in your classroom that's different from what you're fighting against? Can your students read and do math?" I had to examine my work, which was full of passion and effort but deficient in craft. I realized that I needed to take the time to learn how to teach well, or I couldn't extend myself with authority and confidence in organizing efforts. This is essential for caring teachers. We have to get it right for our own students or we can't presume to take on larger systems, no matter how terrible those larger systems are. As educators, we need to root our struggles for social justice in

VOICES
FROM THE CLASSROOM

"Never forget that your passion for your students and your passion for justice are both worthy endeavors. Do not believe you need to forsake one for other. Stay true to your authentic self."

—Dale Weiss

the work we do every day, in a particular community, with a particular group of students.

Third, look around at the many effective ways of teaching children. I don't believe there is a single technique or curriculum that leads to success. Consequently, pick and choose, retool and restructure the best of what you find and make it your own. Most of all, watch your students and see what works. Listen to them, observe how they learn, and then, based on your experience and their responses, figure out how to practice social justice in your classroom.

Fourth, it is not enough to teach well and create a social justice classroom separate from the larger community. You have to be a community activist, a good parent, a decent person, and an active community member as well.

Is all of this possible? Probably not. Certainly it isn't easy and often demands sacrifices. And at the end of the day it might also make you sad, because there is so much more that needs to be done, so many students who don't even have the advantage of a decent classroom and a caring teacher.

This leads to my final suggestion.

Protect and nurture yourself. Have some fun in your life; learn new things that only obliquely relate to issues of social justice. Teachers do a lot of work outside of school hours, yes, and you need to expect that. But daunting though it sounds, you also need to make time for yourself. Walk, play ball or chess, swim, fall in love. Don't forget how to laugh or feel good about the world. Have fun so that you can work hard; and work hard so that you and your students and their parents can have fun without looking over their shoulders.

This is not a question of selfishness but one of survival. Don't turn teaching for social justice into a grim responsibility, but take it for the moral and social necessity that it is.

The above is adapted from the afterword to *Teaching for Social Justice*, edited by William Ayers, Jean Ann Hunt, and Therese Quinn (New York: Teachers College Press, 1998). Reprinted with permission.

12 Tips for New Teachers

by Larry Miller

I was 38 when I started my teaching career, and I thought I knew everything I needed to know. I'd been a community and union activist for years and I'd been political all my life. I figured all I had to do was bring my experience and politics to the classroom and I'd be a great teacher.

Was I wrong. Now I've been teaching high school for more than 19 years and I continue to be humbled. When I work with new teachers, I give them the following suggestions:

1   Keep calm in all situations. Calmness allows you to make rational decisions. If a student is confrontational or out of control, it never ever works to react with anger. Getting into a tug-of-war over who has the last word exacerbates the situation. Let the situation cool down and then try to have a mature conversation with those involved.

2   Make respect central to your classroom culture. A common expression I hear from my students and

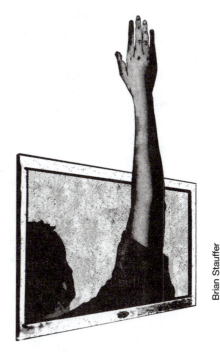

Brian Stauffer

39

parents is "You have to give respect to get respect." They're right. The only way to hold students to high and rigorous expectations is to gain their respect and their acknowledgment that your class will lead to real learning that will benefit them.

3 Base your curriculum on social justice. Frame it with a critical edge. I have four questions for assessing my curriculum:

- Does the curriculum deepen students' understanding of social justice?
- Is the curriculum rigorous?
- Are students learning the skills they need to be critical thinkers, advance their education, be prepared for employment, and become active citizens?
- I am also now forced to ask the question: Does the curriculum increase students' ability to do well on state-mandated standardized tests?

4 Keep rules to a minimum but enforce them. Always have clear consequences and never threaten to take a particular action if you are not willing to carry it out. Talk to students as mature young adults.

5 Whenever possible, connect your classroom discussions and curriculum to students' lives, community, and culture. Learn as much as you can about your students. For example, I use hip-hop lyrics as a means to discuss current trends of thought and worldviews in my citizenship class. Rappers offer plenty to discuss, both positive and negative. I get lyrics from the internet, I borrow CDs from students, and I search for positive rap on TV and the radio.

6 Learn from other teachers and staff. Pay special attention to teachers and staff whose cultures and backgrounds are different from yours. I've always made a point of consulting every day with my colleagues. Their insight can be invaluable.

7   Build students' confidence in their intelligence and creativity. I've often heard my students call kids from the suburbs or those in AP classes "the smart kids." Don't let that go unchallenged. I start the year talking about "multiple intelligences" and how "being smart" can take many forms. I find daily examples of students' work and views to talk about as smart and intelligent.

8   Distinguish between students' home language and their need to know "standard" English. Work with both. This is a huge topic, one you will be dealing with throughout your career. (For a more thorough discussion of home language, see Linda Christensen's book *Reading, Writing, and Rising Up: Teaching About Social Justice and the Power of the Written Word*, which is described on page 358.)

9   Keep lecturing short. Have students regularly doing projects, reading, giving presentations, engaging in discussions, debating, doing role plays, and taking part in simulations.

10   Have engaging activities prepared for students when they walk into the classroom. I might play a piece of music, put an African expression on the board to interpret, or put students in "critical thinking groups" to solve a puzzle.

11   Call students' homes regularly both for positive and negative reports. Visit their homes. Students often belong to nonschool organizations. For example, during Black History Month many churches in the black community have special programs that students perform in. Attend, and go to other presentations given by groups they belong to.

12   Mobilize students to join in new experiences. For example, I sponsor a "polar bear club": We jump into Lake Michigan to celebrate New Year's Day, then we all eat breakfast together.

Teaching in the Undertow

Resisting the Pull of Schooling-As-Usual

by Gregory Michie

As a 7-year-old, I was amazed by the ocean. I remember being awed as I looked out at the vastness of the water off the South Carolina coast. And I recall the cautionary words my mother used each time I tried to wade in deeper than my waist: "Be careful of the undertow."

According to my mom, the undertow was an invisible current beneath the ocean's surface that, if you weren't careful, could pull you down the coastline or out to sea before you knew what was happening. It tugged you along almost imperceptibly, she said, so you had to consciously

Randall Enos

keep your bearings: Pick a recognizable landmark and don't lose sight of it.

I could have used her advice when I began teaching 7th and 8th grade on Chicago's South Side two decades later. I went in with no formal preparation or credentials, and as a white male transplanted from the South, I was an outsider to my students in many ways. My approach at the time grew out of what made sense to me. I thought classrooms should be active spaces where kids had regular opportunities to do and make things. I thought students should be encouraged to express themselves creatively. I thought their voices should be not only heard, but valued. I believed kids should feel a connection between what they studied in school and their lives outside school. And I felt they should be pushed to think critically about the world around them.

Most of all I recognized that a meaningful, quality education was crucial for the young people I would be teaching, whose communities had been largely neglected and abandoned by those in power.

But having beliefs or guiding principles is one thing. Figuring out how to put them into practice, I learned, is another matter altogether, especially if you're teaching at a struggling urban school where the "pedagogy of poverty," as Martin Haberman calls it—characterized by "constant teacher direction and student compliance"—is in widespread use.

In that sort of environment, it's easy to lose your footing as a novice teacher, to begin to drift from your anchorage, to be seduced by the pull of convention or expediency or outside demands. The undertow of schooling, you quickly figure out, can be as strong and stealthy as any ocean's—maybe even more so.

So, how do you resist?

Connections with Colleagues

The first thing to know is, as much as it may seem otherwise at first, you're not alone. I've spent significant time in dozens of Chicago schools during the past 19 years, and although many have their share of adults who have become, at least on the surface, jaded or resigned to mediocrity, I've also found dedicated, caring, even visionary teachers almost everywhere I've been. This is important to understand as a new teacher because it makes it less likely that you'll fall into the trap of seeing yourself as the anointed one, the lone crusader working for justice in an unjust school and world. Heroic teacher memoirs and Hollywood movies notwithstanding, that is rarely, if ever, the way things are.

Although the organizational structures and scheduling at your school may not support alliance-building among teachers (and may, in fact, implicitly encourage you to isolate yourself), one of the best things you can do for yourself as a beginning teacher is seek out allies—both within your school and in the broader community of educators. Fellow teachers with whom you are aligned philosophically and politically can be vital sources of both emotional support and practical ideas, and even those who don't seem to share your views can sometimes prove helpful. A colleague who's been teaching in your building for 25 years, even if "traditional" or "burned out" at first glance, may still have lessons to impart and useful advice to offer, and may, in time, turn out to be not as one-dimensional as you originally thought.

That's not to say that you should expect to be surrounded by hopeful and forward-thinking educators. Cynicism can be deeply entrenched in big-city public schools, and it's also wildly contagious. One of the first temptations for a new teacher is to join this chorus of negativity and begin, however reluctantly, to recite the sorts of excuses you were certain you'd never make: that you can't really get to know your students because there are too many of them, that you can't engage students in group work because they get out of control, that you can't focus on building critical thinking skills when your kids are having a hard enough time just finding a vocabulary word in the dictionary.

I've heard myself say or think all those things at one time or another, and they're all legitimate dilemmas. But

Bill Ayers, longtime educator and author of *To Teach: The Journey of a Teacher*, points out that focusing on all the impediments to your work, although perhaps therapeutic in the short term, is ultimately a dead end for the committed teacher. Ayers suggests turning each obstacle around and viewing it from a more hopeful perspective by saying: "OK, this is my situation, these are the realities. Given that, what can I do?" Maybe you can't do everything you'd planned or imagined—at least not right away—but you can always do something.

Starting Small

It may be that you have to start with something small and seemingly insignificant—like bulletin boards, for instance. In many schools, bulletin boards simply become part of the scenery, wallpapered with routine announcements or seasonal messages that rarely provoke thought or cause anyone—kids or adults—to stop and take notice.

But bulletin boards can be to teachers and students what blank walls are to graffiti artists: an opportunity—the most visible one of all in many schools—to make a statement, to pose questions, to speak out on an issue, to bring kids' lives into classrooms or hallways. In one school I visited last year, I saw a bulletin board that featured the words "They Were Here First" at its center, with the names of a number of Native American tribes radiating around the outer edges. At another school, students displayed what they'd learned about the AIDS epidemic in several African countries. Still another teacher put up a thought-provoking quote along with an invitation for students to attach quotes that they found challenging or inspiring.

Those may not sound like such radical acts when placed alongside the more elaborate proposals of education's critical theorists. But once you're in a classroom of your own, you begin to realize that it's in the details, as much as in the big-picture theorizing, that critical conceptions of teaching find life. Kids can learn about equity and justice from the way community is formed in a classroom, how decisions are made, who is represented on the walls and bookshelves, what sorts of interactions are encouraged and discouraged, whose thoughts and ideas are valued, and, yes, even what's on the bulletin boards. Teaching for social justice, in practice, is as much about the environment you create as it is about the explicit lessons you teach.

The Question of Content

Content does matter, though, and it's another area in which, as a new teacher, you'll be challenged to hold true to your beliefs. For one thing, it's likely that you'll feel the ominous cloud of high-stakes testing looming over every curricular decision you make, dictating your answer to the perennial curriculum question: What knowledge and experiences are most worthwhile for my students? Beyond that, you may be further overwhelmed by all you need to do in order to make what you teach more meaningful and critical: limiting the use of biased and oversimplified textbooks, bringing in primary source documents, connecting topics to real-world issues, reading whole novels instead of chopped-up basal selections, giving students opportunities to write about their lives, weaving the arts throughout your subject areas, inviting your kids to help decide what they want to study, and so on.

The scope of the challenge can be truly paralyzing: Because you can't do everything, you delay doing anything, and instead fall back on using textbooks and following directives until you get your feet more firmly on the ground. But the ground is always shifting when you're a teacher, so your feet may never be fully planted. Instead of waiting for that to happen, why not take on something more manageable: Start with one subject and commit yourself to bringing it to life for your students. Or, if you teach only one subject to several groups of kids, try putting your own spin on things one day a week, and try to build from there. Again, you may not be able to do everything you'd hoped all at once—but you can do something.

Balancing Freedom and Control

If you're coming into the classroom with an orientation toward teaching for social justice, you already understand that, although they have helped many people, in many ways public schools have served as an oppressive force in the lives of poor children and students of color throughout this country's history. I had that shameful legacy in mind when I started out as a new teacher, and I wanted to do my part to interrupt it. But my approach, at least initially, was overly simplistic: If schools were oppressive, I figured, then the antidote to that was freedom, so in my classroom students would be "free." It sounded great in my head, but since I hadn't thought out the specifics of what freedom really meant within the context of a public school—or how I might create the conditions where it could happen—I quickly found myself in the midst of absolute chaos in my classes.

Not only does chaos in your classroom make you crazy, but it directs all your energy toward addressing student misbehavior. Other concerns—such as whether your kids are learning anything—lessen in importance. These skewed priorities are often reinforced by administrators who place a premium on order and control, and who hold up as exemplary those teachers who keep the tightest reins on their students. If you're not careful, you may find yourself falling unwittingly into a similar pattern of thinking: classifying your days as good or bad based solely on how quietly your students sit at their desks or how straight a line they form in the hallway.

Many young teachers think they'll be able to rise above such nonsense once they have a classroom of their own, or they delude themselves with the belief that they'll be viewed as such cool teachers that they won't have to worry about disciplinary issues. Progressive approaches to teaching often encourage such an attitude by glossing over classroom management concerns, or by suggesting that if teachers simply come up with engaging lessons, management issues will largely take care of themselves. But my experience is that, in many urban classrooms, it's far more complicated than that, and if you're blindsided by serious discipline concerns, as I was, you can feel compelled to adopt draconian corrective measures.

The point is not to obsess over order and control as a beginning teacher, but to go in with a specific plan of action rather than vague notions about "freedom." If you really want to have an open and democratic environment in your classroom, you have to be thoughtful and purposeful in creating structures that support it.

These details of practice—creating an environment for learning, rethinking your curriculum, and fostering a democratic community—can all provide opportunities for bringing a social justice perspective into your classroom. But it's also possible to become lost in the everyday details, to get so caught up in the immediacy of your teaching that you don't pay enough attention to its larger contexts. Indeed, the undertow may pull you in such a direction: Professional development seminars and inservice workshops frequently encourage tunnel vision in new teachers by focusing narrowly on specific methods, strategies, or one-size-fits-all approaches.

That's why it's important to remind yourself that methods and other practical matters mean little unless placed within a social, political, and economic context. For beginning teachers at urban schools—especially for those who are coming in as "outsiders" to the communities where they're teaching—committing to continued efforts at self-education on issues of race, culture, and poverty is vital (and also something you're not likely to get at an inservice). Middle-class teachers who lack a personal understanding of poverty and the many ways it can impact children, families, and neighborhoods need to do all they can to increase their awareness. Likewise, white teachers need to work hard to learn about the cultural histories and current struggles of their students of color and, at the same time, to examine their own privilege.

Angela Valenzuela, a professor at the University of Texas at Austin, has written that "a community's best interests are served by those who possess an unwavering respect for the cultural integrity" of the people in that community. Clearly, that requires sincere and sustained effort on the part of "outsider" teachers, but it's far from impossible.

Holding On to Hope

No matter what you do to buoy yourself as a new teacher, you're almost certain to have moments—maybe quite a few of them—when you question the value and effectiveness of what you're doing. One of the most persistent early challenges for a socially conscious teacher—at least it was for me—is fighting the feeling that your work isn't making a difference, or at least not the sort of difference you'd imagined. When your goals are expansive and hopeful, when you believe that teaching is potentially a world-changing act, it can become discouraging to feel continually as if your efforts are falling far short of that vision. As one young teacher I know put it: "You feel like you should be seeing lightbulbs going off in kids' heads every day, like they're suddenly seeing the world differently. But a lot of times, you think, 'this whole week—nothing! I'm not teaching for social justice!'"

At times like those, the undertow pulls in the direction of fatalism, despair, and emotional disengagement. It beckons you to stop trying so hard, to be more "realistic" about the kids you teach, and to abandon your belief that public schools can be transformed in a meaningful or lasting way. Resisting that suffocating pull—and holding on to hope instead—requires a delicate balancing act: acknowledging the grim systemic realities and personal limitations you face as a teacher, but at the same time recommitting yourself to working toward something better. You have to forgive yourself for your failings, then turn around and try to use them to refocus and re-energize your teaching the next day.

You also have to allow yourself to appreciate the good moments that do take place in your classroom—no matter how small they may seem in the grand scheme of things. In the words of the poet and novelist Audre Lorde: "Even the smallest victory is never to be taken for granted. Each victory must be applauded, because it is so easy not to battle at all, to just accept and call that acceptance inevitable." I think every new teacher should have that quote taped to her desk, her classroom door, her rearview mirror, her refrigerator, her alarm clock—to any spot where she might need a little extra strength for the journey.

Becoming a teacher is a journey, after all—one in which you're always learning. One thing I learned while writing this piece is that there's actually no such thing as an undertow. The force of water that pulls you down the beach is called a longshore current, and the one that pulls you out to sea is known as a rip current. Undertow, it turns out, is a colloquialism. Considering that my mother was born on a farm in Georgia and raised in rural Kentucky, it makes perfect sense that that's the term she's always used. Longshore currents and rip currents will probably always be "the undertow" to me.

I learned one more thing, too. If you ever find yourself caught in a real rip current, the best approach is not to try to swim directly against it: You'll exhaust yourself, and the current's force will end up pulling you out anyway. Instead, say those who are knowledgeable in the science of wave motion, you should avoid panicking, swim with the current for a little while, and eventually you'll be free.

The undertow of schools, in my experience, doesn't release teachers from its pull quite so easily. Still, burnout being what it is, there is something to be said for new teachers not trying to fight it at every turn. The best advice, I think, is to choose your battles early on, pace yourself, swim with the current when you have to, and never lose sight of that spot on the shore.

Reference
To Teach: The Journey of a Teacher, by Bill Ayers (New York: Teachers College Press, 1993).

How Jury Duty Saved My Career

by Stephanie Walters

I was so happy with my room. It looked great, if I did say so myself. The word wall was up, the 2nd graders' nametags were all taped down, the first-day activities were all set out.

My teaching partner and I had met several times over the summer to create our plan for the new school year. We were both first-year teachers but we had become really good friends during the time we'd spent together planning our curriculum, and we were really looking forward to meeting and greeting our group of 30 kids.

Randall Enos

We were in our room the day before our students were to arrive, rehearsing, when all my plans went straight out the window.

"Ms. Walters, I need to see you," the voice of our principal said over the PA system. Even as a teacher, being summoned to the principal's office made my heart sink a little.

It sank even more at her office. She told me that due to funding problems, our school couldn't afford to put two teachers in the 2nd-grade classroom. And we hadn't been able to fill our opening in 5th grade. I was now assigned to teach 5th grade.

I was completely dumbfounded. In an instant I saw my diligent work for an entire summer erased. I had invested so many hours in creating a warm, nurturing environment conducive to learning and a well-rounded, appropriate curriculum—for 2nd graders! I had nothing prepared for 5th graders. And they would be arriving tomorrow!

"So what now?" I asked my principal.

"I think you should go up to your new room and get ready for the students," she said, handing me a class list. She told me to work as a team with the other fifth-grade teacher. As I left she added: "Ms. Walters, this will be good for you. It's good to learn flexibility early in your career."

Before that meeting I had been an energetic and eager new teacher, facing a tremendous new challenge, yes, but with a plan in my head and a friend and colleague by my side in the classroom.

Now I was alone, and utterly unprepared. I suddenly felt tired, and scared.

An Audience with "the Queen"

I made my way to "my" room, opened the door and was totally depressed by what I saw. It was naked: nothing on the walls, not a pencil or a single sheet of paper in sight. The maintenance crew had stacked up the desks in one corner when they cleaned the carpets and they were still there in a big, looming pile.

I walked into the room in a fog. I couldn't help thinking about the 2nd-grade classroom I had just left, and all the time and effort I had spent setting it up. I was supposed to start all over. And the kids were coming tomorrow.

I thought I'd start by arranging the room and making nametags. I looked at the class list. Only a handful of the 25 students were reading at or above grade level. Eight of them were students with special needs. I looked at the birth dates: Three had been retained. I really do have my work cut out for me, I thought. Can I do this?

I decided the nametags could wait. First I would introduce myself to my new teaching teammate, the other 5th-grade teacher. Maybe she could help me get started. She was known around our school as "the Queen." She was a good teacher and the principal often raved about her creative ideas in the classroom. But I had learned quickly that the Queen was regarded with great suspicion and cynicism by more than a few teachers in the building. They thought she was arrogant and treated people, students and teachers alike, with disdain. "Steer clear of the Queen," one colleague had warned me. "She's poison."

Unfortunately, this was not an option now. She was officially my partner.

I crossed the hall, knocked on her door, and opened it. Her room was like day to my new room's night. Every wall was covered with brightly colored posters and charts. Her desks were neatly arranged and she had first-day activities ready and waiting for her students. She was leaning against her desk and smiled pleasantly as I walked in.

"Hi, Sandy," I said. "I just wanted to let you know I'm going to be the new teacher in the other 5th-grade room. And I thought you might have some tips for me."

VOICES
FROM THE CLASSROOM

"Teaching is full of successes and failures. Ultimately, although I spent sleepless nights worrying about my mistakes, I learned far more from my failures. You are going to fail throughout your teaching career. If you're not making mistakes, it means that you're not taking risks— you're not attempting new curriculum, new strategies. When you fail you have to reflect on what happened and learn from it."

—Linda Christensen

"Oh, yeah, sure," she said, beckoning me in. She seemed nice enough. She told me about how she was setting up her room, what her standards were for her class, and what she would be doing with her students during the first few days. Then she gave me some puzzle sheets that my kids could do. "In downtime," she suggested. I was starting to think I had this woman all wrong.

We had been talking for a while when she looked at her watch. "Oh, it's getting late and I have to pick my son up from my mom's," she said as she picked up the phone. "Let me just see if I can stay longer. . . . Hi, Mom, can I come and get Jake a little later? I have to stay late helping the new person in the other 5th-grade room. Yeah, she isn't really a teacher yet. . . ."

She continued talking to her mom but I have no idea what she said. All I could hear was the blood pumping in my ears. I wasn't really a teacher? What kind of crack was that? I wanted to pull the phone out of her hand, take her by the wrist and march her down to see my beautiful 2nd-grade classroom—the room that used to be mine, anyway. OK, I wanted to tell her, I'm not ready to teach 5th grade, but that's because I was transferred to the classroom across the hall from yours 20 minutes ago. It's not my fault.

But I didn't make a scene. Instead I sat there for a while longer, waiting for my next chance to escape without being too rude. Finally I headed back to my room, clutching my puzzle sheets, to start unstacking desks and to figure out what to do next.

"This Is Stupid!"

"Michael, Darrin, stop it right now!" I yelled.

It was two months later. The class was supposed to be working on an art project for open house. Soon two of my more active boys had begun to fling paint at each other. Sadly, this was nothing new. Michael and Darrin were constantly pestering other students and each other.

Any group project spelled danger. I had tried a number of times to put my students into cooperative groups, but they always degenerated into little nests of squabbling kids that didn't get much work done. Instead I'd taken to having the kids do individual exercises, which meant stacks and stacks of papers to correct at the end of every day.

In an effort to restore order I told the kids we were done with the art project and tried to get them working on response logs for a book we were reading. Anthony sat at his desk and refused to do any work. Mark also refused, and was very vocal about it. "This is stupid!" he said.

"Is there something else you want to do?" I asked him. I thought maybe I could engage Mark by tapping into something he would enjoy. But he was having none of it. "Nothing you could do," he snapped. "I hate this school and I hate this class. I want Miss Sheffer back!"

I'd heard that refrain before. Many of my students had been in Miss Sheffer's class in 4th grade, after they'd spent 3rd grade with a teacher who called them names and insulted them. Miss Sheffer had been much nicer to them. But she had left before the school year ended, only to be replaced by sub after sub. Pretty soon it became a game for kids: How quickly could they run the new teacher out of the room?

I was determined not to let them do the same to me. But I was having problems. Why weren't my small-group activities working? Was I doing something wrong? I refused to give in to the cynical notion that the kids in my room were too wild to teach. But what could I do?

Now Mark was up and fighting again. I had to call the office and have him removed. During the commotion the Queen suddenly appeared in my doorway.

"Room 20, you have disturbed my class's silent reading," she said sharply. "What are you doing in here?" She surveyed the room, finally fixing her stare on me. "We'd appreciate your help so that we can read our books," she said. I wanted to melt into the floor.

Many times during the past two months I'd found myself running a race at the end of the school day, to get my kids on the bus and beat a retreat to the ladies' room before letting go of the tears that had been building all day.

As the Queen turned on her heel and marched back to her own classroom, I knew today would be no different.

This was not the kind of input from colleagues I had been hoping for. Despite the principal's decree that the Queen and I form a team, I'd gotten very little support from her. There had been a few more stacks of puzzle sheets, but that was about it.

The school district had assigned me a mentor as well, an experienced teacher designated to provide support. I was one of perhaps 20 teachers she was driving from school to school to see. And although she'd been sympathetic, she hadn't been much help with my classroom practice either. It was November, and so she was bringing me handouts about the first Thanksgiving to pass around, with cute little cartoons of turkeys and Pilgrims. We hadn't had a single substantial discussion about teaching. I was still figuring this stuff out for myself.

I was not feeling well. I was tired all the time and I'd been sniffling for a couple of weeks, fighting a pitched battle with some kind of bug. I was always stuffed up and had a hard time hearing the kids. Plus, to make matters worse, now I was losing my voice. But I never dreamed of taking a sick day or making an doctor's appointment. I had not left my class with a substitute, ever. I was too afraid of what they would do.

I was arriving at school at 7 every morning, staying until 6, then going home to tackle an endless stack of individual worksheets. I never got them all done at school. Even when my kids were at art or gym the constant interruptions—from PA announcements to well-meaning colleagues who just wanted to drop by and chat—always kept me from making much headway.

I was always lugging stacks of papers home to correct on the kitchen table. For dinner I'd grab something out of the fridge or cook up a batch of popcorn and eat as I worked. At some point I'd push the papers aside and go to bed, inevitably feeling that I was still behind, and falling behind further still. And then the alarm would go off the next morning and I'd start all over again.

That night as I left school, I tried to take stock. Why was I such a bomb at this teaching thing? Why couldn't I get these kids to respond? And the big one: Why was I still hanging on?

As I drove home, I decided to quit. It's time to admit I'm in over my head, I thought. Give it up. Get a job as a political organizer, or maybe just go back to being a teacher's assistant. Let someone else take the lead in the classroom.

I got home, dumped the mail from my mailbox onto the kitchen table unread, and managed to get undressed before I dropped into bed. My mind was made up. I'd resign tomorrow.

The Letter

I woke up feeling not at all refreshed and began the familiar routine: shower, coffee, worry. Already my mind was racing: Who would get into a fight on the bus and show up in a bad mood? Who would mouth off to me, and how should I respond? My stomach swiftly twisted into all its familiar knots. Even knowing I was going to quit didn't temper my morning dread.

I slumped into a kitchen chair with my coffee cup and glanced down at the pile of mail I had tossed on the table the night before. There was a very official-looking envelope peeking out from under the credit card offers. "Official Jury Summons" was printed on the front.

Jury duty. I was being called for jury duty. A two-day commitment. Two days away from my classroom.

As I examined the summons I thought things over. I knew I could probably get out of serving, but I decided not to try. Somehow leaving the school for a few days to do my civic duty was easier to justify than, say, leaving to go see a doctor about my stuffed-up head. It seemed less selfish, I guess. Besides, I told myself, I'm ready to quit. Maybe jury duty will buy me some time away from the job to rethink my options.

It was a week before my time to serve came up, a week during which all the same terrible things happened to me at school: kids fighting, papers piling up, that sting of failure dogging my steps, the tears welling up inside me as I made my way through the day. I didn't really think two days away from school would change my mind about quitting. But I resolved to hang in there and see what jury duty would bring. Just be patient, I told myself, and get this week over with.

An Amazing Day

The day finally came. I parked in the special free garage for jurors, walked into the courthouse and headed through the doors marked "Jurors Only." It was the first time in months I'd felt like I was being treated special.

I gave my summons to the attendant and she told me to have a seat, they would be calling me shortly. I found a chair and dropped my bulging briefcase next to it with a thud. It was crammed with uncorrected tests and answer sheets I was determined to finish during the next two days.

I settled into my chair and looked around at my fellow jurors-to-be. Some were reading novels, a couple were knitting. One man was doing a crossword. I felt a surge of jealousy. I've always loved crosswords, but I couldn't remember the last time I'd done one. I should be doing a crossword puzzle right now instead of correcting these papers, I thought.

I opened my briefcase and got started. And then, an amazing thing happened. As the wheels of justice turned slowly around me, leaving me completely alone, I corrected every single paper in my case. It took a couple of hours but I never felt overwhelmed. I just did it. When I was done I sat there, trying to figure out why my work hadn't once come this easily since the school year began.

I realized this was the first time I had been able to spend a significant chunk of time grading papers early in the day, instead of trying to tack the chore on to the end of 11 grinding hours at school. And there had been no distractions, no PA system going off every few minutes, no friendly visitors looking to chew the fat.

I was done with my schoolwork! I felt positively giddy as I got up from my chair to get a newspaper. A newspaper! My chance to do a crossword had come a lot sooner than I'd thought.

The paper kept me occupied until lunch. And then an even more amazing thing happened. When I came back to the waiting room I was told my services would no longer be required. My obligation had been met. I was free to go. I had a day and a half to myself.

Walking back to my car, I literally did not know what to do.

I briefly considered going back to school. Maybe I should check on my room, see how the substitute was doing. Or maybe I could sneak in, find some more student work to bring home and sneak out again.

But no, something was happening to me. As I hefted my briefcase full of graded work, I felt some of my old confidence coming back. For the first time in a while I had some spring in my step. I decided I needed some time to think about this, to figure out what had been missing in my life these past few months, and how to get it back.

So instead of going back to work I went home, changed my clothes and took a walk. It was only for an hour, but I savored every stride of it. I felt free. As the knots in my leg muscles beginning to unbunch, I realized just how tight my whole body had become, how little exercise I'd had. I hadn't been getting out like this. Lately all my running had been done on the treadmill my principal dropped me onto the day I was reassigned. I had been pumping away as hard as I could, head down, all alone, afraid to slow down or look around, and never seeming to get anywhere. It had gotten so bad that I'd been ready to quit teaching altogether.

Now, feeling a little looser and a lot less anxious, I realized I could stick it out. I had gotten back in touch with some of my strength. I didn't have to leave teaching. Instead I needed to figure out what was wrong and work on that.

Looking back it seems crazy that jury duty made such a big difference in my life path. But that's how it happened. If I hadn't found that summons in my mail that morning, I would have walked straight into the principal's office and quit.

A New Game Plan

Five years later I was still a teacher, still hanging in there, even feeling proud of myself most days for the job I was doing. I kept my promise to myself to get off that tread-mill and stay off.

Here—with the benefit of 20/20 hindsight—are some things I found it helpful to think about, things that I believe can help you stay in teaching for the long haul:

Take care of yourself. Shortly after jury duty I finally took a day off and went to the doctor for my stuffed-up head, and learned I had a double ear infection. A few doses of antibiotics later, I was as good as new. I shudder when I think of how long I went without seeing a doctor, all those days I struggled to hear what my kids were saying, what might have happened if I'd never been treated. That episode taught me: Pay attention to your body. If you're sick, get the treatment you need. Rest when you're tired.

Eat right. Popcorn is not a well-balanced dinner. It doesn't give your body what it needs. Neither does a steady diet of fat-laden fast food. You don't need to indulge in a macrobiotic seven-course meal every day, but you do need to make sure you're eating properly, getting enough protein, and consuming enough fruits and veggies to supply your body with what it needs to keep running properly. A few small changes in how you deal with food can go a long way. I started making big pots of beans or soup on Sunday to take for lunch during the week. It's a habit I continue today.

Get some exercise. You don't have to run marathons, but putting your body to work on a regular basis will help you release the tension that builds up during the workday.

Pace yourself on the job. Teaching is hard work, and even when you feel you're on the right track the hours can be long, the tasks many. Unless you consciously maintain a reasonable pace for yourself, you won't last long. Don't spend forever at school. Set reasonable limits and when you reach them, stop. That way you'll be strong when it's time to come back.

Don't expect to be perfect. Teaching is not easy. You're going to make mistakes. The trick is to learn from them, and to be forgiving of yourself as you do. It's part of the job to examine your teaching practice, maybe even fret over it a little, in pursuit of doing it better tomorrow. I have friends who've been teaching for 20 years, and I see them struggling in ways I once thought only new teachers struggled: there's one kid in their class they're not sure how to reach, they wonder if they're on target with the message they're trying to deliver, etc. That kind of reflection comes with the territory. Don't let it consume you, but don't fear it either.

Find people who can help you. I realize now that one of my biggest problems when I started teaching 5th grade was a lack of professional support. I got puzzle sheets from the Queen and cute cartoons from my district-assigned mentor, but no real insight into what I was doing in the classroom and what was going wrong.

Now I know there was a reason all my cooperative learning activities failed: No one had ever taught my students how to work cooperatively. And I wasn't teaching them how either, just assigning them work to do as a group and turning them loose. What I needed to do was back up and spend some time with the kids on the specifics of working in a group, and to let them practice the necessary skills. Then maybe my group art projects wouldn't have turned into paint fights quite so quickly. And I wouldn't have felt the need to hand out so many individual worksheets, which left me staggering under the load of all those papers to correct.

As a new teacher, I was not prepared to address practice-related questions like that. Simply put, I didn't know what I didn't know. And I wasn't getting any insight from the people assigned to help me. I found I couldn't rely on them. I needed to seek people out, pick their brains, see what they could teach me.

Start with the other teachers in your building. Contact your union to see what kinds of support or enrichment they might offer. And seek out kindred spirits and talented teachers elsewhere in your community. Are there groups doing political work, for example, that are likely to attract other teachers who might share your interests? Does your union offer professional development activities?

Keep your classroom work relevant to kids' lives. Students are a lot more likely to act up when they're bored. You can address this somewhat by paying attention to your teaching methods: For example, don't just stand by the board and lecture all day. But another critical question to ask yourself frequently is: Are my students learning things that are meaningful to them? Are they being asked to memorize dry facts they will never need again after this class? Or are they being given a chance to learn about things that matter, that have bearing on their lives? This is a very big topic, which is discussed in more depth elsewhere in this book (for example, see "The Best Discipline Is Good Curriculum," page 241, and "Curriculum Is Everything That Happens," page 163). Keep it in mind as you work on curriculum and how you deliver it.

Do what you can to improve new teacher training. Once you've found your feet, start working with your school or your union to ensure that other new teachers get meaningful training and support. Although it's true my mentor wasn't much help, she could have been, if she'd been able and willing to engage me in a real discussion of my teaching practice. Find out who is offering enrichment programs for teachers in your district and let them know what you would find helpful, and what kind of support would help you most in examining and improving your practice.

All students' names have been changed.

Chapter 2

Creating Classroom
Community

Building Community from Chaos

by Linda Christensen

Iread a book on teaching that left me feeling desolate because the writer's vision of a joyful, productive classroom did not match the chaos I faced daily. My students straggled in, still munching on Popeye's chicken, wearing headphones, and generally acting surly because of some incident in the hall during break, a fight with their parents, a teacher, a boyfriend or girlfriend. During this particular year, more than any previous year, they failed to finish the writing started in class or read the novel or story I assigned as homework. Many suffered from pains much

Joseph Blough

bigger than I could deal with: homelessness, pregnancy, the death of a brother, sister, friend, cousin due to street violence, the nightly spatter of guns in their neighborhoods, the decay of a society.

For too many days during the first quarter, I felt like a prison guard trying to bring order and kindness to a classroom where students laughed over the beating of a man, made fun of a classmate who was going blind, and mimicked the way a Vietnamese girl spoke until they pushed her into silence.

Each September I have this optimistic misconception that I'm going to create a compassionate, warm, safe place for students in the first days of class because my recollection is based on the final quarter of the previous year. In the past, that atmosphere did emerge in a shorter time span. But the students were more homogeneous, and we were living in somewhat more secure and less violent times. Although students shared the tragedies of divorce and loss of friendships, their class talk was less often disrupted by the pressure cooker of society—and I was more naive and rarely explored those areas. We were polite to each other as we kept uncomfortable truths at bay.

Now, I realize that classroom community isn't always synonymous with warmth and harmony. Politeness is often a veneer mistaken for understanding, when in reality it masks uncovered territory, the unspeakable pit that we turn from because we know the anger and pain that dwells there. At Jefferson High School in Portland, Ore., where the interplay of race, class, and gender creates a constant background static, it's important to remind myself that real community is forged out of struggle. Students won't always agree on issues, and the fights, arguments, tears, and anger are the crucible from which a real community grows.

Still, I hate discord. When I was growing up, I typically gave up the fight and agreed with my sister or mother so that a reconciliation could be reached. I can remember running to my "safe" spot under my father's overturned rowboat whenever anger ran loose in our house.

Too often in those days, I was in the middle of that anger, and there was no safe spot. My first impulse was to make everyone sit down, be polite, and listen to each other, a great goal that I've come to realize doesn't happen easily. Topics like racism and homophobia are avoided in most classrooms, but they seethe like open wounds. When there is an opening for discussion, years of anger and pain surface. But students haven't been taught how to talk with each other about these painful matters.

I can't say that I found definitive answers, but as the year ended, I knew some of the mistakes I made. I also found a few constants: To become a community, students must learn to live in someone else's skin; understand the parallels of hurt, struggle, and joy across class and culture lines; and work for change. For that to happen, students need more than an upbeat, supportive teacher; they need a curriculum that teaches them how to empathize with others.

Sharing Power and Passion

Before I could operate on that level, I had to find a way to connect with my students. Ironically, violence was the answer. That year none of the get-acquainted activities that I count on to build a sense of community worked in my fourth-block class. Students didn't want to get up and interview each other. They didn't want to write about their names. They didn't want to be in the class, and they didn't want any jive-ass let's-get-to-know-each-other games or activities. Mostly, our 90-minute blocks were painfully long as I failed daily to elicit much response other than groans, sleep, or anger. It's hard to build community when you feel like you're "hoisting elephants through mud" as my friend Carolyn says. I knew it was necessary to break through their apathy and uncover something that made these students care enough to talk, to read, to write, to share—even to get angry.

My fourth-block class first semester was Senior English, a tracked class where most of the students were short on credits to graduate—as T. J. said, "We're not even on the five-year plan"—but long on humor and potential. They came in with their fists up and their chins cocked. They had attitudes. Many of them already had histories with each other.

To complicate matters, our year opened with a storm of violence in the city. The brother of a Jefferson student was shot and killed. Two girls were injured when random bullets were fired on a bus. A birthday party at a local restaurant was broken up when gunfire sprayed the side of the restaurant. So violence was on the students' minds. I learned that I couldn't ignore the toll the outside world was taking on my students. Rather than pretending that I could close my door in the face of their mounting fears, I needed to use that information to reach them.

In the first days, the only activity that aroused interest was when they wrote about their history as English students—what they liked, what they hated, and what they wanted to learn this year. Many of these students skulked in the low track classes and they were angry—not at tracking, because they weren't aware that another kind of education might be possible, but at the way their time had been wasted on meaningless activity. "The teacher would put a word on the board and then make us see how many words we could make out of the letters. Now what does that prepare me for?" Larry asked. But they also hated reading novels and talking about them because novels "don't have anything to do with our lives." The other constant in many of their written responses was that they felt stupid.

For the first time, they got excited. I knew what they didn't want: worksheets, sentence combining, reading novels and discussing them, writing about "stuff we don't care about." But I didn't know what to teach them. I needed to engage them because they were loud, unruly, and out of control otherwise. But how? I decided to try the "raise the expectations" approach and use a curriculum I designed for my contemporary literature and society class, which receives college credit.

During those initial days of listening to these seniors and trying to read the novel *Thousand Pieces of Gold*, by Ruthanne Lum McCunn, I discovered that violence aroused my students. Students weren't thrilled with the book; in fact, they weren't reading it. I'd plan a 90-minute lesson around the reading and dialogue journal they were supposed to be keeping, but only a few students were prepared. Most didn't even attempt to lie about the fact that they weren't reading and clearly weren't planning on it.

In an attempt to get them involved in the novel, I read aloud an evocative passage about the unemployed peasants sweeping through the Chinese countryside pillaging, raping, and grabbing what was denied them through legal employment. Suddenly students saw their own lives reflected back at them through Chen, whose anger at losing his job and ultimately his family led him to become an outlaw. Chen created a new family with this group of bandits. Students could relate: Chen was a gang member. I had stumbled on a way to interest my class. The violence created a contact point between the literature and the students' lives.

This connection, this reverberation across cultures, time, and gender challenged the students' previous notion that reading and talking about novels didn't have relevance for them. They could empathize with the Chinese but also explore those issues in their own lives.

This connection also created space to unpack the assumption that all gangs are bad. Chen wasn't born violent. He didn't start out robbing and killing. Lalu, the novel's main character, remembered him as a kind man who bought her candy. He changed after he lost his job and his family starved.

Similarly, kids in gangs don't start out violent or necessarily join gangs to "pack gats" and shoot it out in drive-bys. Because the tendency in most schools is to simultaneously deny and outlaw the existence of gangs, kids rarely talk critically about them.

A few years ago, scholar Mike Davis wrote an article analyzing the upsurge of gang activity in Los Angeles. He found it linked to the loss of union wage jobs. I hadn't explored Portland's history to know whether our situation is similar to Los Angeles', but I suspected economic parallels. When I raised Davis' research, kids were skeptical. They saw other factors: the twin needs of safety and belonging.

Our discussion of gangs broke the barrier. Students began writing about violence in their own lives and their neighborhoods. T.J. explained his own brushes with violence:

> [T]he summer between my sophomore and junior years, some of my friends were getting involved in a new gang called the Irish Mob. . . . My friends were becoming somebody, someone who was known wherever they went. The somebody who I wanted to be. . . . During the next couple of weeks we were involved in six fights, two stabbings, and one drive-by shooting. We got away on all nine cases. The next Saturday night my brother was shot in a drive-by. The shooters were caught the same night.

Kari wrote that she joined a gang when she was searching for family. Her father lost his job; her mother was forced to work two jobs to pay the rent. Kari assumed more responsibility at home: cooking dinner, putting younger brothers and sisters to bed, and cleaning. While at middle school, Kari joined the Crips. She said at first it was because she liked the "family" feel. They wore matching clothes. They shared a language and nicknames. In a neighborhood that had become increasingly violent, they offered her protection. She left the gang after middle school because she was uncomfortable with the violence.

Students were surprised to learn that Hua, a recent immigrant from Vietnam, was also worried about her brother who had joined a gang. Her classmates were forced to reevaluate their initial assessments of her. Although she had seemed like an outsider, a foreigner, her story made a bond between them.

At first, I worried that inviting students to write about violence might glorify it. It didn't turn out that way. Students were generally adamant that they'd made poor choices when they were involved in violent activities. As T. J. states in his essay: "I wanted to be known wherever I went. . . . But I went about it all wrong and got mixed in. . . . It was nothing I had hoped for. Sure I was known and all that, but for all the wrong reasons."

More often students shared their fears. Violence was erupting around them and they felt out of control. They needed to share that fear.

Through the topic of violence I captured their interest, but I wanted them to critique the violence rather than just describe it. I had hoped to build a community of inquiry where we identified a common problem and worked to understand it by examining history and our lives. That didn't happen. It was still early in the year, and students were so absorbed in telling their stories and listening to others it was difficult to pull them far enough away to analyze the situation. I didn't have enough materials that went beyond accusations or sensationalism, but the topic itself also presented practical and ethical problems, especially around issues of safety and confidentiality.

I want to be clear: Bringing student issues into the room does not mean giving up teaching the core ideas and skills of the class; it means I need to use the energy of their connections to drive us through the content.

For example, students still had to write a literary essay. But they could use their lives as well as Lalu's to illustrate their points. Students scrutinized their issues through the lens of a larger vision as James did when he compared the violence in his life to the violence in Lalu's:

> Lalu isn't a gang member, but some of the folks, or should I say, some of the enemies she came in contact with reminded me of my enemies. Bandits in the story represented the worst foes of my life. In some ways bandits and gangs are quite similar. One would be the reason for them turning to gang life. Neither of them had a choice. It was something forced upon them by either educational problems or financial difficulties. It could have been the fact that their families were corrupt or no love was shown. Whatever the reasons, it was a way of survival.

Finding the heartbeat of a class isn't always easy. I must know what's happening in the community and the lives of my students. If they're consumed by the violence in the neighborhood or the lack of money in their house, I'm more likely to succeed in teaching them if I intersect their preoccupation.

Building community means taking into account the needs of the members of that community. I can sit students in a circle, play getting-to-know-each-other games until the cows come home, but if what I am teaching in the class holds no interest for the students, I'm just holding them hostage until the bell rings.

A Curriculum of Empathy

As a critical teacher I encourage students to question everyday acts or ideas that they take for granted (see "Unlearning the Myths That Bind Us" and "Teaching Standard English: Whose Standard?" in *Reading, Writing, and Rising Up: Teaching About Social Justice and the Power of the Written Word*). But I also teach them to enter the lives of characters in literature, history, or real life whom they might dismiss or misunderstand. I don't want their first reaction to difference to be laughter or withdrawal. I try to teach them how to empathize with people whose circumstances might differ from theirs. Empathy is key in community building.

I choose literature that intentionally makes students look beyond their own world. In the class I co-taught with Bill Bigelow, we used an excerpt from Ronald Takaki's *A Different Mirror* about Filipino writer Carlos Bulosan. Bulosan wrote, "I am an exile in America." He described the treatment he received, good and bad. He wrote of being cheated out of wages at a fish cannery in Alaska, being refused housing because he was Filipino, being tarred and feathered and driven from town.

We asked students to respond to the reading by keeping a dialogue journal. Dirk, who is African American, wrote: "He's not the only one who feels like an exile in America. Some of us who were born here feel that way too." As he continued reading, he was surprised that some of the acts of violence Bulosan encountered were similar to those endured by African Americans. In his essay on immigration, he chose to write about the parallels between Bulosan's life and the experiences he's encountered:

> When I was growing up I thought African Americans were the only ones who went through oppression. In the reading, "In the Heart of Filipino America," I found that Filipinos had to go through a lot when coming to America. I can relate with the stuff they went through because my ancestors went through sort of the same thing.

Dirk went on to describe the parallels in housing discrimination, lynching, name calling, being cheated out of wages that both Filipinos and African Americans lived through.

Besides reading and studying about "others," we wanted students to come face to face with people they usually don't meet as a way of breaking down their preconceived ideas about people from other countries. For example, during this unit, we continued to hear students classify all Asians as "Chinese." In the halls, we heard students mimic the way Vietnamese students spoke. When writing about discrimination, another student confessed that she discriminated against the Mexican students at our school. Our students were paired with English-as-second-language students who had emigrated from another country—Vietnam, Laos, Cambodia, Eritrea, Mexico, Guatemala, Ghana. They interviewed their partner and wrote a profile of the student to share in class. Students were moved by their partners' stories. One student whose brother had been killed at the beginning of the year was paired with a student whose sister was killed fighting in Eritrea. He connected to her loss and was amazed at her strength. Others were appalled at how these students had been mistreated at their school. Many students later used the lives of their partners in their essays on immigration.

Besides making immigration a contemporary rather than a historical topic, students heard the sorrow their fellow students felt at leaving "home." In our "curriculum of empathy," we forced our class to see these students as individuals rather than the ESL students or "Chinese" students, or an undifferentiated mass of Mexicans.

A curriculum of empathy puts students inside the lives of others. By writing interior monologues (see "Promoting Social Imagination" in *Rethinking Our Classrooms, Volume 1*), acting out improvisations, taking part in role plays (see "Role Plays: Show Don't Tell" in *Rethinking Our Classrooms, Volume 1*), and creating fiction stories about historical events, students learn to develop understanding about people whose culture, race, gender, or sexual orientation differs from theirs.

"Things changed for me this year," Wesley wrote in his end-of-the-year evaluation. "I started respecting my peers. My attitude has changed against homosexuals and whites." Similarly, Tyrelle wrote, "I learned a lot about my own culture as an African American but also about other people's cultures. I never knew Asians suffered. When we wrote from different characters in movies and stories I learned how it felt to be like them."

Sharing Personal Stories

Building community begins when students get inside the lives of others in history, in literature, or down the hallway, but they also learn by exploring their own lives and coming to terms with the people they are "doing time" with in the classroom. Micere Mugo, a Kenyan poet, recently said, "Writing can be a lifeline, especially when your existence has been denied, especially when you have been left on the margins, especially when your life and process of growth have been subjected to attempts at strangulation." For many of our students their stories have been silenced in school. Their histories have been marginalized to make room for "important" people, their interests and worries passed over so I can teach Oregon history or *The Scarlet Letter*.

To develop empathy, students need to learn about each others' lives as well as reflect on their own. When they hear personal stories, classmates become real instead of cardboard stereotypes: rich white girl, basketball-addicted black boy, brainy Asian. Once they've seen how people can hurt, once they've shared pain and laughter, they can't so easily treat people as objects to be kicked or beaten or called names. When students' lives are taken off the margins, they don't feel the same need to put someone else down.

Any reading or history lesson offers myriad opportunities for this kind of activity. I find points of conflict, struggle, change, or joy and create an assignment to write about a parallel time in their lives. We've had students write about times they've been forced to move, been discriminated against or discriminated against someone else, changed an attitude or action, worked for change, lost a valuable possession. Obviously, losing a treasured item does not compare to the Native Americans' loss of their land, but telling the story does give students a chance to empathize with the loss as well as share a piece of themselves with the class.

When I was a child, my mother took me to the pond in Sequoia Park on Sundays to feed the ducks. They'd come in a great wash of wings and waves while I broke the bread into pieces to throw to them. I loved to watch them gobble up the soggy loaf, but I began noticing how some ducks took more than others. In fact, some ducks were pushed to the side and pecked at. I've noticed the same thing happens in classrooms. Students find someone who they think is weak and attack them. In my fourth-block class, the victim was Jim. He'd been in my class the year before. I'd watched him progress as a writer and thinker. In his end-of-the-year evaluation, he drew a picture of himself as a chef; his writing was the dough. In an essay, he explained how writing was like making bread. He was proud of his achievements as a writer.

In both classes, Jim was a victim. He was going blind because of a hereditary disease. It didn't happen overnight, but he struggled with terror at his oncoming blindness. Because he was steadily losing his eyesight, he was clumsy in the classroom. He couldn't see where he was going. He knocked into people and desks. He accidently overturned piles of books. Students would respond with laughter or anger. Some days he cried silently into the fold of his arms. He told me, "I know the darkness is coming." Several male students in the class made fun of him for crying as well. One day, Amber was in a typically bad mood, hunched inside her too-big coat and snarling at anyone who came near. When Jim bumped her desk on the way to the pencil sharpener and her books and papers tumbled on the floor, she blew up at him for bumbling around the room. Jim apologized profusely and retreated into his shell after her attack.

A few days later I gave an assignment for students to write about their ancestors, their people. First, they read Margaret Walker's poems "For My People" and "Lineage" and others. I told them they could imagine their people as their immediate ancestors, their race, their nationality or gender. Jim wrote:

> *To My People with*
> *Retinitis Pigmentosa*
>
> *Sometimes I hate you*
> *like the disease*
> *I have been plagued with.*
> *I despise the "sight" of you*
> *seeing myself in your eyes.*
> *I see you as if it were you*
> *who intentionally*
> *damned me to darkness.*
> *I sometimes wish*
> *I was not your brother;*
> *that I could stop*
> *the setting of the sun*
> *and wash my hands of you forever*
> *and never look back*
> *except with pity,*
> *but I cannot.*
> *So I embrace you,*
> *the sun continues to set*
> *as I walk into darkness*
> *holding your hand.*

Students were silenced. Tears rolled. Kevin said: "Damn, man. That's hard." Amber apologized to Jim in front of the class. At the end of the year she told me that her encounter with Jim was one of the events that changed her. She learned to stop and think about why someone else might be doing what they're doing instead of immediately jumping to the conclusion that they were trying to annoy her.

My experience is that, given a chance, students will share amazing stories. Students have told me that my willingness to share stories about my life—my father's alcoholism, my family's lack of education, my poor test scores, and many others—opened the way for them to tell their stories. Students have written about rape, sexual abuse, divorce, drug and alcohol abuse. And through their sharing, they make openings to each other. Sometimes a small break. A crack. A passage from one world to the other. And these openings allow the class to become a community.

Students as Activists

Community is also created when students struggle together to achieve a common goal. Sometimes the opportunity spontaneously arises out of the conditions or content of the class, school, or community. During Bill's and my first year teaching together, we exchanged the large student desks in our room with another teacher's smaller desks without consulting our students. We had 40 students in the class, and not all of the big desks fit in the circle. They staged a "stand in" until we returned the original desks. One year our students responded to a negative article in a local newspaper by organizing a march and rally to "tell the truth about Jefferson to the press." During the Columbus quincentenary, my students organized a teach-in about Columbus for classes at Jefferson. Of course, these "spontaneous" uprisings only work if teachers are willing to give over class time for the students to organize, and if they've highlighted times when people in history resisted injustice, making it clear that solidarity and courage are values to be prized in daily life, not just praised in the abstract and put on the shelf.

But most often I have to create situations for students to work outside of the classroom. I want them to connect ideas and action in tangible ways. Sometimes I do this by asking students to take what they have learned and create a project to teach at nearby elementary or middle schools. Students in literature and U.S. history write children's books about abolitionists, the Nez Perce, Chief Joseph, and others. After students critique the media (see "Unlearning the Myths That Bind Us" in *Rethinking Our Classrooms, Volume 1*), they are usually upset by the negative messages children receive, so I have them write and illustrate books for elementary students. They brainstorm positive values they want children to receive, read traditional and contemporary children's books, critique the stories, and write their own. They develop lesson plans to go with their books. For example, before Bev read her book about John Brown she asked, "Has anyone here ever tried to change something you thought was wrong?" After students shared their experiences, she read her book. Students also created writing assignments to go with their books so they could model the writing process.

Students were nervous before their school visits. As they practiced lesson plans and received feedback from their peers, there was much laughter and anticipation. They mimicked "bad" students and asked improper questions that have nothing to do with the children's book: Is she your girlfriend? Why are your pants so baggy? Why does your hair look like that?

When they returned, there were stories to share: children who hugged their knees and begged them to come back; kids who wouldn't settle down; kids who said they couldn't write. My students proudly read the writings that came out of "their" class. They responded thoughtfully to each student's paper.

James, a member of my English 12 class, was concerned by the number of young children who join gangs. He and several other young men wrote stories about gang violence and took them to our neighborhood elementary school. He strode into the class, wrote "gangs" in big letters on the board and sat down. The 5th-grade class was riveted. He and his teaching mates read their stories and then talked with students about gangs. As James wrote after his visit:

> For a grown person to teach a kid is one thing. But for a teenager like myself to teach young ones is another. Kids are highly influenced by peers close to their age or a little older. I'm closer to their age, so they listen to me. . . . Some of these kids that I chatted with had stories that they had been wanting to get off their chest for a long time. . . . When I came to class with my adventures of being a gangster, that gave them an opportunity to open up. Spill guts. [No one] should object to me teaching these shorties about gang life, telling them that it's not all fun and games. It's straight do or die. Kill or be killed.

The seriousness with which the students understand their lives was in sharp contrast to the seeming apathy they displayed at the year's beginning. Through the year, I came to understand that the key to reaching my students and building community was helping students excavate and reflect on their personal experiences, connecting it to the world of language, literature, and society. We moved from ideas to action, perhaps the most elusive objective in any classroom.

Community and activism: These are the goals in every course I teach. The steps we take to reach them are not often in a straight path. We stagger, sidestep, stumble, and then rise to stride ahead again.

References

A Different Mirror: A History of Multicultural America, by Ronald Takaki (New York: Back Bay Books/Little, Brown, and Co. 2008).

"For My People" and "Lineage" in *This is My Century: New and Collected Poems*, by Margaret Walker (Athens, GA: University of Georgia Press, 1989).

Rethinking Our Classrooms, Volume 1 (Milwaukee: Rethinking Schools, 2007).

Thousand Pieces of Gold, by Ruthanne Lum McCunn (Boston: Beacon Press, 1989).

Q/A How can I start building community in my classroom?

Students spend the most of their waking hours in school, a place that can offer them both an education, in the broadest sense of the word, and a sense of belonging within a classroom community—something that can and should begin on their first school day.

Having a routine to follow in the beginning of the day helps students make the transition from home to school and feel secure. Greeting students at the classroom door, for example, can be a powerful way to communicate the message "I am glad you're here." It's also an opportunity to briefly check in with students: A lot could have happened since they left yesterday.

Another powerful routine is the class meeting, a scheduled time when students get to participate in a classwide discussion. This offers students the chance to share something of importance to them, as well as to practice active listening skills when others are sharing. It can also be a time when conflicts within the classroom can be addressed and collectively solved.

Pay attention to how students are seated. Small group seating—desks arranged in clusters instead of long rows—often helps build collaboration. To encourage students to make new friends, many teachers also find it helpful to periodically change the composition of these groups.

Classroom community also can emerge when students have the means to acknowledge transitions. For example, at the end of a unit of study, offer students time to reflect on what went well for them during the unit and challenges they encountered. Let them share their experiences and offer feedback to one another.

Never underestimate your role in helping to create a classroom community. By being honest and authentic with your students, the seeds of trust will be sown, and classroom community can grow and flourish.

—Dale Weiss

'Brown Kids Can't Be in Our Club'

Raising Issues of Race with Young Children

by Rita Tenorio

I sat down one day with seven of the children in my 1st-grade class. It was early in the year and we were getting to know each other. We talked about how we were alike, how we were different. "Our skin is different," one of the children said. I asked everyone to put their hands together on the table, so we could see all the different colors.

One of my African American students, LaRhonda, simply would not. Scowling, she slid her hands beneath the table top, unwilling to have her color compared to the others.

Susan Ruggles

83

It was a reaction I had seen before. I teach at La Escuela Fratney, an ethnically diverse school in a racially mixed working-class Milwaukee neighborhood. My students typically include black kids, white kids, and Latinos. They have many things in common. Recess is their favorite time of day. Friendships are a priority. They want to "belong" to a group and they are very conscious of where they fit in a social sense.

And they all "know" that it is better to be light-skinned than dark-skinned.

Even though my students have only six or seven years of life experience by the time they reach my classroom, the centuries-deep legacies of bias and racism in our country have already made an impact on their lives. I have seen fair-skinned children deliberately change places in a circle if African American children sit down next to them. An English speaker won't play with a Latino child because, he says, "He talks funny." On the playground, a group of white girls won't let their darker-skinned peers join in their games, explaining matter-of-factly: "Brown kids can't be in our club."

As teachers, we have to acknowledge that we live in a racist society and that children typically mirror the attitudes of that society. Between the ages of 2 and 5, children not only become aware of racial differences, but begin to make judgments based on that awareness. They do this even though they may not be able to understand, in an intellectual way, the complexities of race and bias as issues.

Teachers have a responsibility to recognize the influence of racism on themselves and their students. And we can help children learn the skills and strategies they will need to counteract it in their lives. At Fratney, our 1st-grade teams have put those ideas at the center of our practice.

Are They Too Young for This?

Many people would say that children at this age are too young to deal with these serious issues. I too had real questions at first about what was actually possible with young children. Can you have "real" conversations with 6-year-olds about power, privilege, and racism in our society? Can you make them aware of the effects that racism and injustice have in our lives? Can they really understand their role in the classroom community?

The answer to all of these questions is yes. Even very young children can explore and understand the attitudes they bring, and that their classmates bring, to school each day. They have real issues and opinions to share, and many, many questions of their own to ask. And in this way they can begin to challenge some of the assumptions that influence their behavior toward classmates who don't look or talk the same way they do.

Children at this age can explore rules and learn about collecting data, making inferences, and forming conclusions. They can compare and contrast the experiences of people and think about what it means. They can, that is, if they are given the opportunity.

At Fratney, which serves 400 students from kindergarten through 5th grade, we discuss issues of social justice with all of our students. Teachers in our school have developed a series of activities and projects that help us to discuss issues of race and social justice in a meaningful, age-appropriate way. Here are examples of some of the projects done at the early grades:

We strive to build classroom community by learning about each other's lives and families. We ask our students to collect and share information about their families and ancestry. For example, we might talk about how they got their names; how their families came to live in Milwaukee; which holidays they celebrate and how. And at every step we help the children to explore the nature of racial and cultural differences and to overcome simplistic notions of "who's better" or who is "like us" and who isn't. These activities include:

Me Pockets. This is always a class favorite. Each child takes home a letter-sized clear plastic sleeve, the kind used to display baseball cards. Students are asked to fill the pockets with photos, pictures, drawings, or anything else that will help us know more about them and the things that are important in their lives. The pockets are returned within a week and put into a three-ring binder that becomes the favorite classroom book to read and reread.

The individual pockets reflect the cultural and socioeconomic diversity of the families. Some students put lots of photos or computer images in their pockets. Others cut pictures out of magazines or make drawings. Our experience is that every family is anxious to share in some way, and family members take time to help their children develop the project.

If someone doesn't bring their Me Pocket sheet back, the teachers step in to help them to find pictures or make the drawings they need to add their page to the binder.

I'm always amazed at how quickly the children learn the details about each other's lives from this project: who has a pet, who takes dance class, who likes to eat macaroni and cheese. The children know there are differences between them, but they also love to share the things that are alike.

"Look, Rachel has two brothers, just like me."

"I didn't know that Jamal's family likes to camp. We do too!"

Each of the teachers also completes a Me Pocket sheet. The students love looking at the picture of me as a 1st grader, seeing my husband and children, and learning that chocolate cake is my favorite food.

Partner Questions. Each day we take time to teach the social skills of communicating ideas with others and listening to another person's perspective. We use this time to "practice" those skills with role-playing activities and problem-solving situations they or we bring to the group. For example we might ask such questions as: What is the meanest thing anyone has ever said to you? Why do you think some people like to use put-downs? The children take a few minutes to talk about this with a partner. Afterward some are willing to share with the whole group. We might then role-play the situation as a group and look for ways to respond, such as speaking back to insults.

Remembering Someone Special. By the end of October, during the time of Halloween, Día de los Muertos, and All Souls' Day, we learn about how people remember their ancestors and others who have died or who are far away. We set up a table and encourage students to bring in pictures or artifacts to display. They bring a remarkable variety of things: jewelry, a trophy won by a departed relative, a postcard that person sent them, or perhaps the program from a funeral. And they bring many, many stories. Again, the teachers also participate and share stories of those who have gone before us. We get great responses from our students, and from their families.

Let's Talk About Skin. Another important conversation I have with my students focuses on the varieties of skin color we have in our group. Usually when we begin this discussion, some children are uncomfortable about saying "what they are" or describing the color of their skin. In particular, children with very dark skin—like LaRhonda, who would not even put her hands on the table—are often reluctant to join in. Meanwhile, the white kids often boast about being "pink." Though we've never talked about this in class before, there is definitely a strong implication that it is better to be lighter.

Many children are amazed that this topic is put out on the table for discussion. The looks in their eyes, their frequent reluctance to begin the discussion, tell me that this is a very personal topic.

As part of the lesson, we ask the students if they have ever heard anyone say something bad or mean about another person's skin color. The hands shoot up.

"My mom says that you can't trust black people."

"My sister won't talk to the Puerto Rican kids on the bus."

"Mara said that I couldn't play, that I was too black to be her friend."

They continue to raise their hands and this conversation goes on for a while. We talk about ways we've heard others use people's skin color to make fun of them or put them down. We talk about what to do in those situations.

As we continue to discuss issues of race, we teachers often introduce our personal experiences. I tell them about the first time I realized that black and white people were treated differently. I share my experience being one of the few Latinas in my school. And we try to ask questions that really intrigue the students, that invite them to try to look at things with a different perspective, to learn something new about the human experience and be open-minded to that idea: Did your ancestors come from a cold place or a warm place? Do people choose their color? Where do you get your skin color? Is it better to be one color than another? Lots of our conversations revolve around a story or a piece of literature.

With a little work, we can expand this discussion of skin color in ways that incorporate math lessons, map lessons, and other curricular areas. We've done surveys to see how many of our ancestors came from warm places or cold places. We ask children to interview their relatives to find out where the family came from. We create a bulletin board display that we use to compare and learn about the huge variety of places our students' relatives are from. We graph the data of whose family came from warm places, who from cold, who from both, or don't know.

Skin Color and Science. Our class discussions of skin color set the stage for lots of "scientific" observations.

For example, I bring in a large variety of paint chips from a local hardware store. The students love examining and sorting the many shades of beige and brown. It takes a while for them to find the one that is most like their own skin color.

In the story *The Colors of Us*, by Karen Katz, Lena learns from her mother that "brown" is a whole range of colors. Like the characters in the story, we take red and yellow and black and white paint and mix them in various combinations until we've each found the color of our own skin. Then we display our "research" as part of our science fair project.

In another exercise, inspired by Sheila Hamanaka's *All the Colors of the Earth*, students are asked to find words to describe the color of their skin, and to find something at home that matches their skin color. Then we display the pieces of wood and fabric, the little bags of cinnamon and coffee, the dolls and ceramic pieces that match us.

As we continue these explorations, dealing concretely with a topic that so many have never heard discussed in such a manner, students begin to see past society's labels. It is always amazing to children that friends who call themselves "black," for example, can actually have very light skin. Or that children who perceive themselves as "Puerto Rican" can be darker than some of the African American children.

VOICES
FROM THE CLASSROOM

"Racism is reflected in a hierarchy in which beauty, intelligence, worth, and things associated with whiteness are at the top. The school is one site in which this hierarchical arrangement of skin power is confirmed daily. It is also a site where it can be undone."

—Enid Lee, in "Anti-Racist Education: Pulling Together to Close the Gaps," in *Beyond Heroes and Holidays* (Teaching for Change, 2006)

Writing About Our Colors. As children begin to understand the idea of internalizing another's point of view, they can apply that understanding by examining different ideas and alternatives to their own experiences. As they learn to express themselves through reading and writing, they can learn to challenge stereotypes and speak back to unfair behavior and comments.

Once students have had a chance to reflect on skin color, they write about it. Annie wrote: "I like my skin color. It is like peachy cream." James wrote: "My color is the same as my dad's. I think the new baby will have this color too." And Keila wrote: "When I was born, my color was brown skin and white skin mixed together."

When LaRhonda wrote about mixing the colors to match her skin, she said: "We put black, white, red, and yellow [together]. I like the color of my skin." How far she had come since the day she would not show us her hands.

VOICES
FROM THE CLASSROOM

"Anti-racism is a proactive strategy for dismantling racist structures and building racial justice and equality. It must become a perspective that cuts across all subject areas and institutional practices."
—Enid Lee, in "Anti-Racist Education: Pulling Together to Close the Gaps," in *Beyond Heroes and Holidays* (Network of Educators on the Americas, 1998)

Tackling Issues

These activities have an impact. Parents have spoken to us about the positive impression that these activities have made on the children. Many children have taken their first steps toward awareness of race. They are not afraid to discuss it. They now have more ways in which to think about and describe themselves.

Yet these activities are no guarantee that children have internalized anti-racist ideas. So much depends on the other forces in their lives. We are still working on making these activities better: doing them sooner in the year, integrating them into other subjects, deepening the conversations, finding others' stories or activities to support them. Each year's group is different and their experiences and understandings must be incorporated. I learn something new every time. They challenge my consciousness too.

We rely on our schools to be the place for a multicultural, multiracial experience for our children. We want to believe that learning together will help our students to become more understanding and respectful of differences. Yet so often we do not address these issues head-on. It is unlikely that sensitivity and tolerance will develop, that children will bridge the gaps they bring to school from their earliest days, without specific instruction.

Personally, I want to see more than tolerance developed. I want children to see themselves as the future citizens of this city. I want them to gain the knowledge to be successful in this society. Beyond that, though, I want them to understand that they have the power to transform the society.

When students see connections between home and school, when lessons challenge them to look at the issue of race from multiple perspectives, we take the first steps in this process.

All students' names have been changed.

Resources on Race for Young Children

As the 1st-grade teachers at La Escuela Fratney have wrestled with presenting issues of race and culture to our young students in a meaningful way, we have found these resources helpful:

All the Colors of the Earth, by Sheila Hamanaka (New York: William Morrow and Co., 1994). 32 pp. $5.99.

A beautiful book that describes and celebrates the richness and variety of the many colors of skin. Hamanaka uses images of food, plants, and animals to connect the reader with the text. The message is clear: There is beauty and richness in every color. The children depicted in the book are very diverse and include children with special needs, mixed-race children, and children with albino characteristics.

All the Colors We Are: The Story of How We Get Our Skin Color, by Katie Kissinger (St. Paul, MN: Redleaf, 1997). 32 pp. $9.95.

This is a bilingual picture book—the text is presented in English and Spanish—about how people "get" their skin color. The text explores the basic facts about the roles that melanin, the sun, and ancestors play in making us different. The author uses photographs to explain the concepts in clear, child-friendly language that offers opportunities to explore this scientific concept with children.

Bein' with You This Way, by W. Nikola-Lisa (New York: Lee & Low, 1994). 32 pp. $6.95.

One of the favorite read-alouds in my classroom, this picture book is a joyful, rhythmic chant that celebrates diversity. Familiar, straightforward observations about size, hair texture, and eye and skin color help the reader to dispel the notion of "normal" and recognize that we are all unique. Also available in a well-translated Spanish version.

The Colors of Us, by Karen Katz (New York: Henry Holt, 1999). 32 pp. $12.

When Lena decides to paint pictures of all of her friends she is surprised to learn that brown is not just one color. In this picture book, Lena's mother takes her on a tour of the neighborhood to observe all the shades of "brown" skin. With new labels like "cinnamon," "chocolate," and "pizza crust," she begins to understand how four basic colors combine to make lots of variations. It serves as a great conversation starter on skin color.

We Can Work It Out: Conflict Resolution for Children,
by Barbara Kay Polland (Berkeley, CA: Tricycle Press, 2000).
64 pp. $9.95.

A good resource to supplement the teaching of social skills. Through the use of photos and questions, Polland asks students and teachers to explore such issues as praise and criticism, jealousy, anger, and teasing. Lessons that start with the book can be extended in many ways with role plays, writing, and literature.

Whoever You Are, by Mem Fox (San Diego: Voyager Books, 2001). 32 pp. $12.95.

A wonderful story that we use throughout the school year. With poetic language and mysterious, almost magical illustrations by Leslie Staub, this picture book tells the reader that "there are children all over the world just like you." Our students begin to see how all families experience the universality of love, joy, pain, and sadness.

—Rita Tenorio

What can I do when a student makes a racist or sexist remark?

These kinds of remarks can catch us off guard, and the first instinct is often to respond strongly and cut off the speaker: "That kind of talk is not allowed here." Those of us in early childhood classes might also assume the kids are "too young" to really understand what they are saying.

Neither of these responses is adequate. Remember that curriculum is "everything that happens" at school. Your response or lack of response is just as much of a lesson as the morning math activity. Students will learn so much more if these issues are put on the table instead of under it.

Students also need to be explicitly taught the skills and strategies that they will need to counteract racism and sexism in their lives. And developmentally, students should learn respect and how to take action against unfair behaviors or comments.

Responding properly is a multistep process. You must consider not only who made the remark, but also the effect those words have on others in the classroom. Speak honestly about how the remark makes you feel. Stand up for the person or group that has been insulted. Give the other students the opportunity to respond as well. Beyond that, the whole issue of put-downs and name-calling should be an ongoing focus of the curriculum. These kinds of remarks can become a jumping-off point for meaningful classroom conversations.

—Rita Tenorio

Framing the Family Tree

How Teachers Can Be Sensitive to Students' Family Situations

by Sudie Hofmann

My 7-year-old daughter came home from school with a handmade calico tie for her dad for Father's Day. The oversized tie was carefully cut from the blue and orange fabric and edged using a pinking shears. She had used puff paints to write "I Love You Dad" down the center of the tie. A glob of paint on the corner of the capital D still appeared wet.

"Let's give it to Dad on Father's Day," she said. I told her we would, but I hoped she would forget by Sunday. She didn't. We made the trip to visit her father that day,

Leo Rohn

95

and as I drove the six short blocks, I looked at the mist forming on the windshield and wondered how this could be any more painful.

My daughter grabbed the tie and a roll of masking tape I had put in the back seat. She walked over to the gravestone, which read "If Love Could Have Saved You, You Never Would Have Died." She tried to attach the tie to the smooth granite headstone with the tape, but the rain prevented her from perfectly positioning the tie over her dad's name. Our shared frustration and grief forced us back into the car.

When we reached home, I felt so much anger toward the 1st-grade teacher, who chose to see the world in one unrealistic way. Why did she assume that all 22 children in her class have a dad—or a dad who is present in their lives?

I thought back to an experience of a childhood friend. Her father died when she was in grade school, but the school carried on with its annual 'Draw Your Dad' event. The students drew their fathers on butcher paper, using photos as a guide, and hung the sketches in the gymnasium. On a special night, fathers came to school and attempted to find themselves displayed on the walls of the gym. My friend drew her father, not knowing how to approach the teacher about the dilemma she would face the night of the event. That night she sat quietly on a folding chair, counting the minutes until she could go home.

I never imagined that more than 30 years later I would experience the same insensitivity when my daughter's teacher would ignore the statement I had written on the form I sent to school the very first day: "very sensitive about not having a father."

A Child's Family

Families are groupings of individuals who may or may not be living together, but are perceived by the child to be "family." They may be permanent, temporary, or fluid. Children define their families as units that include adults who make them feel safe and happy. They want stability, tradition, and love. Many children get this in large doses, and for others it's more elusive. Even in cases of abuse, children may still choose to be with their "family." As children from all types of families face challenges at home, the school setting should be one that offers comfort and that validates all family structures.

Teachers can walk a fine line between validating all types of families and singling out students for that validation. By providing appropriate curriculum, media materials, and visual images in the classroom, teachers can send a powerful message about respect and diversity without embarrassing students or violating their privacy.

Although some teacher preparation programs mention the issue of family diversity, not enough teaching practice takes the diversity of families into account. For example, teachers routinely assign family tree projects, possibly without realizing the confusion and pain these projects cause for some children. Issues of adoption or family of origin can present unique and sensitive dynamics in these types of class assignments. Such projects have the potential to engender ridicule or teasing from peers, especially if teachers don't actively intervene in discussions.

Of course, many teachers who assign personal "family" projects are replicating practices that have worked well for some students over the years. The calico tie or family tree project may be more indicative of an organization's unexamined practices than any social statement about families on the part of the teacher.

Advocates for Each Other

Both parents and teachers can support each other in challenging activities and school events that might make children or parents feel unwelcome or uncomfortable. For example, parents should be alert to any forms sent home or letters to parents that are not inclusive or that make assumptions about families. Parents outside of disenfranchised communities need to advocate for other parents who face discrimination. Gay, lesbian, bisexual, and transgender (GLBT) parents will not always feel safe identifying themselves as members of this community, or blended families might not feel any discussion with the school is necessary to explain who the students' biological or stepparents are. Nonspecific, open terms such as "adult at home" or "friends and families" to include, for example, children of partners of single parents should be used on school forms and flyers for school events. This is a school community issue and all parents can promote inclusive language. Images around the school can celebrate a wide variety of families, and school administrators should support the teachers who make the effort to be inclusive.

Even progressive schools, recognizing the diversity in families, will attempt to modify traditional activities to accommodate certain students—like telling students they can pick whom to give their Mother's Day gifts to. Although well-intentioned, this approach has the potential to increase feelings of alienation and discomfort, not minimize them. Telling a student to select someone else in his or her life who is a close approximation to the person that the majority of students in the class will choose does not ameliorate the situation.

I asked an elementary teacher for feedback on how I could address this perceived problem in the most sensitive way. After she thought for a moment she said: "You know, I think we often overlook issues of family diversity because they are not as obvious to us as other issues of diversity. We have leadership and resources for other topics of equity and culture, but because our students are so private in many ways about what is going on at home, we don't necessarily think about it when planning curriculum." She suggested moving away from projects that might single out students and agreed that the "alternative" project for the students who do not fit the norm can be hurtful.

Beyond Mother's and Father's Days

Any classroom activity that requires personal information about a child's family life may need to be carefully assessed.

In addition to the ubiquitous Mother's and Father's Day projects, many teachers in the lower grades have students create family photo albums. Without awareness on the part of the teacher, these projects might create feelings of insecurity or even anguish.

In any case, we should clearly delineate the educational benefits of projects that involve children's private lives. If the goal is to inform students about the diversity in families, maybe students could conduct research and present their work in creative ways such as creating collages of different families. Or teachers could ask students to design their own worksheets for reviewing picture books and popular films.

If the goal is to inform students about the value of their own families, there may be constructive approaches to achieving this goal without requiring that the students divulge personal information. Offering a variety of options—such as personal essays with some measure of anonymity—during a unit on families might give students a welcome alternative. Teachers can offer support and let students know they are available to talk with them or help them find additional help through the school psychologist or social worker.

As we recognize the fluidity of defining families, we can also recognize the ever-changing solutions to addressing social issues in the schools. If we attempt to engage in dialogue with students and other teachers about these issues, we will find that we learn something new about other people's realities and about our own.

Q/A   What do I do when I realize I've made a mistake with a child?

Since you are a person and not some trained robot, chances are that you will make mistakes, such as losing your cool or saying something that you really did not mean to say to a student. We really should try to keep these to a minimum, but when you do make a mistake it is important to acknowledge your error publicly.

One time, for example, I made a comment to a student in front of our class and as soon as I said it, I knew I shouldn't have. I should have been able to control my anger, but I didn't. It was right before lunch, so I had time to consider what I would say upon the students' return to the classroom.

I didn't make a big dramatic scene, but I did apologize in front of everyone. I explained that I had lost my temper. I said that I expected more of the student and his behavior, but more of myself, too. I asked, in front of his peers, if he would accept my apology. He did and we moved on.

It wasn't easy admitting I was wrong in front of 27 kids, but I thought it was important for them to see me as human. It also helped with discipline. When I later had to ask a student to apologize to another for lack of respect of property, feelings, or personal space, the students had already seen me do the same. And they had seen one of their classmates accept an apology rather than continue a cycle of anger and revenge. More often than not, my students were willing to patch things up right there.

—Stephanie Walters

It depends on whether the mistake was made in public and whether it embarrassed or humiliated the student. If you messed up in public in a way that was hurtful to a student, then you have to try to correct it in public—to the extent possible. For example, as a new teacher you will likely struggle with maintaining classroom decorum. Depending on the students, the time of year, the time of day, and how much sleep you've had, you may come down on a student in an unfair way. Apologies can be important, and many students will respect a teacher who can admit that he/she made a mistake. It also may go a long way toward repairing a relationship with a member of your class.

Remember, everything you do in class is education, so how you treat people in public is always more than "classroom management." It's also a vital piece of the curriculum.

—Bill Bigelow

Heather's Moms Got Married

by Mary Cowhey

My 2nd graders gathered on the rug, discussing the impending 50th anniversary of the historic *Brown v. Board of Education* decision. I asked how their lives would have been different without Brown.

"I wouldn't have all these friends . . . 'cause I wouldn't know them," said Sadie.

Michelle raised her hand and said, "I wouldn't exist." Michelle is a biracial girl, with an African American mother and white, Jewish father. Her mother Barbara had stayed for morning meeting that day and she elaborated:

"Because of Brown, I was able to get a good education and went to a college that was integrated. That's where

I met Michelle's dad. We fell in love and decided to get married."

Samuel, who is Panamanian and Pakistani, said, "My mom is brown and my stepdad is white, and they got married." He turned to ask Barbara, "In those days could a brown person and a white person get married?" Barbara said they got married in Massachusetts in 1985, and it wasn't a problem.

Angela, an African American girl, had quietly been following the discussion and finally raised her hand. "Because of that [the Brown decision], things are more fair, like I can go to this school and have all different friends. Still, not everything is fair, and that makes me sad."

Sadie asked Angela what still wasn't fair. "Well, your parents could get married, because you have a mom and a dad, but I have two moms and they can't get married. That's not fair."

Sadie considered this for an instant before asking, "Who made that stupid rule?"

With the honesty and incisive thinking I cherish in 2nd graders, Angela and Sadie had cut to the chase. When it comes to discussing gay marriage in 2nd grade, these are the questions that matter most: Is it fair to exclude some families from the right to marry? Who made that rule (and how is it changing)?

I should pause here to say that I don't teach in Anytown, USA. I teach in Northampton, a small city of 29,000 in western Massachusetts, which has been known as a haven for women and for lesbians. Northampton's status as a refuge from homophobia has been profiled in dozens of newspapers and media outlets around the country and around the world.

Although the numbers vary from year to year, I have always had at least one child in my class with lesbian parents. This year, one third of my students have lesbian parents. Although I probably have more lesbian-parented families than most teachers, the reality is that teachers may not know by looking if they have a child with gay or lesbian parents, aunts, uncles, grandparents, or family friends.

I teach at Jackson St. School (JSS), a public elementary school with about 400 students. Our school is a celebration of economic, racial, linguistic, and family diversity. Families speak a variety of home languages including Albanian, Spanish, Khmer, Vietnamese, Chinese, French, and Hindu. About 39 percent of the students are children of color, with the largest share of those being Puerto Rican. Forty percent of the students receive free or reduced lunch.

The school welcomes family involvement, with a weekly family newsletter and regular potluck dinners. It has a Family Center, which hosts a weekly Parents' Hour with coffee and conversation, as well as a family portrait project, in which a professional photographer takes free family portraits at Open House. These photos are displayed in the front hallway, heralding for all visitors the breadth of the school's diversity. Over the years, many parents have told me that even before speaking to anyone in the school, just looking at those family photos in the front lobby made them feel welcome, like they could fit in.

An Eye-Opener

I began teaching at Jackson St. School when I was fresh out of my teacher preparation program. I decided to start the school year with home visits to my new students and their families. At one of the first homes I visited, a parent greeted me wearing a button that said: "We're here. We're gay. And we're on the PTA." Beth and Karen Bellavance-Grace began talking about being foster parents for the state department of social services and being adoptive parents. As we began talking about family diversity issues, I asked if they would be willing to advise me on good books and teaching ideas. My education in teaching family diversity and learning from my families began on the first day of my teaching career, before I even set foot in my classroom.

When I speak to teachers and future teachers about gay and lesbian issues in elementary schools, they often ask how I can "get away with that." This is particularly ironic in Massachusetts, which was one of the first states to recognize the rights and needs of gay and lesbian youth in schools. In 1993, during the administration of Republican Gov. William Weld, the Massachusetts Governor's Commission on Gay and Lesbian Youth recommended that:

- High schools establish policies protecting gay and lesbian youth from harassment, violence, and discrimination

- Teachers and counselors receive professional development to respond to the needs of these students

- Schools establish support groups (gay-straight alliances)

- Schools "develop curricul[a] that incorporate gay and lesbian themes and subject matters into all disciplines, in an age-appropriate manner"

Despite that progressive policy, established under a Republican governor, teacher self-censorship, often based on the fear of raising potentially controversial topics, remains the status quo in many schools. Another problem, as progressive as the Weld commission's report was, is that it focused solutions primarily at the secondary level, with gay-straight alliances and so forth. Most people still get queasy talking about gay and lesbian issues at middle or—heaven forbid—elementary levels.

Teaching About Same-Sex Couples

In my classroom, issues of family diversity often arise spontaneously. Once a group of my 1st-grade readers decided to act out *The Carrot Seed*, a simple story about a boy who plants a carrot seed and cares for it diligently, despite the discouragement of his brother, mother, and father. After the skit, all the other students wanted a chance to act it out too. I said we could do it once more before lunch. I began pulling sticks with student names at random from a cup, to assign the four roles. After I pulled the first three sticks, a boy had already claimed the part of the brother. One girl had taken the role of the mother and another girl had taken the role of the kid who plants the seed. The last stick I pulled was Natalie's, and the remaining role was for the father. A boy quickly said I should pull another stick. Natalie sprang to her feet without hesitation. "That's OK!" she said, "I'll be the other mom!"

In 2004, same-sex marriage became legal in Massachusetts. Heidi and Gina Nortonsmith, parents of one of my students, had been plaintiffs in the *Goodridge v. Mass. Department of Public Health* landmark lawsuit that resulted in the legalization of same-sex marriage in our state. They were given the first place in line at Northampton's crowded City Hall on the morning of May 17 to get their marriage license.

After the court's decision, my students got "marriage fever." During "sharing time" Maggy reported on how she was the flower girl and her sister was the "ring barrier" at their friends' wedding. Avery Nortonsmith proudly showed the silver ID bracelet that he, his brother, and his moms all got on their wedding day, inscribed with the historic date. Sarah talked excitedly about preparations for her moms' wedding, how she and her sister and six of their girlfriends would be flower girls. I went to the wedding with my daughter and saw about half the families from my class. It was one of the most joyous and supportive celebrations I have ever witnessed.

My 5-year-old daughter caught the fever too, and conducted wedding after wedding in her imaginary play. Each night she'd say, "Come on Mom and Dad, you're getting married tonight." "We got married eight years ago," my husband would remind her. Undeterred, my daughter would say, "No, that was your commitment ceremony, but this is gonna be your wedding."

Even snack time conversations raise the issue of gay marriage. Beth Bellavance-Grace, who now works as an aide at our school, told me about a kindergarten conversation she heard. A girl announced to her table: "I know who I'm gonna marry when I grow up. I'm gonna marry Ella."

"You can't marry a girl," a boy at her table replied.

"That was just in the olden days," she replied. "But now I can."

Discussing Diversity

When we discuss family diversity, I define family as "the circle of people who love you." After I showed *That's a Family* one year, Marisol responded, "Yuck, that is so weird to have two dads!"

James turned to her and spoke with an air of sophistication. "What's the big deal about two dads?" he asked. "I got two dads. I got one in my house and one in the jail. Lots of kids gots two dads."

Marisol considered this a moment, then said, "Oh, I didn't think of that. I have two moms. I have my mom at home and a stepmom at my dad's house."

"See?" James said with a shrug of his shoulders. "I told you it's not so weird."

I had one student who was co-parented by three women. One morning we were having a math exhibition and the students had invited their parents. Thomas' three moms came in one at a time, each from their different jobs. James knew that his parents wouldn't be attending, but he kept looking to the door whenever another parent entered. He finally went over to Thomas and asked, "It be OK if I could borrow one of your moms?"

Margaret Spellings, appointed U.S. Secretary of Education by President George W. Bush, once criticized PBS for producing *Postcards from Buster*, a children's show that included a family with lesbian parents. I wish Spellings could have spent some time in my classroom. And I wish many Americans would approach the issue of same-sex marriage with the same openness as my 2nd graders.

The refusal to extend equal rights to families with gay and lesbian parents hurts children like my students, giving them the message their families are not equal, are somehow inferior. And, as my 2nd graders will tell you: That's not fair.

Most students' names have been changed, except for those presented with last names, who asked to have their real names published in the interest of modeling family pride.

What Can One Elementary Teacher in Anytown, USA Do?

- Do not presume that students live in traditional families with both married heterosexual birth parents. Name a wide variety of configurations that are possible in the diversity of human families. Part of that naming process includes using books and resources that portray family diversity, including the video *That's a Family.* Invite students to respond to the question "Who is in your family?" Allow students to share and display their family stories and pictures.

- Explore and challenge gender stereotypes with your students. Use children's books such as *Amazing Grace, William's Doll, Oliver Button Is a Sissy, China's Bravest Girl: The Legend of Hua Mu Lan, Riding Freedom,* and *Beautiful Warrior* as springboards for discussions. Activities can include students brainstorming lists of stereotypical behavior for boys and girls, then making captioned drawings of boys and girls engaging in nonstereotypical behaviors. These can be made into a class book or hallway display, "Boys Can/Girls Can." Once students learn to question gender stereotypes, they can recognize and reflect on stereotypical characters and behaviors in other books and media. They can extend their understandings of stereotypes to recognize and challenge other forms of bias.

- Teach a lesson on teasing and name-calling. Children's literature, such as *Oliver Button Is a Sissy* or *The Hundred Dresses,* can be an excellent point of departure for discussion and activities. These can help establish a baseline of classroom expectations that we are all respected members of this classroom community and that no put-downs will be tolerated.

- Answer students' questions about gay and lesbian issues in a straightforward, educational manner. Do not ignore or quash their curiosity. Remember that the two main points of reference are respecting differences and equality for all people. Elementary children are not asking about sexuality. When they ask what "gay" means, it's sufficient to say, "Gay is when a woman loves a woman or a man loves a man in a romantic way."

- Replace the phrase "moms and dads" with "parents and guardians" in your classroom and in your school, from informal conversation and classroom teaching to official school documents such as registration forms and emergency cards. Not only is this phrase more inclusive for students with gay or lesbian parents, but also for those being raised by foster parents, grandparents, aunts, and others. It accepts and affirms all of the families in your school.

- Consider showing a video like *Oliver Button Is a Star* as part of a professional development workshop for faculty and staff. Oliver Button Is a Star is a documentary that weaves a reading and musical production of *Oliver Button Is a Sissy* with interviews with adults like arctic explorer Ann Bancroft, author/illustrator Tomie dePaola, and dancer Bill T. Jones, who recall their childhood experiences. It includes scenes (some from my classroom) where 1st and 2nd graders do activities about name-calling and challenging gender stereotypes. *That's a Family* and *It's Elementary* are good choices too.

- In the event that you encounter an intolerant colleague, administrator, or parent, keep the following points in mind:

  - The diversity of families in our school is more beautiful and complex than any one of us could presume to know. Whether we have any self-identified ("out") gay- or lesbian-parented families in our school community or not, it is safer to assume that they are here than not.

  - An estimated one in 10 students may grow up to be gay or lesbian adults.

  - All of our students deserve a safe and supportive school experience.

  - Gays and lesbians are entitled to the same rights as others. We are talking about equal rights, not special rights.

  - We are not talking about "sexuality" when we discuss gay and lesbian issues any more than we are discussing sexuality when we read "Cinderella" or any other story with all heterosexual characters.

—Mary Cowhey

Out Front

by Annie Johnston

My prep period was half over. I still had to prepare for a sub the next day and copy the materials for my next class when a student appeared at my door. Nervously clutching a bathroom pass as her eyes darted from the room number to me, she asked, "Are you the one who does that support group for. . . ." Her voice trailed off.

"The lesbian, gay, bisexual, and questioning youth support group?" I responded. "Yes. They meet Thursdays at

lunch. They are working on a conference of gay/straight alliances around the Bay Area. It's not a large group. . . ." As my explanation continued I could see I had lost her.

"That's not what I want," she said. "I need to talk to someone, right away."

Oh dear, I thought, crisis management. This is not what I can do today. I had to leave early to get my daughter to an appointment. But instead I said, "What do you need to talk about?"

Slowly and hesitantly it came out. A good friend was attracted to her. She might actually be interested. That scared her to her very core. She sought me out because my room number was announced weekly as the location of the support group meetings. I took her name, found out what period she could stand to miss, and spent the rest of my prep period finding someone in the health center who would be positive about the possibility that this child might have feelings for someone of the same sex. I was lucky. More often, I end up playing amateur psychologist.

I teach history at Berkeley High School, considered one of the better schools for queer-identified youth (an all-inclusive term, preferred by the students, for queer and questioning youth).* Yet even at Berkeley, there are limits to the school's openness to queer youth, who tend to graduate early or leave for a semester or two of "Independent Studies." The Independent Studies program is an alternative track in which students only meet with each teacher for one-half hour per week and do all their work on their own.

I have been teaching at Berkeley for years and have been coming out to my classes since my first year. There are a few other staff in this school of 3,000 students who do not hide

VOICES
FROM THE CLASSROOM

"Start teaching before you actually get a job. Begin putting your curriculum together. Decide what subjects or grade levels you'll most likely be teaching—even if you haven't yet been hired—and begin to prepare. With every article you read, think about how to turn it into a lesson, how to bring a particular concept to life for students. Meet with more experienced teachers, raid their files, and build your own before you get a job."

—Bill Bigelow

our sexuality. We know that we have to be seen—that it is important not just for the gay youth but for all the students to have gay role models. We also know that at Berkeley, because of district and city policies forbidding discrimination on the basis of sexual orientation, we won't be fired.

The situation is better at Berkeley than at most schools across the country. But even at Berkeley, homophobia is a constant reality. Girls who are close friends and lean over each other's desk are called "lezzies." Boys who seem in any way weak or "womanly" are called "faggots." Despite advances in the struggle against homophobia in our schools, there is still a long, long way to go.

One teacher described a situation in which a young man, who had been consistently called "faggot" by his peers, took an all-too-typical approach to stop the taunting. He came into her class one day and went up to a shy, relatively unpopular girl and, in front of his buddies, proceeded to make sexually humiliating remarks. He was conforming to teenage male culture, in which "Hey, baby, why don't you suck my. . . ." means, "See, I'm a real man." The club of homophobic ridicule is held over the heads of all young people—it is one of the main means by which gender roles are enforced.

Backlash Era

In this backlash era, out teacher role models are an endangered species. Even in the progressive Bay Area, there have been major flaps over a teacher allowing a brief discussion of the coming-out episode of the TV show *Ellen* in 1997, and a teacher simply letting it be known to her classes that she is lesbian.

At the same time, gay/straight alliances are growing at a phenomenal rate. When students in Salt Lake City formed a gay/straight alliance in 1995, the district banned all clubs rather than allow the alliance to meet. But protesting students walked out en masse and marched to the state capital, forcing the state Legislature to intervene and countermand the district. There have been other significant legal victories since then—in particular the case brought by Jamie Nabozny, which held school administrators in Ashland, Wis., liable when a gay student was harmed by harassment that the administrators had ignored despite the existence of a district antiharassment policy. Many districts have also been more open to training staff on how to create a safe environment for lesbian and gay youth.

At my school, the lesbian, gay, bisexual, and questioning youth support group is an important place for students to find each other and establish a supportive community. It is difficult, however, for those students to be activists around gay issues at school. They face constant harassment and ridicule. It is equally difficult for students who are unsure of their sexual identity to take the radical step of coming to such a gay-identified group.

Take the situation facing Jake, who was ridiculed by other students for the entire semester in my world history class. He came midyear, he said, because he had been so ostracized in his last school. He had a manner about him that just spoke of weirdness and difference. By the end of four months, students would write things on the board about him, no one would work with him, and he would take it all in as if he deserved it. After he brought in a crucifix he'd made in shop class and announced to me that the bloody body hanging from it was himself, I redoubled my efforts to get him seen by a counselor, but to no avail. It was May by that time, the university interns who helped out at the health center were gone for the year, and there was really no one who could help.

Jake spent time hospitalized over the summer for severe depression and on suicide watch, I think. He spent more time hospitalized in the fall. After he left the hospital, he came by to tell me he had known he was gay since he was 7 years old. He'd been in denial, hoping and praying that something would change him.

I'm not sure where Jake got the strength, but he finally decided to stand up for himself, to shove the hatred and ridicule back at his tormentors. He also began reading books about gay male sexuality, and came to a staff development inservice I had organized to speak to teachers about the damage a homophobic environment does to youth.

Jake started to like himself, and it changed his life. He came back to Berkeley High and developed a number of friends. And although he still got gay-bashed, the last time he got kicked and punched he lodged an official complaint rather than just turning the other cheek.

Jake could have been a statistic. According to a study done by Paul Gibson for the U.S. Department of Health and Human Services, gay youth are two to three times more likely to commit suicide and comprise up to 30 percent of all completed suicides.

Help!

As an openly gay teacher, I do what I can to help the Jakes of our school. I talk to the social living classes, work with others to organize staff inservices, get students to speak on panels about their experiences, and advocate for the youth who end up on my doorstep. I struggle with how to make support services available to all students, not just those who come to the lesbian, gay, bisexual, and questioning youth group. This is particularly crucial for students of color, for whom the issue of identity is much more complex.

I know I should do more, but I can't. "Out lesbian teacher" is not my only identity. I can take the lead on these issues for only so long without getting burned out. I need allies, and so do the youth. I need young gay teachers who are supported and encouraged to act as out role models in the schools, instead of being scared that they will be persecuted and driven from their jobs. I need straight teachers to sponsor forums on the issue and push for an "anti-slur" policy.

You don't always get what you need, but you don't get much of anything unless you ask. So here are a few things I would ask of other teachers:

- Set a clear anti-homophobic standard for what is acceptable language and behavior in your classrooms and your schools.

- Incorporate gay issues into the curriculum—not just in social living classes when talking about sex, but in history, English, science, and Spanish.

- Support gay teachers' ability to be out role models for our youth.

Anti-Slur Policy

Establishing policies on language and behavior is sometimes the best place to start. Even at Berkeley, it has been difficult to develop a culture in which antigay language in unacceptable. When I asked a group of queer-identified youth what teachers had done to make a positive difference in combating homophobia, they could not think of a single thing. One year, one teacher tried to make an issue of antigay language, but she was quickly overwhelmed by students' negative responses. For the remainder of the semester, not a single student in her class suffered any consequences for using antigay language.

Once, after a 45-minute argument with students in my class over why antigay language is harmful, Ryanna, still unconvinced, said: "I'll do it, Ms. Johnston, because I respect you. But I just want you to know that none of my other teachers ever has demanded this of me. It is extremely difficult to remember to watch my language here when this is the language I use at home all the time, and when every other teacher in the school considers it acceptable."

Despite her reluctance, however, Ryanna managed to watch her language. Moreover, during the initial class discussion, many other students expressed their disapproval of antigay language, and reevaluated words they had been using.

Such conversations and policies have a ripple effect. One closeted bisexual student told me that he later felt able to raise gay issues in a current events discussion, knowing a large number of the students in the room would take them seriously. In this case, events that affected gay people became a normal, acceptable thing to talk about.

These conversations require a large chunk of class time. Further, policies must be backed up by immediate consequences when students forget or violate the rules. For instance, many students don't understand why calling a test they hated "gay" is insulting to gay people. They don't connect the emergence of "gay" as a slang word meaning "really yucky" to homophobia. It takes teaching to make that connection. Usually a talking-to in the hallway is adequate, although not always. Once in a while, a student will be unwilling to suppress his or her homophobia and will use homophobic remarks to seriously taunt another student. In such cases, teachers need to be aware that gay-baiting is a form of sexual harassment and that state education codes require schools to create a safe place for all students.

Curriculum Issues

An anti-slur policy reduces the amount of negative vibes, but is not sufficient to create a classroom that welcomes the existence of queer people. To take this further step, teachers must include queers and queer issues in their curriculum. It's likely that a tenth of the population is gay in this country, and gay people play a major role in our society. Students must see that fact reflected in what we teach. "Gay" has to be integrated into our picture of current events, historical reality, literary themes, and scientific exploration. We need curriculum in which "gay" is not relegated to the "Sexuality and Sexually Transmitted Diseases" discussion in health and social living classes.

Every subject area has openings for such curriculum, but it takes a conscious effort to develop or access and

VOICES
FROM THE CLASSROOM

"Start small. If there is one teacher with whom you experience pedagogical rapport, consider yourself lucky. Do collaborative projects with each other. Eventually two of you working together will lead to three will lead to four. You will then begin to have a critical mass from which to try out new things."

—Dale Weiss

incorporate the materials. In U.S. history, for instance, when we teach the Civil Rights Movement, we can examine the role of Bayard Rustin, an out civil rights activist who helped organize the 1963 March on Washington. We can include the gay liberation movement as a civil rights movement. We can have students study the Black Panther Party's position on homosexuality. Here is what Huey Newton approved as the official Black Panther position on the subject:

> Homosexuals are not given freedom and liberty by anyone in this society. Maybe they might be the most oppressed people in the society. . . . A person should have the freedom to use his body whatever way he wants to. The Women's Liberation Front and Gay Liberation Front are our friends, they are our potential allies and we need as many allies as possible. . . . We should be careful about using terms which might turn our friends off. The terms "faggot" and "punk" should be deleted from our vocabulary, and especially we should not attach names normally designed for homosexual men to men who are enemies of the people, such as Nixon or Mitchell. Homosexuals are not enemies of the people.

There are countless pieces of literature with lesbian and/or gay themes, ranging from *Coffee Will Make You Black* by April Sinclair, to *Giovanni's Room* by James Baldwin, to *Rubyfruit Jungle* by Rita Mae Brown. A multitude of famous literary icons have been lesbian or gay, such as Sappho, James Baldwin, Adrienne Rich, and E. M. Forster. Biology classes that discuss human reproduction can include the role of artificial insemination in allowing a growing number of lesbians and gay men to become parents. The ongoing "biology vs. environment" debate—i.e., whether sexual preference is determined largely through genetics or environmental factors—can be one of the topics students can choose to research and debate. Physical education teachers can talk openly and respectfully about gay athletes such as diver Greg Louganis and tennis star Martina Navratilova.

If we acknowledge gay people's contributions in every area of our society, young people's perceptions of what it means to be gay can go beyond the often-threatening issue of sexuality.

From elementary school on, teachers need to talk about gay people so children learn they are a normal part of our society. Many students have lesbian and gay family members whom they love. They must not feel they have to hide or be embarrassed by these relationships.

My 8-year-old daughter, for instance, has decided she will not compromise on telling the world she has two moms, no matter what the consequences. Last year, she had a confrontation with a bunch of kindergarten boys who accused her and her friend of being gay because she was leaning on her friend's shoulder for support due to a twisted ankle. She told them there was nothing wrong with being gay. Then she announced that, besides, both her moms were gay.

The boys really went to town on that. The ridicule they subjected her to reduced her to tears. After 10 minutes of crying in the bathroom she returned to class and was given detention—her first—for tardiness. She called it the worst day of her life and said, "And Mom, how am I going to make it through high school?"

In every class, every semester, after I come out I find out about the aunts, cousins, brothers, and friends that young people are normally forced to be silent about. Children desperately need teachers to counter these taboos, to talk about gay people naturally, unabashedly, and positively.

Role Models

A queer-friendly school is one in which there are positive lesbian and gay role models, not just for queer students but also for all students. Whether students are gay or bi or straight, they need to experience gay teachers as people who enrich their lives and care about them. An environment in which lesbian, gay, and bisexual teachers can be out to their students is critical to breaking down the culture of homophobia.

But it is extremely difficult to be out in a school setting. You feel isolated and pegged. In many districts, you can be fired for being out in the classroom. At the least, one risks censure by the administration and homophobic reactions from parents. Every gay teacher fears being targeted and persecuted if word gets out.

Consider my experience with Calley, who was a bright, energetic 14-year-old when she first came to my classroom. She had spent junior high fighting with the Little League coach to be able to play on the all-boys baseball team. She spent her freshman year trying out boyfriends and sporting large hickeys. By her sophomore year, she'd had enough of all that. She began attending the lesbian/gay support group meetings in my classroom and signed up to be a proctor for me. Her mother searched her backpack and read her journal, in which she had a number of poems that made her feelings about sexuality quite explicit. Calley's mother immediately wanted to drag Calley to a therapist. And her mother was looking for someone to blame. I was a handy target.

In a conservative community hell-bent on targeting gays, I'd have been mincemeat. But at Berkeley, where there is no such organized opposition to the rights of gays, and where many straight colleagues and administrators are supportive of gays, Calley's mother could do little about me.

Calley ran away from home that summer, returning to an uneasy truce in the fall. She is out and has a strong circle of friends, but clearly it will be many years before she again feels the support of a loving family.

Gay teachers need to take more risks to provide strong out models of what it means to be gay. We cannot do that, however, without a supportive environment. Straight teachers can help to create such support.

If straight faculty members at my high school would raise a concern about the homophobia they so constantly see in their classes, it would be easier to develop an anti-slur policy. If there were any other teachers developing curriculum that included gay issues (besides when discussing HIV), I would feel supported. These actions do not require a particular sexual orientation. They only require concern and a commitment to act against homophobia.

For many years, "queer" was a pejorative only acceptable when used among gay people. But as the definition of this movement has expanded to include lesbian, bisexual, transgender, and questioning people, many youth openly began using "queer" as an all-inclusive term. This was probably popularized by the short but exciting existence of the group Queer Nation, which did a lot of in-your-face guerrilla theater against heterosexism. "Gay," on the other hand, was an acceptable term in general usage denoting all homosexual people and had a respectful connotation. Among youth now, however, "gay" is a slang adjective with extremely negative overtones. I use "queer" when talking about youth, partly because it covers so many bases, and so many youth aren't sure what base they'll end up playing. I use "gay" when talking about older people because we came of age when "gay" (or lesbian-gay-bisexual-transgender) was the proper term.

References

Coffee Will Make You Black, by April Sinclair (New York: Harper Paperbacks, 1995).

Giovanni's Room, by James Baldwin (New York: Delta, 2000).

Rubyfruit Jungle, by Rita Mae Brown (New York: Bantam, 1983).

Creating Chemistry in Sophomore Chemistry

by Terry Burant

My 10th-grade chemistry classes at an academically rigorous, all-male high school don't exactly provide a host of opportunities to get to know my students. Let's face it, most of our time is devoted to equations, test tubes, beakers, and Bunsen burners. Factor in the typical demands of time made on high school teachers in general, the extra time spent in my extracurricular work as a moderator of student government at my school, and

the pressures of standards and assessments, and I sometimes wonder if it is realistic to think that I really can get to know the students in the classes I teach. However, using my content area as an anchor, I've borrowed, adapted, and developed a few methods for getting to know my students and helping them see that I care about them as human beings. I also work the edges of my classroom life to make connections with my students.

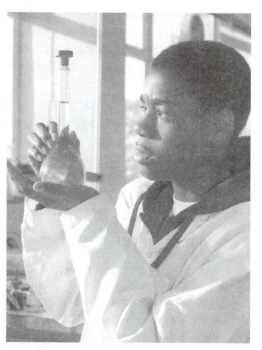

Connecting with Students Via the Content of Chemistry

I begin the school year by asking students to complete two inventories. One asks students about their prior knowledge of the content of chemistry using a simple checklist of key concepts with columns for rating their familiarity with the ideas. The other poses specific questions about their previous experiences in school and their preferences for learning. With these tools, I sneak in a few questions about their personal interests. These basic inventories provide the students with a preview of the content to come and give me a sense of the extent of their background knowledge.

Because chemistry is a science of modeling (just think atoms), my first assignment on the first day of class asks students to create a model of themselves and hand it in the following day. I purposefully leave the description of the product pretty open, requiring only that a model should focus on the "unseen" aspects of who they are and contain at least five key facts about themselves. I also give a few examples of and reasons for models in the sciences (i.e., they help us see what is too small or too big to see, show us the interior of things we can see, and describe relationships between important ideas). I hang on to these models (most of them are drawings) and refer back to them again and again in the first few weeks of school as I learn my students' names. I also like to look at them later in the year for entertainment and to compare the person I now know with the model he once created. Finally, at the end of the year, I pull these models out again and ask the students to make a revised model; this time, of themselves as chemists.

As the school year progresses, I think back to my students' stated interests and the ones I've discovered along the way and rely on these as additional bridges to content. For example, one year I had a number of cross-country runners in my classes and we calculated the weighted average of a cross-country team's personal best times as a way of helping them find the same kinds of weighted averages for the atomic masses of the various elements. I also have a few scuba divers in my classes; when it comes time to talk about the laws governing the behavior of gases, we talk about decompression and the ways that gases find their way in and out of our bloodstreams.

My exams tilt heavily toward problem-solving and calculations, with questions like "How many moles of carbon dioxide are formed when 32 liters of ethanol react with excess oxygen?" These are not exactly the sort of questions in which student responses help me learn about my students, although I certainly do learn about them as learners of chemistry from analyzing their answers and errors. Therefore, to add a human element to my exams, I add optional bonus questions that focus on my students and their lives. I look at it this way—after 40 minutes of punching calculator keys and studying the periodic table, my students deserve a few minutes to relax and ponder different kinds of questions. One year, after using the questions listed below on exams, I developed a decidedly compassionate view of one of my students, Charlie, as one of his memorable experiences first quarter was helping a freshman pick up all of his books off the floor when he dropped them in a crowded hallway. I learned that Steve liked Johnny Cash and thought our theme song should be his classic "Ring of Fire" because we were always making things burn in chemistry. I don't underestimate the power of the connections made in reading and responding to these simple questions. In fact, I've literally been moved to tears by some of the sweet and honest answers my students provide to these questions. My students become people to me when I catch even small glimpses of what would otherwise be hidden aspects of their worlds.

Extra Credit Questions

1. What stands out for you as a memorable experience in this first quarter of the school year?

2. What signals the start of spring for you?

3. If you could designate a theme song for your experience in chemistry so far this year, what would it be and why?

4. What are you grateful for?

5. What would your perfect snow day consist of?

6. If you could invite someone to make a guest appearance in our class, who would you invite and why?

I also keep a classroom library stocked with an array of magazines and books; I like to talk books with kids and help them see that English teachers don't have sole rights and responsibilities for reading. Keying into students' literary preferences is another easy way to get to know them and a good way to broaden the range of reading material I use in my class as well.

Around the Edges

A few days before school starts, I print class lists of my students' names; then, I take those lists out for coffee and read through the names in a leisurely way, savoring the melody they make as I recite them and noting which pronunciations I will need help with when my students arrive. While I do this, I focus on an idea expressed by Gloria Ladson-Billings when I heard her speak at a conference a few years ago. She said something like, "These are somebody's best kids; parents don't save their best kids and keep them at home." My students deserve some precious anticipation on my part just as those on a guest list might be carefully considered before an important event.

The evening before school starts, I pause to ponder the fact that by the time I go to bed the following night, approximately 150 new young people will become a part of my world. I've taught sophomores long enough to know that a lot of living takes place between ages 15 and 16: from grandparent deaths to first driver's licenses, from first dates to beard growth, these simple and profound facets of life (along with some I can't anticipate) will mix it up in my room over the next nine months.

Within the first couple weeks of school, in the margins of my teaching days, I take notes on what I know about my students using an idea I've adapted from Donald Graves, a teacher of writing and reading. I create a simple three-column list with my students' names on it to track my knowledge of each student. As I learn things about each student, I write them on the list (for example, Austin has two beagles, Brandon plays piano, David runs cross-country, Arturo rides his bike to school each day). Some students quickly make their presence known and I can't help but learn about them; keeping this list indicates which students I know very little about and helps me intentionally focus on them and build relationships with them.

Once the school year gets rolling, I attend student events of all kinds. Although I am a big fan of the fall tradition of the Friday night varsity football game in Wisconsin, I mix it up with chaperoning dances, attending JV games of the sports my students participate in (I attended the first hockey game of my life recently), and showing up at other less popular events like our student poetry slam/alternative band night. An added bonus to attending school events is the camaraderie that I've developed with my colleagues while sitting together in the gym at a volleyball game. As time goes on, I typically run into parents of my students (grandparents too!), and some of my best conversations with parents about their teenagers occurs in line for popcorn or just standing on the sidelines of a junior varsity football game. I also move now and then into the wider world to see what my students are up to; for example, this winter I visited a student who rang the Salvation Army bell outside of a mall entrance. I knew he was scheduled to be there and I simply planned my shopping trip accordingly— not to be weird and stalker-ish, mind you; rather, to just to say a quick hello and to offer him a cup of hot chocolate on a really cold night.

Although it is important to create boundaries for your availability as a teacher, I like to use some of my non-teaching time at school to meet informally with students. A couple of days each week, I arrive at school early and I open my classroom door at least half an hour before school begins. In those quiet early mornings, boys come in to show off their new winter boots and ask for my opinion on them, seek help with chemistry problems, talk about their families, or sit quietly in my beat-up reclining chair and eat a muffin or drink a coffee or a Mountain Dew. At lunch, twice per week, I am available for questions or conversation. At the end of one year, one of my quieter students said, "Some of my favorite moments in chemistry happened at lunch when a bunch of us would just sit and talk about random things." For this young man (and for others), my classroom at lunch made a community.

When I have extra time (well, as a teacher, I know this is pretty rare), I make quick phone calls to let parents know that I've noticed something positive about their sons. This might be for the student who suddenly turns on the effort or for the one who steadily makes incremental strides. Regardless of the reason, I've found that these calls usually result in a closer relationship with the student and an ally in the classroom. We all need those student allies, the ones who will go along with our crazier ideas or help diffuse difficult situations.

Cautions

Like building any relationships, getting to know high school students takes time, so don't panic if you feel like it isn't happening fast enough. And, again, just like in other relationships, sometimes my students don't necessarily want to build relationships with me. I don't force it. They are, after all, teenagers; and, as their teacher, I don't always represent someone they want much to do with on a given day. This could, or could not, have something to do with me personally. Sometimes leaving someone alone is the best answer for a while.

In addition to backing off, there are times when I am so tired that I have to almost put myself in "faking" frame of mind in order to be interested in my students. I hate to admit it, but on certain days, some of my students get on my last nerve, and there are definitely some mornings when I feel like I'm living in the song "The Pretender" by Jackson Browne, just "getting up and doing it again" (and yes, I work in a school that just so happens to lie "in the shade of a freeway"). Feigning interest in other people when I really don't feel like listening to them or being around them is one of the best ways I know to get over those grumpy feelings. Listening to a story about a soccer game or helping a student think about a future career direction helps me to recapture the joy of teaching high school chemistry. It's not just the chemistry that matters in my classes; it's the chemists who make it happen.

Creating a Literate and Passionate Community

by Tracy Wagner

I knew that after the last week of classes in Period 3, English 10, I would never see some of my students again. Michael was leaving to live with his mom in Milwaukee; D. J. might be moving back to Chicago and might be taking classes at an area technical college; Janet was opting to leave "regular" high school classes for a work-to-learn program.

Teaching is a strange way to mark the passing of time: Students arrive at the same time every day and, together, we figure each other out. Throughout the year, I felt these students becoming a physical part of my identity.

Katherine Streeter

131

In my first year of teaching, I felt my chest condensing with blows from the administration, other teachers, and policies that I could not control. I survived a twitch under my right eye, stress-induced hives, and endless nights of grading and writing lessons while having to stretch funds to cover my student loans. I felt guilty for not spending enough time with my partner, not doing my writing, and having to go to bed at 9 p.m.

But I also felt my heart widening with more anger and love and concern than I have ever felt before. At the end, I found myself wondering: What will happen when these students are gone?

Although I had enjoyed a spectrum of emotions in all of my English classes during my first year of teaching, my Period 3 class was the hardest for me to let go. Within my high school's tracking system, this class rested at the "regular" level—under the TAG (Talented and Gifted) and ACAMO (Academically Motivated) tracks, but above self-contained special education. The students in that class were an array of ethnicities; all came from middle-class to lower-income homes, and some were labeled as "at-risk." Many students received special education services.

"Remember Me"

On the last day of class, as the students chatted, I laid my own poem on one of the desks in the circle. Earlier in the week, armed with the "Remember Me" lesson plan from Linda Christensen's *Reading, Writing, and Rising Up: Teaching About Social Justice and the Power of the Written Word,* I had placed students' names and mine in a hat. After choosing a name, students were to write a poem, praising what they remembered about this person in our class. The word had spread fast—not a small feat in a large urban school—and students had been able to explain the lesson before I even opened my mouth.

I wondered if the poems would live up to my expectations. I wanted them to be gifts, something that the recipients could take to remember our classroom community and their place in it. As I helped students brainstorm, a small part of me feared that I had not created the community that I had worked for since day one. Listening to their questions—"What if I got the name of someone I don't like?" "What if I've never talked to this person?" "What if there's really nothing good to say?—I thought back on the year's activities and wondered if I had been overly optimistic.

Connecting Students and the World

Throughout the year, I had designed, collaborated on, and discovered hands-on units that use literature to help students explore their lives and connect to the larger community and world. I wanted students to become more "literate," which, to me, meant not only working on basic reading and writing skills, but becoming compassionate members of society, capable of being agents of change. With this in mind, I started the year with a poetry unit inspired by Janice Mirikitani's poem "Who Is Singing This Song?" Mirikitani explains the need to honor our ancestors' work by changing the injustices of the present. She writes: "Who is singing this song? / I am. / pulled by hands of history not to sit / in these times, complacently, / walkmans plugged to our ears, / computers, soap operas lulling our passions to sleep." She then lists specific issues that have moved her and her ancestors to create change. In the end, she dares her readers "to love, to dream" enough to continue their quests. My students seemed to connect to the poem—to the richness of its language, the urgency of its message, and its rap-like flow.

After reading the poem in class, students brainstormed for their own "Who Is Singing This Song" poem by drawing a line down the middle of a sheet of paper. On one side, they named the issues important to their lives. On the other, they listed personal experiences that shaped these concerns. As this is difficult for some students, I supplied examples—racial profiling, the environment, fair treatment of people with disabilities—and told them to talk through why a person might care about each, and then write their own. On the back of the sheet, students listed the books, songs, movies, and role models that represented their beliefs. On the bottom, students filled in the sentence "I am. . . ." Responses ranged from "a student athlete" to "a dark poet," from "rebellious" to "macaroni and cheese." In the following days, students learned literary terms and then began the process of prewriting, then writing a rough draft, soliciting a peer edit, and reworking it into a final poem. On the last day of the unit, students participated in a "read-around" as described in *Reading, Writing, and Rising Up*, listening to each poem and writing positive comments, then passing the comments to each author at the end of class.

I learned many facts about the students through this unit. I learned that I had to deal with the derogatory behavior and assumptions students had created about themselves through the reinforcement of prior classroom experiences. I learned that students could arrive in and disappear from my classes without warning. I learned that many students had not retained "the basics"—sentence structure, how to write a standardized test–ready essay, literary terms—that they would need to move ahead in their academic educations.

So, backed by a selection of 10th-grade books that often felt like choosing the better of many evils, I set out to combine what already existed with resources from the library, my own books, and the collections of other English department teachers. For example, after focusing on the role of conflict in *The Lord of the Flies*, students watched Anna Deavere Smith's video *Twilight: Los Angeles*, based on interviews Smith conducted after the 1992 Rodney King beating. After conducting their own interviews about Rodney King with family members and school personnel and watching the video, my students wrote narratives from their own perspectives about conflicts in their lives. Then students chose the point of view of another agent of conflict in the narrative—a person, nature, fate, society—and inserted that agent's view. Throughout, I sought to help students use writing and literature to feel compassion for people involved in conflicts in the larger world and in their lives.

Making Connections

Next I wanted students to see a connection between literature, writing, and others in their community. Built on a unit designed by Esmé Schwall and Tara Affolter, teachers who were also new to East High School's English department that year, my English 10 students read Sandra Cisneros' *The House on Mango Street* in thematic parts, then responded by writing a personal vignette that shared each theme. At the end, students edited and designed their own books, each with cover, illustrations, and author biography. I delivered the books to Lori Nelson, whose 8th graders had also read *The House on Mango Street*. The middle school kids packed the high schoolers' books with letters and poems responding to what they had written. I remember the silence as the 10th graders read the responses that thanked them for sharing their stories, being brave, and being role models. Martellious, whose book featured stories of losing friends and family to violence in Chicago, told me it was one of the proudest days of his life. I knew he understood how writing about the struggles in his life could help him connect with others. Although I couldn't verbalize it at the time, I now realize that giving the students opportunities to read and write for a larger audience validated them as literate, compassionate members of society.

Throughout the year, I created opportunities for students to experience literacy outside of the classroom. I wanted to take away the mystique of college, and to show them that their lives fit into an academic world. Midyear, I coordinated with graduate student Nikola Hobbel to take a group of my 9th graders to the University of Wisconsin–Madison to be part of her teacher education young adult literature class's discussion on controversies about teaching Harper Lee's *To Kill a Mockingbird*. Bolstered by this experience, I took a carload of Period 3 students to hear Angie Cardamone, a preservice teacher who spent time each week working in my classroom, give a presentation at the university about the effects of tracking in East's English 10 classes. As Michael, Janet, and Charlie listened to Angie, they recognized their voices in her recommendations. I remember Michael, a lower-income, African American student sitting on the side of the room, surrounded by young, white, female preservice teachers. When he participated in a discussion about how white teachers could increase "minority student achievement," I knew his confidence to speak in an academic community showed that he saw himself as a literate member of the discussion.

Near the end of the year, I wanted students to find connections between their lives and a seemingly unrelated text. So to preface the reading of Chinua Achebe's novel *Things Fall Apart*, students studied Nigerian folktales and performed them for our class. Then I asked an African storytelling professor from UW–Madison to speak to the students. Angie agreed to pick the professor up on campus; a student volunteered to videotape the presentation; I organized volunteers to set up the room. When I got sick, I arranged for a sub I knew to cover the class, and trusted that my students could hold the event together.

Sure enough, the students raved and the professor praised the attention and maturity they showed. And though they complained about the difficulty of the reading, the tediousness of text coding (a reading strategy described in Cris Tovani's excellent book *I Read It, but I Don't Get It: Comprehension Strategies for Adolescent Readers*), and the very idea of a "literary analysis" essay, my Period 3 students held on. As I look back on this unit, I realize that the students had gained enough confidence in themselves to tackle—and maybe even enjoy—a difficult read.

Sure, only a few students would routinely do work outside of class, and a lack of computer access caused many projects to be late. Sure, I had to wait for the kids to stop talking at the beginning of every class. Sometimes yelling helped, sometimes walking out, shutting the door behind me, and then walking back in with exaggerated gestures of "Good morning!" did the trick. Things were rarely easy, but by the end of the school year, I witnessed something remarkable that made it all worth the pain.

Conclusions

On the last day of class, I asked the students to read the poems they had written about each other. One by one, the students read loudly and slowly. When Brittany, a quiet, white, middle-class girl who loved the ballet, finished reading her poem about Janet, an extroverted African American girl from a low-income family who loved Tupac Shakur, Janet gave her a hug. The students began a pattern of reading and walking the poems over to the classmates they'd written about, often wrapping their arms around each other. And when their poems were read, I was surprised to see my toughest boys cry.

After the reading, I started to stand but was shushed down by Michael. "Wait, Ms. Wagner," he said, rising, "I've got something to say." Student by student, Michael trailed his finger around the circle, saying one good thing about every one in it. Sometimes I didn't get the jokes, but it was clear that the students understood. He finished, and another student picked up the routine, often walking to the student in the spotlight, hugging, smiling, or hitting a shoulder with a fist. I remember what the students said to each other, and what they said to me.

In the last minutes of Period 3, I sat back and watched the class function as a community of caring individuals. I marveled that I didn't have to say a word.

All students' names have been changed, unless permission was given.

References

The House on Mango Street, by Sandra Cisneros (New York: Vintage Contemporaries, 1984).

I Read It, but I Don't Get It: Comprehension Strategies for Adolescent Readers, by Cris Tovani (Portland, ME: Stenhouse Publishers, 2000).

Reading, Writing, and Rising Up: Teaching About Social Justice and the Power of the Written Word, by Linda Christensen (Rethinking Schools, 2000). See page 358 for details.

Things Fall Apart, by Chinua Achebe (New York: Anchor Books, 1994).

Twilight: Los Angeles, by Anna Deavere Smith (New York: Offline Video and PBS Entertainment, 2000).

"Who Is Singing This Song?," by Janice Mirikitani, in *Yell-Oh Girls! Emerging Voices Explore Culture, Identity, and Growing Up Asian American*, edited by Vickie Nam (New York: HarperCollins, 2001).

Getting Your Classroom Together

by Bob Peterson

S ometimes the top of my desk at school looks worse
than the floor of my teenage daughter's bedroom,
which is quite an accomplishment, really. But
despite the appearance of disorganization on the top
layer of my desk, my years of teaching have taught me
lots of ways to better organize my classroom. Perhaps the
following thoughts will help.

Paying Attention to the Basics

From the start get ideas from other teachers and consult
with them on a wide range of issues. Veteran teachers

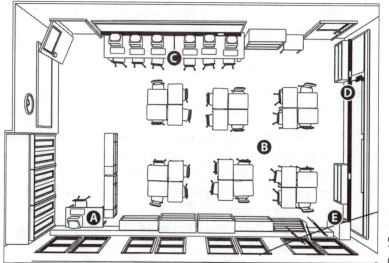

Paul Duquesnoy

139

appreciate being asked for advice. Use only what you think is worthwhile. Take the time to visit as many classrooms as you can and get ideas about everything from wall displays to seating arrangements.

Keep in mind that how you organize your classroom is a reflection on what you think about your students and how you view teaching. For example, displaying students' work on the wall can serve as an affirmation of the importance of student voice in your classroom, but depending on what and how such work is chosen it might also privilege certain groups of students and disadvantage others. (For example, if only the "best" work is always displayed, certain students will rarely have a chance to have their work displayed.)

Similarly a "theater-style" seating arrangement engenders a more lecture-based, teacher-centered approach to teaching, vs. other seating arrangements. Sometimes these things that appear to be invisible are part of a "hidden curriculum" and carry powerful messages to students.

The central questions you should ask when organizing your classroom are "Why am I doing this this way?" and "What purpose will it serve?" For example, in some classrooms it's important that students have access to certain materials, books, or calculators. If that's the case, what's the easiest way these things can be made accessible, yet kept orderly and safe? Similarly, classrooms have bulletin boards. Ask yourself, "Why do I have this display up? What purpose does it serve?

Labeling

I am a great believer in labeling. I label plastic dish pans to categorize different genres and levels of student books; I label boxes and drawers and box shelves so that students not only know where things are, but also where they should be returned. A computer, a printer, and some clear contact paper work wonders when it comes to making neat-looking signs to keep things in order.

Seating Arrangements

The students' seating arrangement is crucial to a successful classroom and reflects how the teacher wants to run the class. I vary my seating arrangements depending on the nature of the particular group of kids, the number of students in my classroom, and my current goals for the class.

For me flexibility is key, because at different times I want students to be facing the overhead projector observing a lesson, facing another student in partners, facing a small group, or facing the whole class for a class discussion or class meeting. Obviously no one seating pattern satisfies all those needs. Many elementary teachers arrange their class so that there's a carpet or meeting area where all student can gather in a circle or group for conversation. Some teachers put desks in groups of four or six for the benefit of having "base" groups in their classroom to help with cooperative group activities and classroom management (for a more detailed discussion, see "The Challenge of Classroom Discipline" on page 251).

Modeling

Regardless of the seating arrangement I may be using at a certain time, I model for my students how we get into other arrangements. For pairing they must sit "eye-to-eye" and "knee-to-knee." For small groups they have to be facing the center point of their table or desks. For classroom meetings, they need to learn how to pick up their desks and chairs and rearrange them in a safe and quiet manner. I model a lot at the beginning of the year, showing students exactly how each of these maneuvers should be performed. I also find it necessary to occasionally model them again throughout the entire school year.

Displaying Materials

The display of educational materials is also central to a successful classroom. I have a book corner, a writing center with various types of paper and story starters, a geography area, an art supply drawer, a dictionary and resource center, computers, and a math manipulative cart. I have a specific space for "the poster of the week" and a special display area for the daily agenda, announcements, and the song of the week.

One way I vastly expand the space that I have for displaying word lists, posters, etc. is by stringing a strong cord at a height of about 8 feet between two perpendicular walls in the front corner of the classroom. Using store-bought skirt hangers (the kind with two movable clamps), I can easily hang 12" x 18" tag board sheets, upon which I list words, math-solving strategies, etc.

Wall displays are always contradictory: Teachers need to strike a balance between displaying student work and putting up challenging questions, posters, maps, and displays. As you strive to strike a balance, remember that care should be taken to ensure that the students "see themselves on the walls," both literally—the walls have pictures of students and their work—and figuratively, so the people students see in posters reflect the nationalities of the classroom and the broader world.

Another way to help students see themselves on the walls: At the beginning of the year, on part of my bulletin board I place a large map of our city, marked with a large sign that says "Where We Live." I have each student place a labeled stickpin in the map to show exactly where they live, and I display essays about the students' neighborhoods nearby.

Organizing the Paper Load

A key part of classroom organization is managing the paperwork—whether it's the school flyers that are to be passed out to the students or homework and class projects that need to be assessed and returned.

Think through a filing system that will grow with you throughout the year, perhaps divided by subject area, unit, or class. If you want to deal with the growing piles of papers on your desk, remember to "handle a piece of

paper only once" as a way to save time and better organize your materials. This requires a filing system that is
broad enough to include all aspects of school life and
flexible enough to allow for new issues.

Talk with other teachers about how they organize
their own crush of papers and how they give helpful
and timely feedback to students' work. It's no easy task.
I have found that occasionally I spend significant time
commenting on students' work, but then don't plan sufficient time for students to read and actually learn from
my comments.

Communication

Clear communication with students and parents is an essential part of classroom organization. Remember that not all
students are auditory, and in particular students learning
English as a second language have special learning needs.
Explain things in writing as well as orally, through frequent
use of the chalkboard, overhead projector, or handouts.
I write down the daily agenda, homework assignments
(which students must copy), and announcements so everyone is aware both auditorily and visually.

Organizing Student Materials

Another crucial part of an organized classroom is helping students learn how to be organized. This is an ongoing task throughout the career of a student. I start by
giving each of my 5th graders a "people's textbook," a
three-ring binder with dividers to organize and maintain
non-textbook materials. I learned this approach from a
high school social studies teacher who gave his students
many supplemental materials but was frustrated by
their inability to hold on to them. I explicitly dictate the
divider categories—songs, poems, words, history, news,
science, and math—and make clear where each handout
should be placed. In addition to dividers I give students
formatted sheets for writing down what goes in some

sections—such as the song or poetry section where students list the singer and song, or poet and title of poem. At the end the year the students are allowed to keep these binders and most do.

Tracking Student Progress

Part of classroom management is not only the grading and managing of papers and other forms of student work, but keeping all that assessment straight. Various forms of record and grade books exist, but what I have found helpful is a clipboard with a sheet of mailing labels. This allows me to take notes on what children are doing and later peel off the label and put it into a three-ring binder of class observations and grades, which has a separate page for each student. Notes range from things such as "counting with fingers to solve problem" to "didn't seem to comprehend passage in independent book." These labels accumulate over time. Assuming I write neatly and in enough detail the first time, they're very helpful when it comes time to write report comments or during parent-teacher conferences. I also use this binder to note any parent contact or student conferences I have.

When more than one teacher is working directly with students, I have found that keeping a "running record" as a word processing file on a shared computer, or a shared file on a file server, is an excellent way to maintain joint records of student progress and contact.

Learning from Doing

Just as we expect our students to learn from their experiences, so should we. Thus spending a little time at the end of the day or week, or even at the end of the school year, to reflect on how to better organize and manage your classroom is worthwhile. Take some notes, keep a file on your computer titled "better ideas for next year" and write down ideas that might improve your teaching next year.

Uncovering the Lessons of Classroom Furniture

You Are Where You Sit

by Tom McKenna

I magine the following scenario: Students enter a classroom with the desk and chairs neatly arranged in straight rows. They hesitate at the door, make a quick assessment of the room and choose a place to sit. They work their way down narrow rows of chairs, careful not to disturb the tight arrangement of furniture. They sit quietly, deposit backpacks under their seats, place a notebook on the desk, and look straight ahead to the front of the room and the much larger teacher desk that stares back at them.

Shortly before the class is scheduled to start, an adult figure enters the room, writes his or her name on the front board along with the name of the class, and assumes a seat at the big desk or the podium standing by its side. School is in session.

Welcome to day one of your first lessons about power, pedagogy, and relationships to physical and symbolic capital.

I have watched students file into my classroom for 35 years. Never have I witnessed students attempt to change the arranged furniture, nor ask to do so. Instead, they arrange themselves according to a prearranged design.

I normally conduct my classes at Portland Youth Builders, the high school completion/GED school where I teach in one of Portland's poorest neighborhoods, with chairs arranged in a large circle. This day, I arrange the chairs in rows. Students walk in the door, stop suddenly, look at me and ask, "What's this all about?"

I simply ask them to take a seat and offer no explanation for our newly arranged room. I take attendance and ask if anyone has any thoughts they want to share before we start class.

Deavon says: "I don't like this. I have to turn around to see who's talking. Can we change the chairs back to the way they usually are, please?"

I ask how other students feel about sitting in rows. Darren says: "I don't like it either. It feels like school."

A chorus of "yeah, I don't like it" affirms Deavon and Darren's comments.

"OK, let's do this." I offer a compromise to my grumbling students. "Let's change the chairs around but I want you to talk about various classroom seating arrangements when we make the change." I hold up architectural drawings of five different classroom arrangements to illustrate what I want them to discuss. "We are going to divide into small groups, each group is going to get one of these drawings, and I am going to ask you to talk about some of the implications of classroom furniture arrangements."

"Tom, you're going deep on us today," says Robert.

"Yeah, what are you up to?" asks Alexxis.

What I'm up to is this: I'm trying to provide students with an opportunity to think about ordinary things in their lives, like classroom furniture arrangements, and push them to find connections between how they sit in a classroom and how they learn to view themselves in a larger political world. I want them to think about what other than math or English is being taught in a classroom divided into rows. What "hidden lessons" are being imparted about power, learning, and equality, what lessons do students learn about who they are from the material shaping of their space?

I ask the students to count off—"one, two, three, four, five"—and put them into five small groups. Then I give each group an architectural drawing of a different classroom design. I give group one a drawing of chairs in rows; group two, chairs in a circle; group three, chairs in a forum arrangement; group four, small groups of four students per group; and group five, chairs facing the wall as one might find in a computer lab.

I ask each group to answer the following questions about its respective classroom arrangement:

- What does your arrangement suggest about student-student relationships in the classroom?
- What does it suggest about teacher-student relations?
- What does it suggest about how learning occurs?
- What does it suggest about power?
- How do you feel when you find yourself seated in your respective arrangement?

At first, students give me quizzical looks. I walk them through the first question about a classroom arranged in rows. "When you were sitting in rows earlier in this class, how did you feel in relation to each other? Remember Deavon's comment that she couldn't see people when they talked? Well, take that comment a step further, how does the arrangement of furniture define how you connect with other students in the room? About how the power is distributed? Chairs aren't arranged by accident or by magic. They are arranged for a purpose. What's the purpose? Who defines that purpose and for what reasons? I want you to think about things you might otherwise take for granted."

Eventually students begin to take their task seriously and engage in thinking about something that they really had never before considered on a conscious level, especially never considered in school—what is the "hidden curriculum" of material school settings?

While the students work, I rotate from group to group, listen to their conversations, take a few notes, and intervene when they get off track.

Group four gets stuck early. Their drawing is one of students seated in small groups.

Emily says: "I'm not getting this. What does how we sit have to do with anything?"

"Let's start with the last question on the handout—yes, I gave you all a handout—'How do you feel when you work in small groups with other students as opposed to sitting in rows?'" I ask.

"I like it."

I ask Emily why she likes it.

"Because I get to talk with my friends rather than listen to some boring teacher. Don't worry, I'm not talking about you, Tom." Emily says.

"How do you and your friends learn things when you work in small groups?" I ask.

Emily shrugs her shoulders, and Kauri answers instead. "We actually learn from each other, we figure it out."

"Right! So, you guys are the source of each other's learning. How is that different from what often happens when you're seated in rows?"

Kauri puts the eraser end of her pencil to her cheek, looks up to the ceiling for a moment, and then says: "You know, I really never paid much attention when I was sitting in rows. I drew a lot instead."

"Do you pay attention in small group settings?"

"Most of the time," says Kauri, "you really don't have much choice but to pay attention. Plus, I want to hear what someone else says. It's a lot more interesting."

"You guys get it. Just think out loud with each other about these questions. I'll check back in on you in a little bit." I move on to another group.

After the students complete their work, they report their thoughts back to the larger group. Before each group begins their sharing, we arrange the chairs in configurations that mirror the particular drawing the group considered. For instance, before group one reports out about the hidden curriculum of chairs arranged in rows, we arrange the chairs in rows. When group two shares their critical reflections of chairs arranged in a large circle, we arrange the chairs into a large circle.

We start with group one, chairs in rows. The group shares that most of their classroom lives have been spent seated in straight rows. Alexxis recalls a time when she was surprised to find a friend who was seated on the far side of the room from her. "I didn't even know she was there for the first couple of weeks of class."

Jason says that he always felt left out. "There wasn't enough room up front for everyone. Only so many students got to sit in the front rows. The rest of us had to fill in the back."

Darren agrees with Jason. "It was like a hierarchy. The same kids go the best seats while the rest of us spaced out in the back."

Deavon added, "I could never talk with anyone, and you know I love to talk."

"Yeah, that was school," added Darren. "The teacher talked and then we were just supposed to listen."

A number of students commented that chairs in rows suggested a classroom where learning begins and ends with the teacher, where power was located up front in a setting that wasn't equal.

"How wasn't it equal?" I ask.

"There was an order," Alexxis says. "Everyone knew who the teacher's favorites were. The kids in the top reading group, the ones who got to monitor recess, they all sat in front. And like Jason said, there was only so much room at the top and that's the way it was."

We move our chairs to form a circle and group two shares its thoughts.

Chance awakes from his slumber. "Is this when we all sing 'Kumbaya'?"

I thank him for his cynicism and ask Jose to begin. "We like circles because you can see who's talking without having to turn around."

"Yeah," says Zong, "I feel a lot less confined. I can breathe."

Slavic says, "It's like there's room for all of us. We can talk if we want or just listen if we want to, like I always do."

Robert looks directly at me. "And you're not controlling everything. We get to talk with each other."

Herman shares that he's not always comfortable in a circle. "I feel exposed."

"I sometimes do too," says Karley, " but I also feel much more together with everyone else in the class. We can all think out loud together. I feel included."

Perhaps the most interesting and the most profound reflection that students discuss is the fact that they never before considered classroom arrangements of furniture as anything more than an arbitrary and benign circumstance of learning. The chairs are where they happen to be. Students adjust themselves and their consciousness to a given reality without giving much thought to, as Paolo Friere writes in *Pedagogy of the Oppressed,* critically "considering reality."

The simple act of moving classroom furniture can offer us a point of critical reflection in regards to the first material reality we experience in a school setting, the room in which we sit. We find that we assume that we don't have the power to arrange the material nature of the room to fit our needs. Someone else owns it. Someone else arranges it. Permission is necessary in order to radically change the relationship of desk to desk, student to student, student to teacher. Permission is needed to change the nature of how we learn to together in an educational community.

The real power of this activity is that it can raise an initial fig leaf of hidden curriculum found in a readily accessible material circumstance. A critical reality can be uncovered in the very chairs in which we sit. The activity is an initial critical exploration of classroom learning. Simple transformation of furniture will not in and of itself change pedagogy but it can provide an easy way to think about the places in which we hope to transform ourselves as teachers and students.

I finish the activity by asking my students the "so what?" question. "Given what we did today, what are the larger lessons to be learned? We spent a whole class period looking at classroom furniture designs. Why? What's to be found when we look beneath our desks? Desks and chairs can be arranged in a variety of ways. So what?"

Chance is the first to respond: "Why don't you tell us?"

Once again, I thank Chance for his contribution to our learning and look to others for answers.

Deavon says, "I just never thought about any of this before. It makes me think, what else did I miss along the way that has somehow shaped me?"

"You know a lot of us never thought we were very smart and we also thought it was our fault that we weren't doing all that good in school. But maybe it wasn't all our fault, maybe being put in the back row had something to do with it. I don't know." Jason shakes his head as he ponders his words.

Jeremiah springs to life and says, "It's kind of like the worksite [students spend time building low-income housing while at Youth Builders]. We're put in crews and have to figure out things by ourselves. I mean, sometimes the boss isn't around, and something happens that you have to deal with. We work in small groups to figure it out ourselves. I was thinking of that when we were sitting in small groups. We could never build a house if we all just sat and listened to someone tell us how to do it. I figure out how to do it when I do it."

"Like I said before," says Darren, "it's about control."

"Tell me more, Darren, how are chairs in rows about control?"

"You learn early on who's in control and who's not when you are just put in rows and told to remember things. You get the feeling that the kids in the front rows deserve to be there and that the kids in back deserve to be in the back," Darren answers.

I direct a question to Jason, "You said earlier that there just wasn't enough room in the front for everyone. How is that similar to what we find in society?"

Jason thinks about my question for a minute before he says, "Now it's like musical chairs out there. Heck, there isn't enough room for all of us in the back row. Forget about the front."

Chance decides to get serious. "What I want to know is who sets up the chairs? I don't mean here, but out there?"

"What do you mean, Chance?"

"For all my time in school I just tried to find a seat in a room arranged by someone else. I feel like I'm trying to do the same now with my life. I want to know who sets up the chairs out there." Chance points out the window. "How do we get to do something else other than try to find a place in the back?"

"Let's start by trying to understand as much as we can about the structure, the arrangement of things, as we can, and then let's see who is making progress turning some of those rows into circles." I know the answer won't satisfy Chance's curiosity, but it's a start.

We can start to uncover a complex system of relationships both in school and "out there" by simply taking stock of where we find ourselves in the world—how we are placed in relation to each other. Once aware, we can try and turn our perspective upside down, to suggest to students like Jason, Darren, Chance, and Deavon that maybe their previous academic and personal failures weren't all their fault, that maybe there are viable strategies that can help students navigate their way through a system that casts them to the rear, a system that teaches them to adjust to a given reality rather than create one. Rather than ending up at the bottom, blaming themselves for their "failure," maybe my students can begin to envision a system, an arrangement, that better suits their collective needs.

And like rearranging classroom furniture, maybe we can think about and change that system one chair at a time.

References
Pedagogy of the Oppressed, by Paulo Freire (London: Continuum, 2000).

Chapter 3

Curriculum, Standards, and Testing

Creating Classrooms for Equity and Social Justice

This essay was published in its original form as the introduction to Rethinking our Classrooms: Teaching for Equity and Justice, Volume I, *and was written by the editors of that book. It was revised by the editors of* The New Teacher Book.

A s teachers, we begin from the premise that schools and classrooms should be laboratories for a more just society than the one we now live in. Unfortunately, too many schools are training grounds for boredom, alienation, and pessimism. Too many schools fail

Diana Craft

to confront the racial, class, and gender inequities woven into our social fabric. Teachers are often simultaneously perpetrators and victims, with little control over planning time, class size, or broader school policies—and much less over the unemployment, hopelessness, and other "savage inequalities" that help shape our children's lives.

But *The New Teacher Book* is not about what we cannot do; it's about what we can do. Brazilian educator Paulo Freire writes that teachers should attempt to "live part of their dreams within their educational space." Classrooms can be places of hope, where students and teachers gain glimpses of the kind of society we could live in and where students learn the academic and critical skills needed to make it a reality.

No matter what the grade level or content area, we believe that several interlocking components comprise what we call a social justice classroom. We argue that curriculum and classroom practice must be:

- **Grounded in the lives of our students.** All good teaching begins with a respect for children, their innate curiosity and their capacity to learn. Curriculum should be rooted in children's needs and experiences. Whether we're teaching science, mathematics, English, or social studies, ultimately the class has to be about our students' lives as well as about a particular subject. Students should probe the ways their lives connect to the broader society, and are often limited by that society.

- **Critical.** The curriculum should equip students to "talk back" to the world. Students must learn to pose essential critical questions: Who makes decisions and who is left out? Who benefits and who suffers? Why is a given practice fair or unfair? What are its origins? What alternatives can we imagine? What is required to create change? Through critiques of advertising, cartoons, literature, legislative decisions, military interventions, job structures, newspapers, movies, agricultural practices, or school life, students should have opportunities to question social reality. Finally, student work must move outside the classroom walls, so that scholastic learning is linked to real-world problems.

- **Multicultural, anti-racist, projustice.** In the publication *Rethinking Columbus,* Rethinking Schools used the discovery myth to demonstrate how children's literature and textbooks tend to value the lives of Great White Men over all others. Traditional materials invite children into Columbus' thoughts and dreams; he gets to speak, claim land, and rename the ancient homelands of Native Americans, who appear to have no rights. Implicit in many traditional accounts of history is the notion that children should disregard the lives of women, working people, and especially people of color—they're led to view history and current events from the standpoint of the dominant groups. By contrast, a social justice curriculum must strive to include the lives of all those in our society, especially the marginalized and dominated. As anti-racist educator Enid Lee points out in an interview in *Rethinking Our Classrooms*, a rigorous multiculturalism should engage children in a critique of the roots of inequality in curriculum, school structure, and the larger society—always asking: How are we involved? What can we do?

- **Participatory, experiential.** Traditional classrooms often leave little room for student involvement and initiative. In a "rethought" classroom, concepts need to be experienced firsthand, not just read about or heard about. Whether through projects, role plays, simulations, mock trials, or experiments, students need to be mentally, and often physically, active. Our classrooms also must provoke students to develop their democratic capacities: to question, to challenge, to make real decisions, to collectively solve problems.

- **Hopeful, joyful, kind, visionary.** The ways we organize classroom life should seek to make children feel significant and cared about—by the teacher and by each other. Unless students feel emotionally and physically safe, they won't share real thoughts and feelings. Discussions will be tinny and dishonest. We need to design activities where students learn to trust and care for each other. Classroom life should, to the greatest extent possible, prefigure the kind of democratic and just society we envision and thus contribute to building that society. Together students and teachers can create a "community of conscience," as educators Asa Hilliard and Gerald Pine call it.

- **Activist.** We want students to come to see themselves as truth-tellers and change makers. If we ask children to critique the world but then fail to encourage them to act, our classrooms can degenerate into factories for cynicism. Although it's not a teacher's role to direct students to particular organizations, it is a teacher's role to suggest that ideas should be acted upon and to offer students opportunities to do just that. Children can also draw inspiration from historical and contemporary efforts of people who struggled for justice. A critical curriculum should be a rainbow of resistance, reflecting the diversity of people from all cultures who acted to make a difference, many of whom did so at great sacrifice. Students should be allowed to learn about and feel connected to this legacy of defiance.

- **Academically rigorous.** A social justice classroom equips children not only to change the world but also to maneuver in the one that exists. Far from devaluing the vital academic skills young people need, a critical and activist curriculum speaks directly to the deeply rooted alienation that currently discourages millions of students from acquiring those skills. A social justice classroom offers more to students than do traditional classrooms and expects more from students. Critical teaching aims to inspire levels of academic performance far greater than those motivated or measured by grades and test scores. When children write for real audiences, read books and articles about issues that really matter, and discuss big ideas with compassion and intensity, "academics" starts to breathe. Yes, we must help students "pass the tests" (even as we help them analyze and critique the harmful impact of test-driven education). But only by systematically reconstructing classroom life do we have any hope of cracking the cynicism that lies so close to the heart of massive school failure, and of raising academic expectations and performance for all our children.

- **Culturally sensitive.** Critical teaching requires that we admit we don't know it all. Each class presents new challenges to learn from our students and demands that we be good researchers, and good listeners. These days, the demographic reality of schooling makes it likely that white teachers will enter classrooms filled with children of color. As African American educator Lisa Delpit writes in her review of the book *White Teacher* in *Rethinking Our Classrooms*, "When teachers are teaching children who are different from themselves, they must call upon parents in a collaborative fashion if they are to learn who their students really are." They must also call upon culturally diverse colleagues and community resources for insights into the communities they seek to serve. What can be said about racial and cultural differences between teachers and students also holds true for class differences.

We're skeptical of the "inspirational speakers" administrators bring to faculty meetings, who exhort us to become superteachers and classroom magicians. Critical teaching requires vision, support, and resources, not magic. We hope the stories, critiques, and lesson ideas here will offer useful examples which can be adapted in classrooms of all levels and disciplines and in diverse social milieus. Our goal is to provide a clear framework to guide classroom transformation.

References

Rethinking Our Classrooms: Teaching for Equity and Justice, Volume I (Milwaukee: Rethinking Schools, 2007).

Rethinking Columbus: The Next 500 Years (Milwaukee: Rethinking Schools, 1998).

'Curriculum Is Everything That Happens'

An Interview with Veteran Teacher
Rita Tenorio

Rita Tenorio has spent more than 25 years teaching children in the early elementary grades. Since 1988 she has taught at La Escuela Fratney, a public school in Milwaukee that she helped to found. Fratney features two-way bilingual education—all students learn in both English and Spanish—and a curriculum that emphasizes anti-racist, social justice education. In this interview by Leon Lynn, she offers encouragement and guidance to those just starting out in the teaching profession.

Rob Dunlavey

Do you think that the average person coming out of a teacher education program in college is ready to be a teacher?

I would say this to them: You've spent a lot of time in school, you've had some experiences, you've been able to accumulate a lot of information, and lots of it is probably very, very good. But there are also a whole bunch of other things, important things, that you may not know yet. You need to be open to that and ready to learn things.

Like what?

Well, to begin with, if you haven't been around teachers who have a political consciousness, who have experience with the social and political effects of things that take place in the schools, you definitely have to learn about that. You can't be thinking that your classroom is a safe little place that's separated from the rest of the world. Schools are impacted by larger social forces, by the dynamics of who has power in our society, how decisions are made. These forces determine so many things, including whether schools are adequately funded, whether the students and their families are comfortable or struggling to make ends meet, so many things that affect what happens in the classroom.

I like to think that the people who have worked with us at Fratney have a sense of that, because we try to make it a real up-front issue. Fratney is built on the principles of anti-racism and multiculturalism, the idea that we're not just preparing students to take and pass tests, we're not just preparing them academically but also to play a conscious and active role in society, to recognize and combat racism, to actively pursue social justice. These are things that many new teachers may not have been exposed to.

What advice would you give to a new teacher who finds a job in a school where the students are from a culture the teacher doesn't know well?

I think all teachers, especially new teachers, have to work very hard at getting to know who their students are. I don't just mean what their favorite colors are, but understanding things about them and their families. When I was first teaching, I knew very little about African American history and culture. My stereotypes were that the African American children came from very poor families who didn't have much education, that they were city-bound kids. But then I began listening to the children, the stories they told, and I began to realize just how stereotyped and limited my understanding was. I remember hearing children talking about going camping with their families and realizing that I never would have imagined them doing that. That's just one small example.

How can the teacher start bridging those gaps?

It's the teacher's job to invite the students to bring that information into the classroom, to tell stories about their families, to feel valued for making that contribution and for who they are. And we need to make sure this applies to all the children, not just the cute and verbal ones who are acclimated to the culture of school. That tends to happen a lot: There's this picture in the teacher's mind of the ideal kid and this notion that things would be better "if you could just be more like so-and-so." And that's so limiting, so unfair.

Curriculum is everything that happens. It's not just books and lesson plans. It's relationships, attitudes, feelings, interactions. If kids feel safe, if they feel inspired, if they feel motivated, if they feel capable and successful, they're going to learn important and positive things. But if those elements are not there, if they feel disrespected or neglected in school, they're learning from that too. But they're not necessarily learning the curriculum you think you're teaching them.

VOICES
FROM THE CLASSROOM

"Locate the cultures, the history of the community around your school. Who are the local heroes? What groups are working for justice in your school's neighborhood? Who are your allies? Who can your students research? The media puts forward athletes and movie stars as contemporary heroes. Where can they find alternative models in your community?"

—Linda Christensen

Teachers are under ever-increasing pressure to "teach to the test," to drill everyone on the same narrow band of curriculum and keep test scores up. And in many places there is increased support for very strict, scripted curriculum and teaching, such as Direct Instruction. How can a teacher do the kinds of things you are saying are crucial, while coping with these pressures?

It's a paradox, to be sure. In school you learn all about multiple intelligences, and different ways and styles of learning, and then you start teaching and more often than not they hand you a curriculum and say, "This is how to do it." And you can't just walk away from that. But you have to try and find ways to go beyond what is being scripted. Maybe you have to follow a very narrow instructional model in reading, for example, but maybe there are ways you can integrate a broader vision of reading into other subjects, like science or math.

And there's another element: You have to be part of a culture that stands up and asks: "Is this the best thing for our children?" There are schools where those questions are never asked. It's up to teachers to play a role in changing that, in raising holy hell if necessary to advocate for the children.

How can a new teacher, new in the building and district, do that?

It may seem overwhelming for people who are newer in the profession, but in some ways I think it's actually easier for them. I know I had a lot more energy for this stuff when I was younger and didn't have children of my own at home to care for. When you're young and new, you can establish who you are and what your priorities are.

One thing that really helped me was getting together with a network of people, searching out people who felt the way I did, and staying connected with them. You want to find the people in your own building whom you feel you can communicate with, whom you can raise questions with. You want to start looking in your district: I found some terrific people in the teacher union and through some professional development activities. There are networks and groups that stretch all across the country that address some of these issues, like multiculturalism, and you can tap into those. If you have friends from the university, and other people you've known for a while, you stay connected with them. Find people in the community, people who aren't teachers, who are interested in education issues. Get on the web and start hunting for good websites and list-servs. Then it's not just your voice out there in the wilderness. And together you can make good things happen.

Q/A

Where can I look for curriculum materials?

Start by asking around at school to find out who is widely recognized as an excellent teacher. Some teachers will be on almost everyone's list. Call or email these teachers and ask if there would be a convenient time for you to come by and talk curriculum and raid their files. Make sure you go to their classrooms so that they'll have materials handy. It's fine to get "greatest hit" lesson plans, but it's more useful to have an experienced teacher walk you through a full unit. Ask that teacher who else you should talk with, and whether or not there are networks of social justice teachers in the area.

One of the most comprehensive sources for social justice teaching materials is the Teaching for Change online Busboys and Poets bookstore: http://bbpbooks. teachingforchange.org/. This site also links to the resources we review and recommend in *Rethinking Schools* magazine. For history and social studies materials, check out the Zinn Education Project site, www.zinnedproject. org, which not only features lots of published resources, but also offers free downloadable lessons, most of which first appeared in *Rethinking Schools*. The Zinn Education Project facebook page is also a daily "people's history" calendar and curriculum guide. And, of course, every issue of *Rethinking Schools* includes excellent stories on social justice teaching. Subscribe at www. rethinkingschools.org

And to bring life and justice to classroom walls, check out the great posters in the Syracuse Cultural Workers catalog at www.syrculturalworkers.com.

—Bill Bigelow

Standards and Tests Attack Multiculturalism

by Bill Bigelow

Proponents of "higher standards" and more testing promise that students will learn more and schools will finally be held "accountable." In practice, their reforms are hostile to good teaching and pose a special threat to multiculturalism

The state where I teach, Oregon, joined the national testing craze well before No Child Left Behind became law. In the late '90s, the Oregon Department of Education gave a glimpse of the test mania to come when it field-tested its first-ever statewide social studies assessments. The tests were a multiple-choice maze that lurched about helter-skelter, seeking answers on World War I, constitutional amendments, global climate, rivers in India, hypothetical population projections, Supreme Court decisions, and economic terminology. From a close reading of these tests, social

David McLimans

169

studies knowledge is little more than the acquisition of disconnected facts about the world.

The version of standards pressed by "accountability" proponents threatens the development of a multicultural curriculum—one that describes and attempts to explain the world as it really exists; speaks to the diversity of our society and our students; and aims not only to teach important facts, but also to develop citizens who can make the world safer and more just.

In a sense, the entire effort to create fixed standards violates the very essence of multiculturalism. Multiculturalism is a search, a "conversation among different voices," in the words of Henry Louis Gates, to discover perspectives that have been silenced in traditional scholastic narratives. Multiculturalism attempts to uncover "the histories and experiences of people who have been left out of the curriculum," as anti-racist educator Enid Lee emphasizes. Because multiculturalism is an undertaking that requires new scholarship and constant discussion, it necessarily is ongoing. Yet as researcher Harold Berlak points out, "standardization and centralization of curriculum testing is an effort to put an end to a cacophony of voices on what constitutes truth, knowledge, and learning and what the young should be taught. It insists upon one set of answers." Curriculum standardization is, as Berlak indicates, a way to silence dissident voices, "a way to manufacture consent and cohesion."

Creating an official, government-approved social studies is bound to be controversial, whether at the national or state level. Thus, according to the Portland *Oregonian,* from the beginning, state education officials "tried to stake a neutral ground," in order to win approval for its version of social reality: "We have tried so hard to go right down the middle between what teachers want, what parents want, and what the [Republican-dominated] Legislature wants," according to Dawn Billings, a Department of Education curriculum coordinator. Not surprisingly, this attempt to be "neutral" and inoffensive means that the standards lack a critical sensibility—an emphasis on conflict and diversity of interpretation—and tend toward a conservative "Father Knows Best" portrait of history and society. For example, one typical 10th-grade benchmark calls for students to "Understand how the Constitution can be a vehicle for change and for resolving issues as well as a device for preserving values and principles of society."

Is this how, say, Frederick Douglass or the Seminole leader Osceola would have seen the Constitution? Shouldn't students also understand how the Constitution can be (and has been) a vehicle for preserving class and race stratification and for maintaining the privileges of dominant social groups? For example, in the 1857 *Dred Scott* case, the Supreme Court held that an enslaved person could not sue for his freedom because he was property, not a human being. Chief Justice Roger Taney declared that no black person in the United States had "any rights which the white man is bound to respect." The abolitionist William Lloyd Garrison called the Constitution an "agreement with Hell" for its support of slavery. And in 1896 the Supreme Court ruled in *Plessy v. Ferguson* that segregation—"separate but equal"—did not violate the 14th Amendment.

Almost 40 percent of the men who wrote the Constitution owned slaves, including George Washington and James Madison. In my U.S. history classes we look at the adoption of the Constitution from the standpoint of poor white farmers, enslaved African Americans, unemployed workers in urban areas, and other groups. Students create their own Constitution in a mock assembly, and then compare their document to the actual Constitution. They discover, for example, that the Constitution does not include the word "slave" or "enslaved person," but instead refers euphemistically to enslaved African Americans, as in Article 4, Section 2: "No person held in service or labor in one state, under the laws thereof, escaping into another, shall in consequence of any law or regulation therein, be discharged from service or labor, but shall be delivered up on claim of the party to whom such service or labor may be due." It's a vicious clause, that sits uncomfortably in the "preserving values and principles" rhetoric of Oregon's standards.

It is probably inevitable that school curricula will reflect the contradictions between a society's myths and realities. But although a critical multicultural approach attempts to examine these contradictions, standardization tends to paper them over. For example, another benchmark—"Explain how laws are developed and applied to provide order, set limits, protect basic rights, and promote the common good"—similarly fails the multicultural test. Whose order, whose basic rights, are protected by laws? Are all social groups included equally in the term "common good"? Between 1862 and 1890, laws in the United States gave 180,000,000 acres (an area the size of Texas and Oklahoma) to privately owned railroad companies, but gave virtually no land to African Americans freed from slavery in the South. Viewing the Constitution and other U.S. laws through a multicultural lens would add texture and depth to the facile one-sidedness of Oregon's "neutral" standards.

Indeed the "R" word, racism, is not mentioned once in any of the seven Oregon 11th-grade field tests nor in the social studies standards adopted by the state board of education. Even if the only yardstick were strict historical accuracy this would be a bizarre omission: the state was launched as a whites-only territory by the Oregon Donation Act and in racist wars of dispossession waged against indigenous peoples; the first constitution outlawed slavery but also forbade blacks from living in the state, a prohibition that remained on the books until 1926. Perhaps state education officials were concerned that introducing the concept of racism to students could call into question the essentially harmonious world of "change, and continuity over time" that underpins the standards project. Whatever the reason, there is no way that students can make sense of the world today without the idea of racism in their conceptual knapsack. If a key goal of multiculturalism is to account for how the past helped shape the present, and an important part of the present is social inequality, then standards and tests like those adopted in Oregon earn a failing grade.

Despite the publication of state social studies standards and benchmarks, throughout the country, teachers or parents don't really know what students are expected to learn until they see the tests. MetriTech, an out-of-state assessment corporation, developed Oregon's. As Prof. Wade W. Nelson pointed out in a delightfully frank *Phi Delta Kappan* article, "The Naked Truth About School Reform in Minnesota," "The content of the standards is found only in the tests used to assess them. Access to the tests themselves is carefully controlled, making it difficult to get a handle on what these standards are. It seems ironic to me that basic standards—that which every student is expected to know or be able to do—are revealed only in tests accessible only to test makers and administrators. This design avoids much of the debate about what these standards ought to be"—a debate that is essential to the ongoing struggle for a multicultural curriculum.

It's when you look directly at the tests that their limitations and negative implications for multiculturalism become most clear. Test questions inevitably focus on discrete facts, but cannot address the deeper, multifaceted meaning of facts. For example, in the Oregon social studies field tests, one question asked which constitutional amendment gave women the right to vote. Students could know virtually nothing about the long struggle for women's rights and get this question right. On the other hand, they could know lots about the feminist movement and not recall that it was the 19th and not the 16th, 17th, or 18th Amendment (the other test choices) that gave women the right to vote.

Because there is no way to predict precisely which facts will be sought on state tests, teachers will feel pressured to turn courses into a "memory Olympics"; teachers won't be able to spend the time required to probe beneath the headlines of history. For example, in my U.S. history class at Franklin High School in Portland, students perform a role play on the 1848 Seneca Falls, N.Y., women's rights conference, the first formal U.S. gathering to demand greater equality for women. The original assembly was composed largely of middle- to upper-class white women. I wanted my students to appreciate the issues that these women addressed and their courage, but also to consider the limitations imposed by their race, class, and ethnicity. Thus in our simulated 1848 gathering, my students portrayed women who were not at the original conference—enslaved African Americans, Cherokee women who had been forcibly moved to Oklahoma on the Trail of Tears, Mexican women in the recently conquered territory of New Mexico, poor white New England mill workers—as well as the white middle- and upper-class reformers like Elizabeth Cady Stanton and Lucretia Mott who were in attendance. In this more socially representative fictional assembly, students learned about the resolutions adopted at the original gathering and the conditions that motivated those, but they also saw firsthand how more privileged white women ignored other important issues such as treaty rights of Mexican women, sexual abuse of enslaved African Americans, and the workplace exploitation of poor white women, that a more diverse convention might have addressed.

The knowledge that my students acquired from this role play consisted not only of "facts"—although they learned plenty of these. They also exercised their multicultural social imaginations—listening for the voices that are often silenced in the traditional U.S. history narrative, becoming more alert to the importance of issues of race and class. However, this kind of teaching and learning takes time—time that could be ill-afforded in the fact-packing pedagogy required by multiple-choice tests. And after all their study, would my students have recalled whether it was the 16th, 17th, 18th, or 19th Amendment that gave women the right to vote? If not, they would have appeared ignorant about the struggle for women's rights.

In a demonstration of its own shaky grasp of the material on which it tests students, Oregon shows that the reverse is true as well: One can master isolated morsels of fact and remain ignorant about the issues that give those facts meaning. For example, in a test question repeated throughout the seven pilot tests, the state uses the term "Suffragette," an inappropriate and dismissive substitute for "Suffragist." Someone who had actually studied the movement would know this. As Sherna Gluck points out in her book *From Parlor to Prison*, women in the suffrage movement considered this diminutive term "an insult when applied to them by most of the American press."

My global studies students spend the better part of a quarter reading, discussing, role-playing, and writing about the manifold consequences of European colonialism. They read excerpts from Okot p'Bitek's poignant book-length poem, *Song of Lawino,* about the lingering psychological effects of colonialism in Uganda; role-play a trial on the colonial roots of the potato famine in Ireland; and examine how Asian economies were distorted to serve the needs of European ruling classes. But when confronted with Oregon's multiple-choice question that asks which continent was most thoroughly colonized in 1914, would my students answer correctly?

As these examples illustrate, in a multicultural curriculum it's not so much facts as it is perspective that is important in nurturing a fuller understanding of society. And sometimes considering new perspectives requires imagination as much as or more than memory of specific facts. For example, my history students read about the people Columbus encountered in 1492, the Taínos—who themselves left no written records—in excerpts from Columbus' journal and articles like José Barreiro's "Taínos: Men of the Good." I ask students to write a story or diary entry from the point of view of a Taíno during the first few days or weeks of their encounter with Spaniards that draws on information in the readings, but goes further. It's necessarily a speculative undertaking, but invites students to turn the "Columbus discovers America" story on its head, encourages them to appreciate the humanity in the people usually marginalized in tales of "exploration." In response, students have written pieces of startling insight. Sure, a multiple-choice test can assess whether students know that Columbus first sailed in 1492, the names of his ships, where he landed, or the name of the people he encountered. But these tests are ill-equipped to assess what students truly *understand* about this encounter.

Necessarily, the "one best answer" approach vastly oversimplifies and misrepresents complex social processes—and entirely erases ethnicity and race as categories of analysis. One question on an Oregon social studies test reads: "In 1919, more than 4.1 million Americans belonged to labor unions. By 1928, that number had dropped to 3.4 million. Which of the following best accounts for that drop?" It seems that the correct answer must be A.: "Wages increased dramatically, so workers didn't need unions." All the other answers are clearly wrong, but is this answer "correct"? Since when do workers leave unions when they win higher wages? Weren't mechanization and scientific management factors in undermining traditional craft unions? Did the post-World War I Red Scare, with systematic attacks on radical unions like the Industrial Workers of the World and deportations of foreign-born labor organizers, affect union membership?

And how about the test's reductive category of "worker"? Shouldn't students be alert to how race, ethnicity, and gender were and are important factors in determining one's workplace experience, including union membership? For example, in 1919, professional strikebreakers, hired by steel corporations, were told to "stir up as much bad feeling as you possibly can between the Serbians and the Italians." And, as Howard Zinn points out in *A People's History of the United States*, more than 30,000 black workers, excluded from AFL unions, were brought in as strikebreakers. A multicultural awareness is vital if we're to arrive at a satisfactory answer to the above test question. But tests like these reward students for choosing a historical soundbite that is as shallow as it is wrong.

This leads me to an aspect of standardized tests that is especially offensive to teachers: They don't merely assess, they also instruct. The tests represent the authority of the state, implicitly telling students, "Just memorize the facts, kids. That's what social studies is all about—and if teachers do any more than that, they're wasting your time." Multiple-choice tests undermine teachers' efforts to construct a rigorous multicultural curriculum because they delegitimate that curriculum in students' eyes: If it were important it would be on the test.

At its core, multicultural teaching is an ethical, even political, enterprise. Its aim is not just to impart lots of interesting facts, to equip students to be proficient Trivial Pursuit players, but also to help make the world a better place. It highlights injustice of all kinds—racial, gender, class, linguistic, ethnic, national, environmental—in order to make explanations and propose solutions. It recognizes our responsibility to fellow human beings and to the earth. It has heart and soul.

Compare that with the sterile fact-collecting orientation of Oregon's standards and assessments. For example, a typical 49-question high school field test includes seven questions on global climate, two on the location of rivers in India and Africa, and one on hypothetical world population projections in the year 2050. But not a single question in the test concerns the lives of people around the world, or environmental conditions—nothing about increasing poverty, the global AIDS epidemic, disappearance of the rainforests, rates of unemployment, global warming, etc., or efforts to address these crises. The test bounds aimlessly from one disjointed fact to another. In the most profound sense it's pointless.

Indeed the test's random amorality may reveal another of its cultural biases. Oregon's standards and assessments make no distinction between knowledge and information. The state's version of social education would appear to have no *raison d'être* beyond the acquisition of large quantities of data. But for many cultures, the aim of knowledge is not bulk, but wisdom—insight into meaningful aspects about the nature of life. Writing in the winter 1998–99 issue of *Rethinking Schools*, Peter Kiang makes a similar point about the Massachusetts Teacher Test that calls into question the validity of enterprises such as these. He writes that:

> by constructing a test based on a sequence of isolated, decontextualized questions that have no relationship to each other, the underlying epistemology embedded in the test design has a Western-cultural bias, even if individual questions include or represent "multicultural" content. Articulating and assessing a knowledge base requires examining not only what one knows, but also how one knows.

Students "know" in different ways, and these differences are often cultural. Standardized social studies tests nonetheless subject all students to an abstract data-heavy assessment device that does not gauge what or how they have learned. As Kiang points out, test makers address multicultural criticism by including individual questions about multicultural content—for example, by highlighting snippets of information about famous people of color like Martin Luther King Jr., Cesar Chavez, and Harriet Tubman. But these "heroes and holidays" additions cannot mask the fundamental hostility to multicultural education shown by standards and assessments like those initiated by Oregon.

Spelling out an alternative to culturally biased, superficial "accountability" plans would require another article. In brief, I want the states to abandon the effort to treat teachers as cogs in a delivery system of approved social information. I want departments of education to support me and other teachers as we collaborate to create curriculum that deals forthrightly with social problems, that fights racism, social injustice, and environmental destruction. I want them to support teachers as we construct rigorous performance standards for students that promote deep thinking about the nature of our society. I want them to acknowledge the legitimacy of a multicultural curriculum of critical questions, complexity, multiple perspectives, and social imagination. I want them to acknowledge that wisdom is more than information— that the world can't be chopped up into multiple-choice questions, and that you can't bubble-in the truth with a No. 2 pencil.

A number of the lessons mentioned here are described in greater depth in the Rethinking Schools books *Rethinking Globalization: Teaching for Justice in an Unjust World* and *Rethinking Columbus*, www. rethinkingschools.org; and at the Zinn Education Project website, www.zinnedproject.org.

References

"Multiculturalism: A Conversation Among Different Voices," by Henry Louis Gates Jr., in *Rethinking Schools: An Agenda for Change* (New York: The New Press, 1995) p. 7.

Song of Lawino & Song of Ocol, by Okot p'Bitek (Portsmouth, NH: Heinemann, 1984).

"Standards and the Control of Knowledge," by Harold Berlak, in *Rethinking Schools*, Vol. 15, No. 4.

"Taínos: Men of the Good," by Jose Barreiro, in *Rethinking Columbus: The Next 500 Years* (Milwaukee: Rethinking Schools, 2003).

"Taking Multicultural, Anti-Racist Education Seriously: An Interview with Enid Lee" in *Rethinking Our Classrooms, Vol. 1* (Milwaukee, WI: Rethinking Schools, 2007) p. 9.

"Trivial Pursuit Testing," by Peter Kiang, *in Rethinking Schools*, Vol. 13, No. 2.

Q/A My students don't bring back their homework. Should I keep assigning it?

First ask yourself some questions: Why are you giving homework? Is there a school policy, or is it up to the teacher? In many places it is a timeworn tradition that students have homework, or it may be that parents demand it or have banned it.

What is the purpose served by homework? Is it a real opportunity for students to review or practice a skill? Is it meant to let families know what is going on in class? Or is it just "busy work"? What happens to the work that students bring back? Who looks at it? How is it used or not used?

These questions are just the beginning.

If you really want your students to take homework seriously, spend time on it and return it. Be sure the content is meaningful and connected to their lives, the classroom, or both.

Homework has to be thought through and planned like any other part of the curriculum. Involve students in the development and use of the information in their homework. Let them know that you and they will need the data they collected, or the words of the person they interviewed, to continue the work in the classroom during the coming days.

Homework can be an opportunity to learn about the lives and perspectives of students and their families. It can be a chance for kids to practice collecting data, to experiment with materials and ideas, to gain expertise in conducting surveys and interviewing others. Asking for the knowledge, ideas, and perspectives of students and their families will give you and your students the rich beginnings of many classroom conversations.

You also have to be sensitive to the circumstances students face outside of school. Is there a place for the student to do work at home? Will there be another person available to help with the work or to see that it's done? What resources does your student have outside of school? Does the family have access to computers or other technology, for example? Don't assume that all your students do or do not have resources. Ask.

If you have students who can't or don't do homework, you can also find ways for them to complete the work at school.

Here are some examples of homework assignments that invite students' lives into the classroom.

Interview someone in your family about:

An upcoming holiday, a current event, experiences that they may have had.

Respond to the question:

What is peace? What is justice? What is your best advice to me? What do you know about _____?

—Rita Tenorio

Working Effectively with English Language Learners

by Bob Peterson and Kelley Dawson Salas

As communities across the United States are becoming more diverse, many new teachers are finding that their responsibilities include teaching both academic content and language skills to English language learners.

There are many different types of bilingual ed/ESL programs (see the box on page 184), and great differences can exist between programs that purport to serve students in similar ways.

Regardless of the type of program you're in, remember that it's your responsibility to deliver instruction to

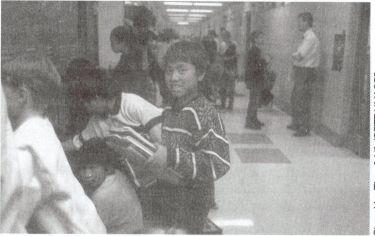

these students in a way that is understandable. That means organizing your teaching practice in a way that meets their needs, as well as "working the system" to ensure that these students are getting the services, such as extra support for taking tests, that they need.

As a starting point, find out what kinds of services your school offers to support English language learners—and to

Types of ESL and Bilingual Programs

English as a Second Language (ESL)

Emphasis is on learning and using English in the classroom and on preparing English language learners to function in "mainstream" English-language classrooms. English language learners may be placed in an English as a second language class, "sheltered English" classes, or they may participate in a pullout ESL class. ESL teachers may also support classroom teachers in their classrooms. Other languages typically are not used in ESL programs.

Transitional Bilingual Education

(Also referred to as "early exit bilingual education")

Students' native language is used in classrooms to help students learn academic content while they are learning English. As soon as possible (usually two or three years), students are moved into instruction in English only. The goal is proficiency in English, not continuing to develop the student's native language skills.

Developmental Bilingual Education

(Also referred to as "maintenance bilingual education" or "late exit bilingual education")

These programs develop and maintain proficiency in students' native language as well as English. Students entering developmental bilingual programs as kindergartners are typically taught to read and write in their native language first, and then literacy skills are transferred to English. Once students function in both languages, they continue to learn language and content in both languages.

Dual Language Education

(Also referred to as "two-way bilingual" or "two-way immersion")

These programs serve a mix of English language learners and native English-speaking students. They teach language and content in both English and in a target language (for example, Spanish, Japanese, etc.) The goal is for all students to become literate in both English and the target language, and to develop and maintain both languages.

support you as their classroom teacher. Ask your administrators, colleagues, or district bilingual/ESL office. Then do
a little of your own research about English language learners and how their needs can best be served. (See the resource
list on page 187 for some places to start.)

Strategies for Improving Instruction for English Language Learners

Speak slowly, audibly, and clearly in whatever language you
use in the classroom. Avoid asking students in front of the
whole class if they understand. Instead, ask students to volunteer to repeat the instructions in their own words, in English, or in the students' native language.

Prepare English language learners for challenging whole-
class lessons ahead of time. In a small group, teach the sec-
ond-language vocabulary that students will need to know.
In addition to vocabulary, introduce the concepts that the
whole class will be learning. Use materials that are geared
for the specific group of English language learners (i.e., use
materials in the students' home language and/or materials in
English that are appropriate for the students' English reading level). That way when you teach the whole-class lesson,
English language learners have a head start because they
already had one comprehensible lesson on the topic.

Use lecture and verbal instruction as little as possible.
Use visual cues such as posters, overhead pictures, slide
shows, videos, and illustrated books. Use active methods
of learning such as games, skits, songs, partner interviews,
and structured conversation with classmates. When necessary, explain concepts in the students' home language (have
a colleague, parent volunteer, or student help if you are not
able to do this). Finally, be prepared to spend additional
time helping English language learners do the work. To keep
things in perspective, try thinking about how your performance on the assignment would change if you were doing
it in a language in which you were not yet fully proficient.

Use whole-class instruction as little as possible. English
language learners sometimes get lost and/or tune out during this kind of lesson. Whenever possible, work with small

groups of children, or get students working on an assignment and circulate among them as they work.

In reading class, use literature—in English or the students' home language—that features the students' language/cultural groups. Give English language learners lots of attempts to be successful in a low-stress environment. Choral reading, echo reading, and partner reading all allow students to work on fluency and pronunciation without putting them on the spot. Rehearsing a sentence, paragraph, or page before reading it aloud to a group can help students to improve fluency one chunk of text at a time. Plays and skits provide a wonderful excuse to encourage students to practice the same lines over and over until they master them, and presenting a play or skit in their second language gives students a great sense of accomplishment.

Encourage students to maintain and develop their first language at school, at home, and in the community. Research shows that students learn English more effectively, and don't lag as far behind their English-speaking classmates in other subject areas, when they do more academic work in their native language. And when students are pushed to learn English only, and aren't given the chance to continue learning their home language, they lose the opportunity to be bilingual, a skill that's increasingly valued in society.

Don't assume students have special education needs just because they're struggling academically. It could just be that they lack the language skills to successfully complete more academic work in English. At the same time, don't ignore potential special education needs either. Seek out resources in your school, district, and community to help you determine what is going on with a particular student.

Strategies for Becoming More Culturally Competent

If you do not yet speak the languages of the children you work with, start learning. Even if you do not master a student's language, learning a few words and courtesy phrases is a sign of respect and effort on your part. If you already speak your students' languages, congratulations! Continue to work at improving your skills.

Learn about the cultures of the children you teach. Listen to your students and show interest in their cultures while being careful not to put students on the spot or assume that they're experts on their cultures. Plan assignments that bring students' cultures, families, languages, and experiences front and center. Talk with colleagues, parents, and friends who share the students' backgrounds. Read, see movies, listen to music, travel to the students' home countries if possible. This is a lifelong process.

Find ways to communicate with parents in their first language unless they ask you to speak with them in English. For example, find out if an interpreter is needed and arrange for one ahead of time.

Resources for Working with English Language Learners

Dual Language Instruction: A Handbook for Enriched Education, edited by Nancy Cloud, Fred Genesee, and Else Hamayan (Philadelphia: Heinle & Heinle, 2000).

Help! They Don't Speak English: Starter Kit for Primary Teachers, (Oneonta, NY: Eastern Stream Center on Resources and Training [ESCORT], 1998).

Learning and Not Learning English: Latino Students in American Schools, by Guadalupe Valdés (New York: Teachers College Press, 2001).

The Power of Two Languages: Literacy and Biliteracy for Spanish-Speaking Students, edited by Josefina Villamil Tinajero and Alma Flor Ada (New York: McMillan/McGraw Hill, 1993).

Dr. Jim Cummins' ESL and Second Language Learning Web, http://iteachilearn.org/cummins/index.htm

This site offers details about Cummins' work researching second language acquisition and literacy development, and links to other web resources.

Stephen D. Krashen's Website, www.sdkrashen.com

Information about Krashen's many informative articles and other writings about language learning.

Rethinking Schools Special Collection on Bilingual Education, www.rethinkingschools.org/special_reports/bilingual/resources.shtml

This site provides a more in-depth listing of articles and resources for teachers working with English language learners.

Q/A

I hate the textbook I've been given to use. What can I do?

In order to present students with multiple perspectives on any topic, it is likely that you will need more than one resource. Part of the challenge in becoming a social justice teacher is finding the materials you will need to supplement the books you have available in your school. Then there is also the trick of finding the time and opportunities in the weekly schedule to use them. It is not easy, but it is worth the energy you expend.

Take the time to review the textbooks you're given, then determine where you will need to add on to what you've got. Start with your school library. Tap the public library as well, for classroom literature. If you have access to a university, see if it has collections of curriculum materials available for lending. Then get on the internet: Start with the resources and web links you'll find at www.rethinkingschools.org.

Monthly book clubs like Scholastic or Troll often offer quality literature at a great price. They are an inexpensive way to begin collecting multiple copies of books for use in reading instruction. Don't be afraid to ask if there is money in the school budget to add to your classroom collection.

Songs and poetry are great sources of alternative perspectives too. And you can use data and information from the news to help students explore concepts in math, science, and other curricular areas.

If you still feel you're "stuck" with poor resources, remember that you have the ability to help your students look critically at what they are reading and see the shortcomings for themselves. Help them find ways to "talk back" to the textbook and teach them how to find other perspectives that are not represented in its pages.

—Rita Tenorio

If your principal has told you to use the textbook, defying a direct order from him/her will generally be considered insubordination and will land you in trouble, or even the unemployment line. However, perhaps there are other people in your school or department who don't like this book. Ask around to find out. Get together with those people. Write up a critique of the book and propose alternative curriculum.

In the short term, go ahead and use the book but use it critically. Invite students to read between the lines: Whose perspectives are missing? Was America "discovered" or "invaded"? See "Students as Textbook Detectives" in *Rethinking Our Classrooms, Volume 1*, or *Rethinking Columbus* for lots of ideas on how to engage students in a critique of their textbooks. (See page 359 for details.)

In a nutshell: If you feel like you have to use the assigned text, use it, but find other materials as well. Even if you "use" the textbook, any good administrator will expect you to supplement it with lots of other materials.

—Bill Bigelow

Q/A How do I get started planning a teaching unit?

Often a unit begins with a central piece of literature or history. I examine the piece to uncover what lens, what approach, I will take with the material. I construct a question that I want students to answer by reading, writing, and discussing from the central text as well as a variety of other texts—movies, poetry, first-person narratives—including their own lives. For example, when I teach Alice Walker's *The Color Purple*, we ask about the roles of men and women in society. We read the novel, but we also look at images of women and men in advertising. We read "Jury of Her Peers" and "The Yellow Wallpaper," and poems by Sharon Olds, Ethelbert Miller, and Anne Sexton. We watch *Defending Our Lives*, a documentary about abused women who are in prison for killing their abusers. We interview men and women in our lives.

At other times, the question is the central focus of the unit, and I find a variety of texts with diverse voices to answer it—again including the students' voices. For example, in my unit on the politics of language, I begin with the question "Is language political?" Over the years, I have varied the first text I use depending on the students in the classroom. I know I want to get to Ebonics, or Spoken Soul, but I discovered along the way that *Pygmalion* is a better way to start—far away from Portland, Ore.

Either way I begin, I outline the key reading and writing tasks I want students to complete during the unit; I am concerned with the content I am teaching as well as the literacy skills the students are developing. Typically, a unit in my class will take five or six weeks, and I want to make sure that students are writing a personal narrative, some poetry, and an essay during that unit.

—Linda Christensen

'I Just Want to Read Frog and Toad'

by Melanie Quinn

One mid-September night, when I was tucking my 5-year-old son Eamonn in bed, the standardization madness came home to roost. With quivering lip and tear-filled eyes, Eamonn told me he hated school. He said he had to read baby books that didn't make sense and that he was in the "dummy group."

Then he looked up at me and said, "I just want to read Frog and Toad."

I am an experienced elementary teacher and college professor, with a long-standing disdain for "ability" grouping, dummied-down curricula, and stupid, phonics-driven stories that make no sense. And yet here I was, seemingly unable to prevent my own child from being crushed by a scripted reading program of the type so beloved by No Child Left Behind (NCLB).

Heidi Younger

What's So Bad?

Eamonn had left kindergarten happy and confident, even requesting his own library card that summer. His older brother and sister were wonderful role models who had enjoyed sitting at the kitchen table on dreary Northwest days writing and illustrating their own books and, when they were older, reading chapter books in bed before they fell asleep.

But then the desire to quickly "fix" struggling readers and standardize curricula descended on the primary grades at his school.

When my son had been in kindergarten, the 1st- and 2nd-grade classroom teachers, with the principal's strong urging, had looked at two scripted programs: SRA/McGraw-Hill's "Open Court Reading" and "Houghton Mifflin Reading." When I heard about this, I spoke to the Site Council, principal, and teachers in an effort to persuade them to instead focus on improved teaching using authentic literature. The principal assured me that a decision to buy either program was on hold.

That fall, however, I opened the *Welcome Back to School Newsletter* and read that the Houghton Mifflin program would be used for the 1st and 2nd grades. Mixed in with feelings of dismay and anger, I felt guilty that I had not fought harder to ensure that the scripted curriculum was not adopted.

After Eamonn's lament about Frog and Toad, I decided to do further investigation. I grabbed Eamonn's backpack and found a wad of photocopied "books" and a 20-page chunk of stapled-together workbook pages.

Limiting Vocabulary

One of the photocopied "books" was *The Big Pig's Bib*. I'd give a synopsis of the tale, but it makes no sense and is little more than a collection of unrelated words. The story begins by introducing the human characters and saying, "It is Tim and it is Mim." In standard English, the word "this" would be used to introduce Tim and Mim—i.e., "This is Tim and this is Mim." Unfortunately, the program has not yet presented the word "this," so instead it introduces the characters using clumsy, nonstandard English: "It is Tim and it is Mim."

At one point, the story says the pig is not big but then at the end, Tim and Mim fit it with a "big pig's bib"—even though there are no events or clues as to how the pig, who was not big, can now wear a "big pig's bib."

Then there's the story of *Can Pat Nap?* The simplistic line drawings show a child sitting down under a tree. In the tree is a bird that one assumes is a woodpecker. The text reads, "Pat can nap. Tap, tap, tap. Pat can not nap. Tap, Tap, Tap. Sap on the cap. Can Pat nap? Not here, Pat!"

I am confused. Can Pat nap or can't he? Better still, who cares?

A Waste of Resources

The workbook pages, meanwhile, are supposed to coincide with the books but are little more than simplified skills. One asks the student to circle short "I" sounds; another asks the children to draw a diagonal line from one part of a compound word to another. All of the writing and thinking is done by the publisher, and the children merely fill in disjointed

VOICES
FROM THE CLASSROOM

"Teachers can be agents of change. We shouldn't accept the idea that we don't have the power to do anything in the situation. Even if you don't see yourself as a political person or someone with control over what you're doing, in reality, you're making thousands of political decisions every day.

"Not intervening when a student makes a racist comment is a political decision. Teaching from textbooks that emphasize only the European American experience is another one. Those are political decisions that hurt students. You can also make choices that help students—choose to intervene when you hear a homophobic slur, choose to find books that represent the experiences of many different kinds of people, etc."

—Kelley Dawson Salas

blanks. Once they identify the pattern, there is no need to even read the surrounding text.

There are a few pages that ask for some sort of thought process, for example to write an alternate ending for a story. Unfortunately, those exercises have been crossed out. Apparently, having children actually think and write takes up too much time.

After a few days, I cooled down enough to approach the principal, classroom teacher, and reading teacher. I asked that Eamonn be allowed to read real books and during workbook time, to write his own stories in a journal. I was assured accommodations would be made. (It turns out, however, that they weren't.)

Life continued at its hectic pace. Eamonn stopped crying about reading, and he seemed relatively happy with school. Weeks, then months, passed.

Capitalizing on Students' Interests—or Not

The following spring, as we sat on the couch one afternoon, Eamonn offered that reading was beginning to be fun. I asked why. "Well, since it is the end of the year, we are getting to read words like 'about' and our reading workbook and worksheet packets ask us to fill in the blanks with bigger words," he explained. "All year until now the blanks have been for little words like, 'I,' 'I,' 'I.'"

Eamonn hopped up excitedly and ran to his backpack to show me a book he had just gotten. He pulled out a photocopied book, Number 71, titled *White Knight*. On the cover was a whimsical knight dressed in armor with a large "W" on his shirt and a banner with WK on it. Then Eamonn said, "See, it is a knight!"

Eamonn explained that the students were also excited because the teacher had handed out the book to the class a while earlier, but then taken it back. "She goofed up," he said. "See, she had all these books copied and ready and she passed out the wrong number. We had other ones we had to read first before we could get to this number. We had not read numbers 69 and 70 yet."

While the Houghton Mifflin program boasts of quality stories from well-known children's authors, those apparently are sparingly dispersed in the classroom. The photocopied books sent home for children to read and add to their "library" are boring both textually and visually, filled with black-lined drawings of androgynous human characters.

And then there is the case of the white knight with the large W on his chest, perpetuating stereotypes of the damsel in distress being rescued by the white knight who "always does what is right."

Eamonn opened up the four-page book and read:

> (Page 1) White Knight said,
> I am brave. I fight for what is right!"
> (Page 2) Miss Moll was up high. She called, "White Knight! White Knight!"
> (Page 3) White Knight climbed high to get Miss Moll, but he did not hang on tight. He fell on his thigh.
> (Page 4) Miss Moll came down to White Knight. She said, "You might like some pie." White Knight sighed.

At the end of the reading, Eamonn's head dropped and he looked up with disappointment. "Well, that wasn't very good," he admitted.

But then he proceeded to tell his own story:

> It could have been that the White Knight is going by a dragon and he pulls out his sword—this might be bad but there could be blood—and he kills the dragon and then he goes to the castle and battles the guards. Then he runs up a bunch of stairs, and he rescues Miss Moll. When they are running down the stairs, there are new guards and he battles them. Then they get on horses and ride past the dead dragon, ride off down the road and get to their castle and live happily every after.

"That could be a good story," he says proudly.

What could I say? I affirmed what he already knew: that stories need to be complete, not exercises in the "long i spelled igh." And Eamonn's story actually had a plot. It had a beginning, middle, and end, a problem and a solution, a protagonist and an antagonist. Unfortunately, the main lesson he took from White Knight was the reinforcement of the damsel in distress stereotype.

I am angry that Eamonn did not get to write his own knight story, and that he and his classmates were denied the opportunity to critically think about the stereotype being perpetuated in White Knight. Instead he had his time wasted by filling in "about" on a workbook page while the teacher tried to distribute the next book in chronological order.

When Eamonn started 2nd grade, his teacher granted my request that he be allowed to read actual books during reading time, not photocopied nonsense. He has become an avid reader and falls asleep every night with a book in his hand. He prefers reading real books with real stories—the kind you find in public libraries and bookstores but, increasingly, not in our nation's elementary classrooms.

References

Frog and Toad Are Friends, by Arnold Lobel (New York: HarperCollins, 1979).

How can I get started using poems with my students?

Poetry fits into every nook and cranny of the school day and school year. Sometimes a poem helps students learn about each other. A poem like George Ella Lyon's "Where I'm From" acts as a model for students to write similar poems using the details of their lives. Lyon's poem uses a repeating line and a list, which is a powerful but easy way to help students write their own poetry. (See *Reading, Writing, and Rising Up*.)

And sometimes a poem creates a word and emotional picture so that students can understand a contemporary or historical situation. The poem "teaches" an event from a different perspective. For example, Martín Espada's poem "Federico's Ghost," included in *Rethinking Globalization*, illuminates the effects of pesticide sprays on farmworkers and their children.

Students also can use poetry to demonstrate their understanding of a historical or literary character or situation: I often recycle Lyon's "Where I'm From" poem and have students write from a particular character's point of view.

Dialogue poems (see *Rethinking Our Classrooms, Volume 1*) are effective when controversy or different opinions may arise. For example, students may write about the integration of Central High School in Little Rock, Ark., from the point of view of either a segregationist or an integrationist on the first day of school. These help students get inside the heads and hearts of people from literature and history.

But poetry shouldn't be limited to the reading and writing of poems. Poetry is also the play of language in essays and narratives. It encompasses hearing the heartbeat of a sentence, finding and using strong verbs, sliding metaphoric language into an analytic essay, surprising the reader with an unexpected analogy.

—Linda Christensen

The books mentioned here are published by Rethinking Schools. Details can be found beginning on page 357.

Teaching Controversial Content

by Kelley Dawson Salas

A classmate in my master's degree program explained to our class: "I really want to talk with my students about why it's wrong to discriminate against gay people. I had one conversation with them about it, but then my principal found out, and ever since then he's been watching every move I make. I feel like I can't teach about this anymore."

After working for weeks to write units on such topics as gender bias, racism, and the criminalization of youth, our class discussed what it would be like to actually teach these units in our classroom. We wanted to teach the lessons we'd written—in fact, we had chosen

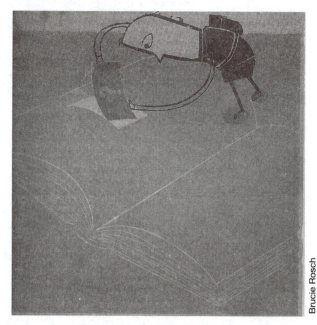

Brucie Rosch

this master's program because it explicitly focused on anti-racist teaching. But although many of my classmates strongly believed in the lessons we wrote, at the same time most expressed doubts about actually being able to teach these lessons in our classrooms.

Our professor prompted us: "Tell me about your fears. What do you think could happen if you were to teach these units in your classrooms?" We called out our concerns and our professor wrote our list on the board:

- I'll get fired.

- My principal won't fire me but will retaliate against me in other ways.

- Other teachers in the building won't want to work with me.

- I'll end up being totally isolated at my school.

- Parents will challenge me.

These fears are very real for teachers who decide that curriculum needs to integrate a strong social justice focus, one that helps kids learn about multiple perspectives and develop critical thinking skills.

Even after completing my fifth year of teaching, I still experience fears and insecurities when it comes to implementing a social justice curriculum. But it's gotten a little easier each year.

Out on a Limb

During my first year of teaching, I was inspired by an article in *Rethinking Schools* by Kate Lyman about teaching the Civil Rights Movement to elementary students. Using Kate's article as a starting point, I decided to teach a unit on the Civil Rights Movement and have my 3rd-grade students write and prepare a class play for presentation at our February all-school assembly, which had a "Black history" theme.

I knew that I was going out on a limb, because I wrote the unit myself, and I really didn't know whether I was "allowed" to deviate from the 3rd-grade social studies textbook I was supposed to be using. As I began teaching the unit I felt isolated: I had asked my partner teacher to plan the unit with me and to teach it simultaneously in his classroom, but he'd decided he wasn't interested in doing that.

Despite my feelings of uneasiness, I went ahead with my teaching and found that the students responded very well to the content and the projects that we did. But I still wondered what consequences I might face if someone walked into my classroom and began to question what we were studying.

The story had a happy ending. My partner teacher—although he politely declined my request to co-teach the unit—saw that I needed some help, and so after school one afternoon we built a life-sized "bus" for the play. The kids wrote the play, learned their parts, and in the process showed a good understanding of the events of the Montgomery, Ala., bus boycott.

The students presented their play at our February assembly, and as a final touch after the performance, they sang Bob Marley's "Get Up, Stand Up" and got the whole school up and singing along. A strange feeling washed over me. I had embarked on this unit with a sense of fear and insecurity, yet with a kind of determination that what I was doing made sense. Things turned out much better than I had expected. It was a far cry from "What if I get fired for this?"

This was a good lesson for me. I was at a school that was not particularly progressive, yet I learned that it wasn't repressive, either. It was mostly a "teach and let teach" environment. I never took any flak for teaching about the Civil Rights Movement, though neither did I get any earth-shattering compliments. Teachers didn't start knocking down my door asking to team-teach social studies units with me, but neither did my principal ask me to go back to the textbook. In short, what I had done was OK.

Seeking "Permission"

Since then, I have talked to lots of veteran teachers and asked how I should go about teaching from a social justice perspective, given that I am a new teacher with many things to learn. I want to teach my students to think critically, analyze our world, and learn to change it, but I am not always as confident about my approach as I wish I was. And I often second-guess myself, wondering whether I am "allowed" to teach the way I want to teach. At the end of my first year of teaching, I asked veteran social studies teacher Bill Bigelow a question that had been on my mind all year: "Who has the authority to decide what I teach?"

He answered simply: "You do."

It was a critical moment for me. All year I had been searching for someone who would grant me permission to teach the way I wanted to. In my school community, I had not experienced resistance, but I was looking for more than the absence of resistance. I needed someone to tell me that it was OK to do the kind of social justice teaching I was trying to work toward. My conversation with Bill made me understand that the person who has the greatest control over what happens in my classroom is me. Waiting for someone else to give me permission or authority to teach the way I wanted to was not necessary.

But that's not to say that those of us who wish to teach from a social justice perspective don't need to explain our curriculum and methods to others in our school community. We need to be prepared to respond to questioning or criticism from other teachers, administrators, or parents who don't want us to teach in this way. Peter Brown, a teacher-educator from California, gave me some great advice that he said he shares regularly with those he mentors: "Before you start a unit that you think may be controversial, inform the parents and principal about what you'll be teaching and explain how it fits into the school's curriculum and standards."

For example, the Milwaukee Public Schools' Teaching and Learning Goal #1 states: "Students will project anti-racist, anti-biased attitudes through their participation in a multilingual, multi-ethnic, culturally diverse curriculum." This provides an excellent rationale for many of the activities I do in my classroom, and since my district is formally committed to it, it's hard for principals and parents to argue.

At times I have used an approach of notifying parents and my principal ahead of time. Other times, when I was fairly certain there wouldn't be resistance to my teaching, I have followed a philosophy of "teach first, answer questions later." For example, I used this approach with a video called *That's a Family*. The video is an excellent resource for teaching about family diversity. It presents several types of families, including adoptive families, single-parent families, foster families, gay and lesbian families, and divorced families.

Before I began using this video with my class, I cleared it with my principal (I needed her permission to purchase the video for our school library). I also considered whether I should notify parents that I would be teaching about different kinds of families, including gay and lesbian families. I predicted there could be some resistance from parents who are opposed to homosexuality. I asked one parent what she thought I should do. "Do you notify parents of every single thing you teach?" she asked. " If not, it would be inconsistent to notify them about this, and could raise more alarm than necessary." I agreed with her analysis and have taught the video two years in a row without complaint from anyone.

Other Suggestions

Part of the process of deciding whether to use a video (or any other material or lesson) also involves having an understanding of the school community where you work. After my first year, I switched schools and I now work at a very progressive school with teachers and families who are, for the most part, committed to diversity and social justice. At this school, people are much more likely to be tolerant.

As with any kind of curriculum you teach, a unit you write yourself should be of high quality and well prepared. In planning units that address specific issues of social justice, I have found it useful to start by researching what other teachers have done in this same area. There is lots of social justice curriculum out there. Rethinking Schools and Teaching for Change are two great resources, where I have regularly found and "borrowed" from other teachers' teaching ideas.

Another very important rule of thumb is to always preview any materials that you are going to use, even if they have been recommended by other teachers. I found that when I taught my unit on the Civil Rights Movement, much of the PBS *Eyes on the Prize* video series was useful and appropriate for my 3rd graders. Other parts were not as crucial and some, such as graphic images of the corpse of lynching victim Emmett Till, were not age-appropriate.

In my first few years as a teacher, I have taught about several different issues that some people might consider controversial. They include immigrants' experiences and rights, union organizing, the Civil Rights Movement, Mexican American organizing, resistance to slavery, the U.S. government's removal of Native Americans from their ancestral lands, the U.S. war on Iraq, the budget shortage in our schools, bullying, stereotypes, xenophobia, homophobia, racism, and sexism.

By no means have I done a full "unit" on each of these topics. Some, such as slavery and the removal of Native Americans from their lands, I teach through literature. Others, like stereotypes and racism, require a long-term conversation with my students. And some, like our study of the U.S. war on Iraq and the budget shortage in our schools, come up during our regular classroom discussions of current events.

Each year I try to improve and add on to the units or concepts that I've taught in the previous year, but I still feel I have a long way to go to reach my goal of having a year's worth of solid curriculum that integrates a social justice perspective and teaches about specific issues of justice.

Knowing that I am making progress and that I have the support of like-minded teachers keeps me energized to continue working toward my goals.

Engaging my students in social justice issues is, for me, at the heart of my teaching. I have learned that developing curriculum is a long-term process that often happens very slowly. But I wouldn't do it any other way.

References
Eyes on the Prize (Washington, DC: PBS, 1987).

"From Snarling Dogs to Bloody Sunday," by Kate Lyman, in *Rethinking Schools*, Volume 14, Number 1.

That's a Family (Harriman, NY: New Day Films, 2000).

Q/A

How do I get a student to redo an assignment?

Redoing or revising an assignment is key for students who lack academic skills. When we allow students to slide by with shoddy, inferior work, C or D papers, we set them up for future failure.

Establishing clear criteria for each assignment—and going over those criteria with students before they get started on their work—helps with the revision process. Students need to know specifically what the teacher's expectations are. No guessing. Students need both clarity and models when possible.

Prior to assigning a poem, literary analysis, or response to a film or book, I hand out criteria sheets, which list the traits of the genre, and examples of student work from previous years.

If I don't have examples, I write a sample model to distribute.

If the criteria are clear, then students can use them as a guide when they revise. For example, I have my students color-highlight their papers for different narrative criteria; when they have no dialogue or character description to highlight, they know that is a place where they need to revise. The revision is part of the process of writing, and I build it into each assignment. (See "Childhood Narratives" and "Essay with an Attitude" in *Reading, Writing, and Rising Up: Teaching About Social Justice and the Power of the Written Word*. For more information on this book see page 358.)

Sometimes, especially in an untracked classroom, some students will complete the assignment thoroughly, while others will attempt the assignment but get bogged down or run into roadblocks. It's easy to blame students at this point: to say they are lazy, or "slow," or lack a serious interest in school. Instead of bemoaning what they've done incorrectly, we can use their papers to figure out where their comprehension broke down. This is when the real teaching begins. Students are more likely to return to a task when they understand it.

—Linda Christensen

Even First-Year Teachers Have Rights

by Bill Bigelow

I t began with a call that I was to report to the vice principal's office as soon as possible. The voice at the other
end indicated that it was urgent.

I was a first-year teacher at Grant High School in Portland, Ore. The call gave me the creeps. From the moment
we met I'd felt that Lloyd Dixon, the curriculum VP, could
look deep into my soul—and that he didn't like what he saw.
Whenever we passed in the hall he smiled at me thinly, but
with a glance that said: "I've got your number, Bigelow." He
had a drawl that reminded me of the Oklahoma highway

patrolman who gleefully arrested me in 1971 for not carrying my draft card.

It was my first year as a teacher. And I must confess, my classroom difficulties made me a tad paranoid.

Dixon's secretary ushered me into his office when I arrived. "It seems we have a problem, Bill," he said. He paused to look at me and make sure I was duly appreciative of the serious nature of the meeting. "The mother of a student of yours, Dorothy Jennings, called to say that you had given her smutty material, a book that discusses oral sex. What's the story?"

I explained to the vice principal that the "smutty" material was Studs Terkel's *Working*, a book that includes interviews with dozens of people—autoworkers, hotel clerks, washroom attendants, musicians—who describe what they do for a living and how they feel about it. I told him that it was a text the school had purchased and that I issued it to my 9th graders for some in-class reading during our career education study.

"Well, Bill, Dorothy apparently took the book home. And her mother's upset because of a section Dorothy read her about a prostitute, where she describes having oral sex."

I told him that I had not assigned that chapter and that students didn't have permission to take the books home, as I taught two sections of the class but had only 35 copies of the book. I didn't mention that indeed I had considered using the chapter, "Roberta Victor, Hooker," because it was filled with insights about sexism, law, and hypocrisy. (The alleged oral sex description was a brief reference in a long interview.)

Dixon ordered me to bring him a copy of *Working* so that he could read the passages I assigned, and to meet with him the next day. "You should be aware that I regard this as a serious situation," he said. And with that, New Teacher was waved out the door.

I went to see my friend Tom McKenna, a member of a support group I'd helped organize among teachers in the area. Tom suggested I talk to our union rep. My visit with Thurston Ohman, a big-hearted man with an easy from-the-belly laugh, was a revelation. "You haven't done anything wrong," he assured me. "If they try to come after you in some way, the union will back you 100 percent."

Solidarity

It was a delicious moment, and I realized how utterly alone I'd felt up until that point. Ironically, in my history classes and my freshman social studies classes we'd recently studied the rise of labor unions, but until that instant I'd never personally been a beneficiary of the "injury to one is an injury to all" solidarity.

Buoyed by my talk with Ohman, I returned to VP Dixon's office the next day. He wasn't worried about Mrs. Jennings anymore. But he was still upset. "Bill, I read over the pieces that you assigned. Very interesting. Pretty negative stuff. My daughter is an airline stewardess. She doesn't feel like the gal in that book.

"Do you know that the reading on the autoworker uses the s-word five times and the f-word once?"

"The s-word?" I asked.

"Yes. On pages 258, 259, 261, and twice on page 262. The f-word is used on page 265."

I didn't want to laugh, but I didn't know what to say. His complaint was about an interview with Gary Bryner, president of the United Auto Workers local at the Lordstown, Ohio, General Motors plant. Given Mr. Dixon's comment about his daughter, I had a hunch that his ire was aimed more at Bryner's "negative" critique of the plant's deadening working conditions and his descriptions of workers' resistance than at his occasional use of s- and f-words. But this wasn't the time or place to argue politics. "I guess I didn't realize, Mr. Dixon."

"No. Well, Bill, here's what I'd like you to do. Get a black marker and every time this gentleman uses the s- and f-words, darken them so students won't be exposed to that kind of language. Will you do that for me, Bill?"

I know some people would have fought it. Had it not been my first year as a teacher—a temporary teacher, no less—I would have fought. Instead I made one of those compromises that we're not proud of, but that we make so we can live to fight another day. After school, marker in hand, I cleansed Gary Bryner of his foul language—in all 35 copies of *Working*.

Twenty-some years later, the censored books are still in circulation in Portland high schools.

I offer this instance of curricular interference as a way of acknowledging that administrative repression can be a factor limiting the inventiveness of a new teacher. But in my experience, the intrusions of the Lloyd Dixons of the world are exceptions that prove the rule. And the rule is that we have an enormous amount of freedom.

Even as a first-year teacher the Jennings affair was my only brush with administrative censure. I frequently brought in controversial guest speakers, films, and additional readings. It was 1978–79, the year of Three Mile Island, the final months of the Sandinista revolution in Nicaragua, and a growing U.S. awareness of the injustices of South African apartheid. In class, we studied all of these.

No doubt, it's important for individuals early in their teaching careers, as well as those of us further along, to make an assessment of the political context in which we work. After all, if we lose our job, we don't do anyone any good. But generally, I believe that the most powerful agent of censorship lives in our own heads, and we almost always have more freedom than we use. The great Brazilian educator Paulo Freire once wrote that in schools we should attempt to fill up all the political space we're given. But we rarely do.

That said, a few years ago a school district in an affluent Portland suburb terminated a good friend of mine at the completion of her third year of probation, spouting nonsense about her failure to teach critical thinking skills and the like. The obvious irony for those of us at her hearing was that she was fired precisely because she was successful at teaching her students to think critically. She had the misfortune of being one of the only nontenured teachers in a progressive, pedagogically adventurous social studies department during the rise of the ferociously conservative

Oregon Citizens Alliance. The political environment had shifted to the right; it was sacrificial lamb time.

It's worth mentioning that during my first years at Jefferson High School, following my year at Grant, I was gifted with supervising vice principals who were extraordinarily supportive and even enthusiastic about livelier, risk-taking teaching. Shirley Glick was one of several VPs who offered nothing but encouragement as I felt my way toward a more critical and multicultural curriculum. The Lloyd Dixons of the world exist, but so do the Shirley Glicks.

Incidentally, I never met Mrs. Jennings. But she left her mark. For a long time I subconsciously imagined a Mrs. Jennings sitting at every student's home, hoping for a chance to chew me out for some teaching crime I'd committed: "You snake, why'd you use that book/film/article/poem with my innocent child?"

In my imagination, parents were potential opponents, not allies, and I avoided calling them to talk about their children or what I was trying to teach. This neglect was a bad habit to fall into. Even from a narrow classroom management standpoint, my failure to call moms, dads, or grandparents from time to time made my quest for classroom order a lonely campaign. Parents could have exerted a bit of pressure on the home front. But they also could have told me something about their son or daughter, offered a fuller portrait than what I saw in my daily slice of 47 minutes.

And that would likely have made me a more effective teacher.

References

Working, by Studs Terkel (New York: The New Press, 1997).

Q/A

How do I prepare for a substitute teacher?

Don't ever assume that the person who will take your class will come prepared. Sometimes that happens. Lots of times it doesn't. Put together a folder that the substitute can find easily. Include basics like a class list and seating chart, procedures for the day, duties that the sub may have to cover for you, and bus lists and dismissal information so no one gets lost when school lets out.

And include worksheets for your kids to do. Sometimes the work that a substitute plans to give your students will be in direct conflict with the way you've been teaching. Don't take the chance of your kids spending the day coloring worksheets about holidays, copying paragraphs to practice penmanship, or playing hangman. Instead, make sure that the worksheets or games are ones that will connect to your students and the work you do in your classroom.

Find a colleague who will agree to check in with a sub on the days you are gone and vice-versa. The colleague can alert the sub to specific information that might be needed that day.

As wonderful as your students might behave for you on a daily basis, know that they will probably give the substitute a hard time. Having things prepared for them that they like to do, that will challenge them a bit, will make their day without you at least somewhat productive.

It's important that you find out later how the day with the sub went. Some schools have the secretary ask subs to complete a form before they leave. Find out what the students thought too. Take note of subs who do a good job and keep their names for future reference. Likewise, alert your principal to those substitute teachers you wouldn't want to use again.

—Rita Tenorio

Testing Kindergarten

Young Children Produce Data —Lots of Data

by Kelly McMahon

You may not believe how many tests kindergartners take—and what they are missing as a result.

I remember my kindergarten experience from decades ago. Way back then, kindergarten focused on letters, sounds, counting, coloring inside the lines, cutting straight along the solid black line, and learning how to get along with others. I remember looking forward to rest time, recess, snack, and show and tell. That was kindergarten before the days of No Child Left Behind. Kindergarten post-No Child Left Behind results in many children disliking school and feeling like failures.

I started teaching 5-year-old kindergarten for Milwaukee Public Schools (MPS) in 2003. Since then, I have seen a decrease in

Randall Enos

213

district initiatives that are developmentally appropriate, and an increase in the amount of testing and data collection for 5-year-olds. Just when I thought the district couldn't ask for any more test scores or drills or practice, a new initiative and data system popped up for my school to complete. When my school did not meet its Adequate Yearly Progress (AYP) goals three years, it became a School Identified for Improvement (SIFI), with Level Two status.

The students in my classroom during the 2008–09 school year completed more assessments than during any of my prior years of teaching kindergarten:

- Milwaukee Public Schools' 5-Year-Old Kindergarten Assessment (completed three times a year)
- On the Mark Reading Verification Assessment (completed three times a year)
- A monthly writing prompt focused on different strands of the Six Traits of Writing
- 28 assessments measuring key early reading and spelling skills
- Chapter pre- and post-tests for all nine math chapters completed
- Three additional assessments for each math chapter completed
- A monthly math prompt
- Four Classroom Assessments Based on Standards (CABS) per social studies chapter (20 total)
- Four CABS assessments per science chapter (20 total)
- Four CABS assessments per health chapter (20 total)

My students were also expected to complete four benchmark assessments beginning in the 2010–11 school year.

This list does not include the pre- and post-Marzano

vocabulary tests (which I refuse to have my students complete because the assessment design is entirely developmentally inappropriate) or the writing and math portfolios we are required to keep.

In 2008, the literacy coach at my school handed us a copy of the new MPS Student Reading Portfolio, which included a list of 10 academic vocabulary words per semester that kindergartners would be expected to know. My students would have to complete pre- and post-tests each semester. When I brought the MPS Student Reading Portfolio to the Milwaukee Teachers' Education Association's (MTEA) Early Childhood Committee, the members were surprised and disgusted. This new reading portfolio asked kindergarten students to define terms like *Venn diagram, sound out, understand, poetry, tracking, sight word, expression,* and *describe*; it also expected kindergartners to produce 20 different sounds, including the blending and digraph sounds *ch, qu, sh, th,* and *ing* at a proficient level. This developmentally inappropriate assessment tool was designed without the input of early childhood educators. The MTEA Early Childhood Committee submitted our comments and recommendations for proposed changes to both the MPS Reading and Early Childhood Departments. We never got a satisfactory response.

> **VOICES**
> **FROM THE CLASSROOM**
>
> *"It's in the classroom where we mainly do our activism, instilling in the kids a sense of justice and acceptance of different cultures and races. Whenever someone says a put-down about someone else, and we sit down and talk about it, that's activism to me."*
>
> —Floralba Vivas

Kindergartners Need to Play

One negative impact of continued assessment-crazy data collection on my school has been the total disregard for the importance of children's social and emotional development. As more and more of my students spend less time interacting with their peers outside of school, I am forced to severely limit the amount of time dedicated to play centers in my classroom. Without the opportunity to interact with their peers in structured and unstructured play, my students are losing out on situations that allow them to learn to problem-solve, share, explore, and deepen their learning.

As Edward Miller and Joan Almon point out in their book *Crisis in the Kindergarten: Why Children Need to Play in School*, "Research shows that children who engage in complex forms of socio-dramatic play have greater language skills than nonplayers, better social skills, more empathy, more imagination, and more of the subtle capacity to know what others mean. They are less aggressive and show more self-control and higher levels of thinking."

Apparently young children stopped learning through play the moment the bipartisan No Child Left Behind bill passed Congress and was signed into law by President George W. Bush.

Sleepless in Milwaukee

The issue of allowing young children in kindergarten to rest has been a battle since MPS issued a guideline for rest time for early childhood programs. The district guidelines proposed a maximum 45-minute rest time in the fall for all day 4-year-old kindergarten, followed by a maximum of 30 minutes rest in the spring. The guidelines suggested a maximum of 30 minutes to be used for rest in the fall in 5-year-old kindergarten classrooms, and for rest to be *entirely phased out* in the spring.

These policies fly in the face of brain research, which suggests that sleep allows the brain to cement the learning that has taken place. As Marilee Sprenger writes in her book *Learning & Memory: The Brain in Action*, "Through prior knowledge or interest, the new information may be added to the old and form more long-term memory. The process may have to be repeated several times before long-term memory is formed. The brain will process some of this information during sleep. Studies have shown that while rats are in the sleep stage called REM (rapid eye movement) sleep, their brains reproduce the same patterns used for learning while awake."

But MPS insists that I wake up a sleeping child who might have only gotten five or six hours of sleep each night.

My administrators allotted my students 20 minutes of rest time each day for the 2009–10 school year. However, by the time my students finish using the restroom and get a drink of water after their one and only recess for the day, they will have roughly 10 minutes to rest. Every year I have at least one child in my classroom who is not getting adequate sleep every night.

There was a young boy in my classroom who went to daycare directly from school and stayed there until 11 p.m. By the time his mother picked him up, drove home, and gave him a snack, it would be 1 a.m. before he finally got to bed. This child would then be up roughly five hours later to start his day all over again. He entered my classroom exhausted and in need of additional sleep. When he allowed himself to fall asleep at rest time, it was nearly impossible to wake him.

When district officials came into my classroom, I had to defend my professional judgment in allowing this child to continue to sleep after I began afternoon instruction. I have multiple students in my classroom this year with similar sleeping schedules at home, yet they are allowed only 10 minutes for rest. I am experiencing far more behavioral problems in the afternoon this school year due to the decrease in time my students are allowed to rest.

I'm left wondering how much more testing and data collection I might be expected to do, and how many more developmentally inappropriate initiatives I will be asked

VOICES
FROM THE CLASSROOM

"We have to teach from a global perspective. We work in the biggest superpower on the planet. Given increased global inequality, global warming, and poverty, and the devastation of mother earth, we have responsibilities to address that. We need to teach for global justice. And if we don't, who will?"

—Bob Peterson

to implement. I also wonder exactly how much longer I can continue to "teach" under these circumstances.

References

Crisis in the Kindergarten: Why Children Need to Play in School, by Joan Almon and Edward Miller (College Park, MD: Alliance for Childhood, 2009).

Learning & Memory: The Brain in Action, by Marilee Sprenger (Alexandria, VA: Association for Supervision and Curriculum Development, 1999).

How can I prepare my students for a field trip?

First, remember that many families simply can't afford extra fees for field trips. Try to find free or inexpensive activities. One of my schools was right on a major university campus, so there were a lot of low-cost cultural events available. I also sought out trips that were significantly discounted to students through arrangements with our school district.

Second, have a clear idea of what you expect your students to accomplish on the trip. I've worked with colleagues who would create elaborate learning packets for students to complete on field trips. Then they would give the students grades and even test them on the material.

I view field trips in a much different light. I told my students to be aware that people are watching them. I told them, "Some people will have a negative opinion of you and low expectations of your behavior." We discussed whether it's right for others to judge them like that, and of course they said no. So I posed the question: "How will we make sure that people see us differently?"

The first time I asked this question, one student raised her hand and replied, "Be good."

"OK, fine, but what does it mean to be good?" I responded.

That was a more difficult question; kids don't always know what we want, so they say "be good" as their catch-all answer.

We discussed specific appropriate behavior before each field trip. For example, if we were going to see a play, there should be plenty of applause for the actors, no talking during the performance, no kicking the seat in front of you, and no screaming when they dim the lights!

For practice, in class before a trip I would ask students to demonstrate "good" and "not-so-good" behavior. Once in a while there would be a slipup on a trip, but we would discuss it and figure out how the students could improve their behavior. And almost every time they did improve.

—Stephanie Walters

Dealing with Standardized Tests

by Kelley Dawson Salas

I began teaching elementary school in 1999, and since then there has not yet been a single year when my school did not require me to do some amount of "test prep" to get my students ready to take standardized tests.

It's a fact of life in today's schools: Kids have to take standardized tests and teachers are expected to prepare them. Federal legislation makes sure that schools whose students do poorly on tests face strict consequences: Parents must be informed that they can transfer to a different

school, funds may be taken away, administrators and staff can be replaced. Fear of being punished drives many schools to place a high priority on helping students score well on tests.

But, you may ask, what's wrong with wanting our students to score well on tests? For most of us, it only makes sense that if we are going to ask our students to do something, we want to help them be as successful at it as possible.

There are lots of potential problems with standardized tests and with the activities we use to get students ready for them. If not kept in check, a narrow, obsessive focus on standardized tests can dumb down the curriculum and make school a boring, lifeless place for both students and teachers. I've learned that this can happen even in a school where educators are committed to rigorous, child-centered curriculum and opposed to excessive standardized testing. I have found that even though it's difficult, I have to speak up when my colleagues and administrators discuss testing. Otherwise, testing and test prep activities can eat up a large part of the school year and leave little time for real teaching and learning.

Here's how that happened one year in my classroom.

A School 'in Need of Improvement'

In September, I learned that my school was on the "schools in need of improvement" list. The test was coming in November, and we needed to get the kids ready fast, so they could do well on the test and we could get off the list. We immediately undertook a drastic change in our 4th-grade program (the grade I teach and the most heavily tested grade in my school). We scrapped what we were doing in reading and math, recruited every additional support staff person available, and began to provide small group test prep activities in math and reading for two hours a day.

To make room for test prep, we put the district's own math curriculum on hold for two months: Instead we needed to teach an "overview" of all the concepts that would be on the test. We stopped teaching reading as a subject that integrated content in science and social studies, because we needed to group our students across classrooms, strictly by reading level, to help them make the most progress possible before the test.

Hands-on activities and science and social studies content had no place in this test prep program. There was very little time left each day once the test prep groups were done, and we had to cut back on the activities that we normally do in the fall, including our study of water quality in the Milwaukee River and our beach cleanup at Lake Michigan.

During the entire fall of that school year, I came to work each day infuriated and demoralized, and went home each night feeling even worse. I hated wasting class time on test prep. I hated feeling like we were racing the clock, cramming as much information as possible into 9-year-old brains before the day of the test.

I resented the fact that I had to participate in all of this simply because I was a 4th-grade teacher. I was angry that I had only had a small voice in the process by which our entire curriculum was hastily revised and our school year was derailed. I felt that our school administrators had made decisions under pressure. I felt trapped because I didn't agree with those decisions, and yet I was the person that had to carry them out. I thought about transferring to a different grade and even about leaving teaching all together.

I also felt an overwhelming responsibility to my students, especially those who were learning English as a second language. This was the first year they were required to take their tests in English, and on top of everything else, teachers had been instructed to make whatever accommodations they needed, so the test would be as reliable a measure as possible of their academic knowledge. This amounted to translating the test into Spanish, allowing extra time, and spending lots of time reminding students that they are intelligent even though taking a test in their second language might make them doubt that. I thought the system was horribly unfair for second language learn-ers, and I felt like it was my responsibility to protect them from this unfairness.

We started the testing process in November. It lasted eight school days—almost two entire weeks. By the time Thanksgiving rolled around, the test was over, and on December 1, we were ready to start what we considered our "real school year."

The million-dollar question: Did it work? Well . . . we got off the list, but not exactly because of our scores that particular year. While we had been busy doing test prep, our school had filed an appeal based on data from the previous year, and we succeeded in having the "schools in need of improvement" label removed.

A Different Approach

During those three months (nearly a third of the school year), many of my colleagues and I came to the conclusion that the test prep activities took up too much classroom time and that some of them were not helpful. We met. We debated. And in the end we decided to take a different approach the following year—one that was far less intrusive into the life of our classroom and, happily, one that allowed us to return to our normal math and science curriculum.

We decided to teach reading as we normally would, but to include a few multiple-choice, "practice test"–type activities, and with some instruction on how to do those kinds of test activities successfully. And we decided that try-ing to cover a year's worth of math curriculum in two months is just not possible. We went back to using the district's cur-riculum and pacing schedule but added a strong focus at the beginning of the year on how to solve word problems and how to explain mathematical solutions—something important to getting good test scores, but also something we definitely want our kids to know how to do regardless.

Through these experiences I learned that striking a bal-ance is key. I know that I cannot ignore the tests or the need to prepare my students for them. I know I need to do some things to familiarize my students with the test format and the types of questions they will encounter. I also think it's reasonable to have students experience a simulated testing environment prior to the actual test: Practice runs will help cut down on nervousness when the real testing starts.

What I am not willing to do is to spend every day of the year using multiple-choice, worksheet-type activities simply because "that's what they'll see on the test."

Every school is different and there is no magic formula for how much test prep to do or how to do it. What is crucial is that teachers and administrators talk with each other about the testing that occurs at each grade level and that they agree on a plan that prepares students sufficiently without overtaking the entire curriculum.

The staff at my school discusses testing often. As a new teacher, I sometimes find it difficult to stand up for what I believe. Even though many of my colleagues are philosophically opposed to the testing craze, there is nonetheless an enormous amount of pressure to demonstrate academic proficiency and sufficient "adequate yearly progress," and that can lead to all sorts of curriculum changes that aren't necessarily good for kids.

As teachers, we must advocate for our students and insist upon their right to real, rigorous curriculum. If we don't stand our ground, we run the risk of allowing our curriculum to wither away into endless and meaningless worksheets and practice tests—which won't keep kids engaged in learning, and won't keep good teachers engaged in teaching!

In Wisconsin, for example, teachers, parents, and community activists formed the Coalition for Responsible Assessment to advocate for curbs on the use of standardized tests and to link issues of testing to broader issues about the quality of education available in public schools. This coalition has given teachers a way to connect with their peers, as well as a broader spectrum of the community, around issues of testing and teaching.

As a new teacher, it can be hard to decide when to stand up and advocate for something and when to close your door and quietly teach the things you believe will engage children and help them learn. It is worth the effort, though, to craft an approach for dealing with testing and test prep that works for you at your particular school. Hopefully, such an approach can allow you the opportunity to teach a rigorous, interesting, high-quality curriculum for many years to come.

For Further Information

FairTest: The National Center for Fair & Open Testing, www.fairtest.org
FairTest provides information, technical assistance, and advocacy on a broad range of testing concerns, and works to end the misuse of standardized tests and to promote responsible alternatives. The website offers fact sheets, links to more comprehensive resources, and information about the *Examiner*, the group's newsletter.

Susan Ohanian Speaks Out, www.susanohanian.org
Ohanian, a prominent and well-respected researcher, uses this website to dispense news and information on the standardized testing craze. Her presentation is often entertaining, as when she presents her "Outrage of the Day" or warns that you could take all the sincerity among standardized testing advocates, "place it in the navel of a fruit fly and still have room for three caraway seeds and the heart of a member of the Business Roundtable." But the information she collects on testing is serious, deep, and a real boon to teachers seeking alternatives to fill-in-the-blank assessment.

Pencils Down: Rethinking High-Stakes Testing and Accountability in Public Schools, edited by Wayne Au and Melissa Bollow Tempel (Rethinking Schools, 2012), www.rethinkingschools.org

This powerful collection takes high-stakes standardized tests to task. Through articles that provide thoughtful and emotional critiques from the frontlines of education, *Pencils Down* exposes the damage that standardized tests wreak on our education system. Better yet, it offers visionary forms of assessment that are not only more authentic, but also more democratic, fair, and accurate.

Reading Between the Bubbles

Teaching Students to Critically Examine Tests

by Linda Christensen

Tests today are high-stakes. Based on test scores, students are retained, placed in summer school and remedial classes; schools are reconstituted or otherwise penalized; and in some instances, teachers' and principals' salaries rise and fall. Students, especially those who fail the tests, may internalize the failure, and question their ability and their intelligence. They learn to blame themselves, and some come to believe they will not succeed because they are not capable enough.

As my daughter said after receiving a 3 ("not competent") on an oral Spanish test one year, "Maybe I don't have what it takes." The test took away the experience of animated conversations with her host family in Cuernavaca, as well as her ability to navigate Mexico City. Instead of questioning the validity of the measurement tool as an "authentic assessment," especially compared to her experience in Mexico, she questioned herself.

My friends at low-achieving elementary schools have been counseled to redesign their regular curricula so that students can get accustomed to multiple-choice questions. But in a classroom where we try to develop students' capacity to think critically and imaginatively, that's not easy. How can a role play about an important historical or social issue be reformatted into a multiple-choice activity? How does an A-B-C-D answer format encourage students to imagine themselves as an interned Japanese American or a Cherokee Indian facing government-ordered removal?

Teachers are also asked to mimic the more "authentic" assessments in fairly inauthentic ways. A kindergarten colleague, for example, was asked by the 3rd-grade teachers to prepare students for the state's six-trait analysis scoring guide by giving them scores of 1 to 6 on everything from lining up at the door to tying their shoes and counting.

Clearly, this isn't the kind of teaching we want in our classrooms. To achieve real gains in knowledge and skills, students need a rich curriculum with varied opportunities to use their learning in real-world activities. This material will generate growth that may or may not be reflected in test scores, but will increase the likelihood of students seeing themselves as readers, writers, historians, scientists, mathematicians, and thinkers.

However, I live in Oregon, a state that has filled our classrooms with tests. As a teacher and mother who has patched up the wounds test scores have left behind, and as a victim of a school that was reconstituted in part due to low test scores, I am a firm advocate in fighting against the overassessment of students. But I also believe we must create an opportunity to teach students to critique the tests as we coach them on how to increase their performance.

Examining the Origins and Purpose of Tests

We may have contempt for the tests, but learning how to take them is a survival skill in today's society. Thus, I want to support and even deepen students' critiques of the tests, but in a way that equips them to succeed on the tests. The question for new and veteran teachers alike is: How do we establish a critical stance on assessments while preparing students to be successful on them? How can we prepare students to take tests and at the same time equip students to be critical of them?

One of my most important aims as a teacher is to encourage my students to think critically about aspects of life that they might otherwise simply take for granted. Unfortunately, testing is a piece of school life that students accept as part of their education. From the time they are in 3rd grade in Oregon, students sit through batteries of tests. Their scores are sent home, informing their parents where they stand in the education pecking order of other 3rd graders in the district. Students come to expect that, like beef, they will receive a ranking from the government: exceeds, meets, conditionally meets, does not meet. They move through school dragging these test scores behind them.

If I don't interrupt this routine, I allow students to internalize the state's labels. Students, particularly students whose test scores lag behind, may accept placement in non-college track courses, and otherwise lower their expectations. Counselors won't recommend them for the higher-level math and science classes needed for acceptance into a four-year university. Of course, some students break out of the rut test scores have carved for them. But for many, their scores mark their place, not only in school, but in life after school.

One way to prevent this internalization is to take the time to critically examine the origins of the testing movement and the tests themselves, to get students to honestly appraise their own abilities instead of accepting the judgment of the exams, and to help them develop an interior monologue that talks back to the labels.

In my classes, I begin by tackling the tests with students, and then teaching them to create new ones. Although my junior and senior students at Portland's Jefferson High School weren't saddled with the reading, writing, and math tests that Oregon 3rd, 5th, 8th, and 10th graders currently take, my students had their behinds kicked by the SATs. After their encounters with these grueling tests, they fumed at me and their math teachers. "Those tests might as well have been written in Greek!" Shameka said after her Saturday was ruined by the exams. For my students, an investigation of the history of the SATs was as critical as teaching them how to improve their scores.

To help students understand the origins of the exam and help them put their scores in perspective, my class read the chapter "The Cult of Mental Measurement" from David Owen's book *None of the Above*. Students were shocked by what they discovered about the founder of the SATs, Carl Campbell Brigham: According to Owen, he published in the same eugenics journal as Adolph Hitler and was convinced that there should be stronger immigration laws to protect the "contamination of the American intellect" by "Catholics, Greeks, Hungarians, Italians, Jews, Poles, Russians, Turks, and—especially—Negroes."

But even without this gem of a chapter, getting students to investigate the origins and uses of tests in their school district or state is a good place to start. (See Bill Bigelow's "Testing, Tracking, and Toeing the Line: A Role Play on the Origins of the Modern High School," in *Rethinking Our Classrooms, Volume 1*, to help students develop a critique of the historical motivation behind the testing industry.)

Many teachers may choose not to take on an in-class study of tests, but even then it's important for us as teachers to familiarize ourselves with this history, so that we can talk with students when they encounter the tests.

Examining the Tests

Once students cast a critical eye on the origins of the tests, I help them improve their performance by examining both the content and the format of the tests themselves. The more they know about how the questions are put together, as well as the vocabulary of the material, the better prepared they are to meet the challenge.

In my sophomore language arts class at Grant High School in Portland, students demystified the state tests and used their knowledge to teach others about their discoveries. We examined practice reading tests that I downloaded from the Oregon Department of Education's website. We looked at the instructions and the content. We looked at the test's text passages and asked: "Whose background knowledge is honored here? Whose culture is represented? Whose culture and knowledge is missing? How would that make a difference in test results?"

Most of my sophomores agreed with their classmate Greg's critique of the test's reliance on short, random passages: "I thought the stories would be things we could relate to. We drift off when they don't interest us. They are disconnected. We'd be more likely to stick with it if we cared about what we read." They were quick to note that this test did not really measure their ability to read—which for them meant reading novels and short stories. As Greg so aptly described, tests are disconnected short passages followed by five or six questions. Students may have defined "reading" too narrowly, but they grasped an essential point neglected by the test makers: Reading is sustained and cumulative. Our understanding of the text builds over time.

My students also pointed out that the tests had more items about rural life than about urban life. Test selections included a snippet from Mark Twain about mosquitoes, a piece by Gary Paulsen about sled dogs in Alaska, and a Barry Lopez essay about wolves' howls. They also included a legal index, a chart about global gold production, and a calendar of upcoming events in Alaska. Students didn't find any of these particularly interesting or useful. Mostly, they were puzzled by the selections: Why these and not others? Students discussed how when they got bored and lost focus, they stopped taking the test seriously. Some reported bubbling in the rest of the test without reading the items; others just quit. A few students at Jefferson, who sensed the test's disrespect for African American experience by omission, simply bubbled obscenities on the answer sheets.

This is important information for me as teacher. The value of the test scores—which I have doubts about to begin with—becomes negligible. Students' discussion also helps illuminate the huge discrepancy between their past test scores and their abilities. Although some might attribute the students' refusal to mere laziness, I understand that, in part, it's a form of survival: They need to be able to say "I didn't try" if they receive a low test score. But resisting these tests can sabotage their own futures.

Developing Test-Taking Strategies

After students discuss their reactions to the content of several tests, they practice taking one of the sample tests. When they complete the exercise, I divide them into small groups and ask them to share their answers to the test questions and discuss what evidence from the reading informed their choices. I want them to understand that although they might disagree about the answers and the questions might be poorly worded, they have a better chance of getting more answers "correct" if they go back to the text to find support for their choice.

I also let them know that I have given the test to a number of teachers, and that they disagreed on some of the answers. In other words, the test answers are not perfect and even good readers come up with conflicting answers. During this activity, students also share their strategies—if they used any—for taking the sample test.

Then I give students the "correct" answers, according to the Oregon Department of Education (ODE), and I ask them to note in the margin the type of question, based on ODE's Reading and Literature Content Standards: word meaning, locating information, literal comprehension, inferential comprehension, evaluative comprehension, literary forms, or literary elements and devices. I do this for two reasons: I want students to understand the types of questions they will be asked, and I also want to poke holes in the questions themselves.

Students put up a fuss about the state's categories. "That's not a literary form!" one student fumed after I told them that's how the state had classified a legal index. The point of this activity is for students to understand that the questions vary based on the reading and literature content standard the test is attempting to cover, and sometimes the state's labels are confusing. I want students to cut the tests down to size, to know that the tests are not infallible; that humans, not gods, make them.

Then I ask students to note if they missed a certain kind of question more often—locating information vs. literary elements, for example—because it does indicate the kinds of strategies individual students need to use. Word meaning questions, for example, often involve using context clues. And missing literary forms most often means that a student needs to brush up on that category.

We also discuss and create a class list of the strategies to use on the test. After our final round of working with the tests, students in my sophomore class at Grant came up with the following list:

- Read question first.

- Locate key words in question.

- Note type of question:
  - In passage—word meaning, graph.
  - Throughout passage—inference based on gathering clues.
  - Not in passage—your conclusion based on evidence in passage.
- Be a detective—look for clues.

- Use the process of elimination.

- 50/50—guess when you can eliminate two choices.

By engaging in this process, students learn to critique the tests, but also how to maneuver within them.

Once students have the basic format down, I give them a test I construct using high-interest material. I have used "Doin' the Louvre" from master slam poet Patricia Smith as well as poems by Jimmy Santiago Baca and Martín Espada. I collect articles by and about teens in the *Oregonian* and in magazines—"Eggs and Twinkies," about race in the Asian community, or "I Love Skratching," a critique of a Gap ad. I follow the test question format from the state, using their categories—word meaning, inferential comprehension, literary elements, and the like.

When I give students my test, I also pass out highlighters and ask them to read with a highlighter in hand. We discuss what to highlight based on our previous discussions: key words in the questions, for example, and key sections of the passage that correspond to the question. After students take my test, we once again scrutinize the types of questions and refine their strategies.

Creating Tests: Thinking Like a Test Maker

Then I turn students loose to create their own tests in small groups. Each group has to create a test using the kinds of items typically found in the Oregon tests: a poem, a graph, a passage from a short story or essay. Then they create questions, typically five, to go with their passage. Afterward I find the best models, copy their tests, and students once again practice their test-taking skills.

When students think like a test maker, certainly their ability to read the test is enhanced, but something else happens as well: They realize that these are just questions about a reading. There is nothing magical, nothing omnipotent about them, nothing that marks these as the questions one must answer in order to be "smart." In other words, this process helps demystify the power of the test makers.

The work I've described here may raise student scores by a few points, and help students question the legitimacy of the tests as well as their results. But teaching students to examine the history and motives of local and state tests, and preparing them for the big day(s), is no substitute for fighting to end the encroachment of assessments in our classrooms. As teachers and parents we can organize against the broader attack on public education that allows fill-in-the-bubble tests to dominate our classrooms, and makes students question their abilities.

References

None of the Above: The Truth Behind the SATs, by David Owen with Marilyn Doerr (Lanham, MD: Rowman & Littlefield, 1999).

Rethinking Our Classrooms, Volume 1 (Milwaukee: Rethinking Schools, 2007). See page 359 for more information.

Q/A

I'm totally nervous about being evaluated. And I just got a letter from my principal informing me I'm going to be observed! What should I do?

The first thing you should do is relax. That might sound easier said than done, but it is important to keep in mind that evaluation is a component of the teaching profession (any profession, for that matter) and observations are necessary in order for a principal to provide you with a valid evaluation. So you can't have one without the other. And it is much better to have your principal see what is going on in your classroom herself than to make up a story in her head.

The observation is the ideal opportunity for you to show off your work. As a new teacher no one expects you to be Teacher of the Year, but observations are the best way for principals to determine if you may very well be on your way to accepting that title one day.

Sometimes observations are announced and sometimes your evaluator may just "drop in" to sit in on part of a class or lesson. Again, don't be alarmed; both observation methods can be instructive when it comes to rating lesson planning, classroom management, and knowledge of content. And as a teacher you can use both methods to help you think critically about your practice. Here's what I mean:

For example, after your principal drops in for an informal observation, consider scheduling a follow-up meeting with her. Send her an email acknowledging her stopping in and tell her that you want to know what she thought were strengths in what she saw as well as any tips for improvement.

If you receive a note from her indicating time and duration of the observation, request a pre-observation meeting. This meeting needn't be long, but it should be time where you provide an overview of what you expect your principal to see during the time frame in which she's present (this is especially important because she might walk in in the middle of the lesson or leave before you are finished). Bonus points: provide a lesson plan at the meeting for discussion. By doing that, you are demonstrating your ability to plan ahead. She will be able to ask questions of you that would be impossible for you to answer while you are teaching.

Whether the observation is formal or informal, always schedule a post-observation conference. At this meeting you should be reading from a written summary your principal provides. There should be some key indicators of strengths (commendable job of building background knowledge, establishes high expectations) and weaknesses (could move around the room more to assess understanding of all students). Ask questions about observations noted and request concrete suggestions for what you can do to improve the lesson. Being an active participant in the discussion shows that you are open to constructive critique and are committed to improving your practice. Sometimes as new teachers we want to defend the choices we make and are resistant to taking suggestions. We are afraid to show what we don't know and instead want to present ourselves as the greatest thing to teaching since chalk! Be careful of being too confident. If we fail to recognize that there is always room for improvement we shut ourselves off from the potential we have to be truly great in our profession.

If you haven't seen your principal since the first day of school, and it is nearly Thanksgiving break, this is cause for alarm. If your principal is MIA, drop her a line inviting her to your class to observe a lesson you think your students will enjoy. Request specific feedback: what were the strengths, and what were areas that could be improved.

After any post-observation conference you may also want to enlist the assistance of your mentor to discuss the suggestions your evaluator made to you. Together you can devise a plan to build on the positives of your lesson and reshape the areas where there is need. (By the way, it isn't a bad idea to invite your mentor to sit in on your lesson as well.)

You might be thinking that there is a lot of writing, meeting, and discussing that go on in this process, and you would be correct if that's what you are thinking. The evaluation process is an active one, not a passive one. If done correctly, observations are meant to be instructive, not intrusive. Evaluation is meant to improve a teacher's instruction, not to create insecurity. However, if you feel that your principal is using the process as a "gotcha" game it is important to discuss your feelings and concerns with you mentor or another trusted colleague. That person can help you figure out a way to address your concerns directly with your principal, and may even sit in with you while you do.

Keep in mind that evaluation is more than someone coming into your room, telling you you're doing a great job, and handing you a piece of paper at the end of the year and then walking away. At least it should be more than that. If done with fidelity and honesty, the evaluation process is one of the best tools to assist new and veteran teachers alike to improve their practice.

—Stephanie Walters

Chapter 4

Discipline: Rescuing the Remains of the Day When Class Doesn't Go as Planned

The Best Discipline Is Good Curriculum

by Kelley Dawson Salas

During my first year of teaching, I tried everything to get my students to behave. Behavior charts, individual plans. Class incentives, class conse-quences. Tricks, threats. Rewards, punishments. Strict atti-tude, friendly attitude. Yelling, reasoning, sweet-talking, pleading for sympathy.

Barbara J. Miner

One day, I wrote the word "celebration" on the board and promised the class they could have a party if they behaved for the whole day. I crossed each letter off one by one. By noon we all knew they'd never make it. In short, I was desperate.

Discipline is an exhausting part of the job that never really goes away. The message that most of us get is that to be a good teacher, you must first be a good disciplinarian. You must control your students' behavior. Only then, when your classroom is under control, can you begin to teach. I disagree.

No teacher has to wait until the students are "under control" to start teaching them worthwhile stuff. It's actually the other way around. Over and over again, I have found that the moment I start to teach interesting, engaging content, I experience immediate relief in the area of discipline.

During my first year, my classroom was pretty wild. (Don't hold it against me; I know you've been there!) But it made sense to me that my students acted the way they did. I was a brand-new teacher, totally inexperienced. My students wanted more than I could offer them, and they were bored and confused much of the time. I didn't really see how forcing them to behave would change that.

It took some time, but eventually I quit working so hard at controlling my students' behavior and started focusing on my own: What was I teaching? What methods was I using? What was I doing to engage, to teach students so that they would not be bored and disruptive?

I looked at what I was doing in social studies: plodding through a textbook that was inaccurate, boring, and disconnected from my students' lives. I decided to teach some lessons about the Civil Rights Movement, and to have the class write and perform a play about the Montgomery bus boycott. It was an extremely rough first attempt at writing and teaching my own curriculum, but for our purposes, it worked. I was engaged, the students were engaged, and we all spent a lot less time dealing with discipline.

In my subsequent years of teaching, I've had similar experiences. Every time there's a slump in my teaching—yes, even though I work hard, it happens—kids get bored (I get bored, for that matter) and discipline gets hairy. It's like a rumbling that slowly turns to a roar and ultimately demands action: If you don't plan some good curriculum, things are really going to get out of control here.

Of course, it's important to have rules and consequences, and to apply them consistently while teaching interesting content. I find it works well to remind kids frequently why an ordered environment helps them learn, to show them how rules and consequences help create a classroom where real learning can happen. Also, when I'm teaching something I really believe is worth my students' time, I feel more authority to demand a high standard of behavior.

Even the best curriculum can't magically solve all behavior issues. Our society creates a lot of pressures and problems for kids, and they often bring these to school. Students witness violence, live in poverty, struggle to help hardworking parents, and watch a ton of TV, much of it inappropriate. Some students have serious problems that will not go away without specific intervention. It may help to work with the school psychologist, social worker, or administrators in these cases. Teachers can also push for schoolwide preventive programs like anti-bullying, anger management, or peer mediation. These can have a great impact on behavior.

VOICES
FROM THE CLASSROOM

"Set clear, high expectations for all students. Don't feel sorry for kids. They don't need your pity; they need you to give them tools and knowledge to navigate the education system. Don't excuse them from homework or higher-level skills or more challenging work. They need clear and consistent high expectations."

—Linda Christensen

I'm now in my fourth year of teaching, and I'm still struggling to create all the curriculum I need to motivate and engage my 4th graders for six hours a day. Whenever I feel overwhelmed by the size of that task, I try to remind myself to think small: I go back to my first year and remember that back then, even one good lesson was sometimes enough to tip the scales from boring, intolerable, and out of control to what I could at least call "manageable."

Each year, I am building upon those lessons and offering better and better curriculum to my students. I know discipline issues will never completely disappear from my classroom. But I also know good curriculum goes a long way toward making my classroom run smoothly. And engaging curriculum is more than just a fix for behavior headaches. It can also get kids to think deeply, care about our world, and help them learn to make positive changes.

As a bonus, I feel less foolish now that I don't have to stand at the front of the class and take away my students' celebration one letter at a time.

Discipline: No Quick Fix

by Linda Christensen

Creating a climate of respect is easy to talk about and hard to practice. Ideally, we want a space where students listen respectfully and learn to care about each other. A sign in our hallway reads "No Racist or Sexist Remarks." I've often said, "I just don't tolerate that kind of behavior." But this year, it was like saying, "I don't tolerate ants." I have ants in my kitchen. I can spray chemicals on them and saturate the air with poison and "not tolerate" them, or I can find another solution that

Mark Fisher

245

doesn't harm my family or pets in the process. If I just kick kids out of class, I "don't tolerate" their actions, but neither do I educate them or their classmates. And it works about as well as stamping out a few ants. I prepare them for repressive solutions where misbehavior is temporarily contained by an outside authority, not really addressed. Sometimes, I am forced to that position, but I try not to be.

Dealing with Name-Calling

One year, students in the class Bill Bigelow and I co-taught were often rude to each other. Their favorite put-down was "faggot." (This in a class where a young woman came out as a lesbian.) During the first weeks, several young women complained that they had been called names by boys in class. They felt the hostility and wanted to transfer out. They didn't feel comfortable sharing their work or even sitting in the class because they were pinched, hit, or called names when our backs were turned. As one of the main, but certainly not the only, instigators, Wesley wrote in his end-of-the-year evaluation, "I started the year off as I finished the last year: bad, wicked, and obnoxious. I was getting kicked out of class and having meetings with the deans about my behavior every other day."

For critical teachers trying to build community, this creates a serious problem. Do we eliminate this student? When, after trying time-outs, calling his home, talking with his coach, and keeping him after class, we finally kicked him out—his friends said, "They're picking on him." Which wasn't true. But it set us up as the bad guys and divided us from the students we wanted to win over.

Increased police presence in the area has created situations where students gain honor by taunting the cops in front of peers. This carries over to class, where we represent the same white authority as the police until students get to know us. Although Wesley was not skilled academically, in other respects he was brilliant. He was an artist at toeing the line technically and creating total chaos in the process. He'd raise his hand and make perfectly nice comments about someone's paper in such a way that the entire class knew he was mocking the whole procedure. Even with two of us in the classroom, he defeated us at every turn. Clearly, we were playing on his terrain, and he knew the game better than we did even if we'd taught longer than he'd been alive.

Here we were teaching about justice, tolerance, equality, and respect, and yet when we had a problem with a talented student who didn't want to go along, we turned him over to the deans. Ultimately, what lesson does that teach our students? That we talk a good game, but when pushed, we respond like other traditional teachers? It's a complex issue. I don't want to keep the class from progressing because of one or two students, but I don't want to "give up" on students either. On bad days, I threw him out. On good days, I tried to look behind his behavior and figure out what motivated it.

Looking Beyond the Words

In teaching critical literacy, I tell students to look behind the words to discover what the text is really saying; in working with "problem" students in class, I need to look behind the students' behavior. What is motivating this? How can I get to the root of the problem? In my experience, the more negative students feel about themselves and their intellectual ability, the more cruel or withdrawn they are in the classroom.

Tyrelle, Wesley's classmate, wrote early in the year that he felt stupid. "My problem is I don't like to read out loud because I don't think the class would like it. Every time I try to write or do something my teachers told me that's stupid, you did it wrong, or you can't spell. My friends [who were classmates] say it too. I don't say anything. I just act like I don't hear it, but I really do."

One day I overheard his friends teasing him about his spelling. After class I talked with him about it. I arranged for him to come in so we could work privately and I would teach him how to write. Because so many of his friends were in the class, he was afraid to ask for help. His way of dealing with the problem was to close down—put his head on his desk and sleep—or make fun of people who were trying to do their work. This did not totally stop, but once he found a way into his writing he would usually settle down and work.

During the second semester he wrote, "You guys have helped me become a better person because you were always after me, 'Tyrelle, be quiet. Tyrelle, pay attention.' After a while I learned how to control myself when it was time to." He'd also learned to separate himself from his friends so he could work.

Wesley, who admitted to being "bad, wicked, and obnoxious," was also a victim of poor skills and low academic self-esteem. He'd sneak in after school for help with his writing, or I'd go over the homework readings and teach him how to "talk back" to the author. Sometimes he'd call me at home when he was stuck. At the end of the year his mother said, "He told me that he didn't think he could write. Now he says he knows how." With both of these students, recognizing the cause of the behavior—embarrassment over poor skills—and helping them achieve success helped to change their behavior. Once the withdrawn or antisocial actions stopped, they contributed to the community rather than sabotaging it. This was not a miraculous, overnight change. On some days, the behavior backslid to day one, but most times there was steady improvement.

I have yet to discover a quick fix for out of control behavior. I try calling my students' homes in September to establish contact and expectations. I usually ask, "Is there anything you can tell me that will help me teach your child more effectively?" Parents know their child's history in schools and can give important insights. When my daughter didn't turn in a project, her teacher called me. I discovered that her class had long-term work that students needed to complete at home. I appreciated the call because Anna insisted that she didn't have homework. Her teacher made me realize how much parents need to hear from teachers—not only for keeping track of homework, but also so we can work in tandem.

Often working with a coach or activities advisor helps because they've established strong one-on-one relationships. They also have access to an area where the student feels successful. One coach, for example, told me that "Jeremy" just realized that he would play high school ball, maybe college ball, but he'd never be pro. He'd turned from gangs to sports in the 7th grade, and the vision that fueled him was the NBA. Suddenly, that dream came against reality. He practiced hours every day, but he knew he wouldn't make it. His attitude had been sour and nasty for weeks. He needed a new vision. This information helped me to understand Jeremy and allowed me to get out the college guide and talk about choices. His final essay was "Life After Sports."

Mostly, I call students at night and talk with them after the day is over, their friends are no longer around, and both of us have had a chance to cool down. Students joke about how they can't get away with anything because Bill and I call their homes. I overheard one student say, "Man, I got to go to class today otherwise they'll call my uncle tonight." Perhaps it's just letting them know we care enough to take our time outside of school that turns them around.

Q/A

How can I help my students stay organized?

Organization is a skill that's learned. That means we must plan for it, just as we plan to teach a lesson on rhyming words or writing persuasive paragraphs.

First, I wrote into our daily schedule "clean desks" about every two weeks, so that my students were prepared for it, just like any other activity during the day.

I explained why we did this: It made it easier for them to keep their work neat and find it easily. Then our days moved more smoothly: We didn't have to stop because half of us couldn't find our math folders or journals.

Students kept a homework folder, an assignment book, and a journal in their desks. Other than their textbooks, a pencil, and a 24-count box of crayons, that was it. The less there was in the desks, the less chance there was for clutter to take root.

Next, we went through the cleaning process step by step: Remove all texts and put them in a pile. Remove all loose papers, file the ones you need to keep and recycle the ones you don't. And so on.

Finally, I practiced what I preached: I forced myself to clean my desk and I shared with my kids that I had done so. Afterall, how could I expect them to listen to me if my desk was a complete mess?

—Stephanie Walters

The Challenge of Classroom Discipline

by Bob Peterson

One of the most challenging tasks in any elementary classroom is to build a community where students respect one another and value learning. Too often, children use put-downs to communicate, resolve conflicts violently, and have negative attitudes toward school and learning. These problems often are based in society. How can one tell students not to use put-downs, for example, when that is the predominant style of comedy on prime-time television?

Barbara J. Miner

But schools often contribute to such problems. Approaches based on lecturing by teachers, passive reading of textbooks, and "fill-in-the-blank" worksheets keep students from making decisions, from becoming actively involved in

251

their learning, and from learning how to think and communicate effectively.

Involving Students in Decision-Making

If a teacher wants to build a community of learners, a number of things have to happen. Students need to be involved in making decisions. They need to work regularly in groups. They need a challenging curriculum that involves not only listening but actually doing as well. They need to understand that it is OK to make mistakes, that learning involves more than getting the "right" answer.

At the same time, teachers need to make sure that students are not set up for failure. Teachers need to model what it means to work independently and in groups so that those who have not learned that outside of school will not be disadvantaged. Teachers need to be clear about what is and what is not within the purview of student decision-making. And teachers need to learn to build schoolwide support for this kind of learning and teaching.

The parameters of students' decision-making range from choosing what they write, read, and study, to deciding the nature of their collaborative projects, to helping establish the classroom's rules and curriculum.

Each year I have students discuss their vision of an ideal classroom and the rules necessary in such a classroom. I explain how certain rules are made by the state government, by the school board, by the school itself, and by the classroom teacher. I let kids know that I will be willing to negotiate certain rules, but that my willingness to agree to their proposals (because ultimately I hold authority in the classroom) is dependent on two things: the soundness of their ideas and their ability as a group to show that they are responsible enough to assume decision-making power. I also tell kids that if they disagree with rules made outside of the classroom, they should voice their concerns.

Things don't always go smoothly. One year while discussing school rules the kids were adamant that anybody who broke a rule should sit in a corner with a dunce cap on his or her head. I refused on the grounds that it was humiliating. Eventually we worked out other consequences including time-outs and loss of the privilege to come to the classroom during lunch recess.

The cooperative learning technique of the "T-Chart" is helpful in getting kids to understand what a community of learners looks like during different activities. The teacher draws a big "T" on the board and titles the left side "looks like" and the right side "sounds like." Kids brainstorm what an outside visitor would see and hear during certain activities. For example, when we make a "T-chart" about how to conduct a class discussion, students list things like "one person talking" under "sounds like" and "kids looking at the speaker" and "children with their hands raised" under "looks like." We hang the T-chart on the wall; this helps most children remember what is appropriate behavior for different activities.

Classroom organization is another essential ingredient in building a community of learners. The desks in my class are in five groups of six each, which serve as "base groups." I divide the students into these base groups every nine weeks, taking into account language dominance, race, gender, and special needs, creating heterogeneous groups to guard against those subtle forms of elementary school "tracking."

Dividing Students into Base Groups

Throughout the day children might work in a variety of cooperative learning groups, but their base group remains the same. Each group has its own bookshelf where materials are kept and homework turned in. Each group elects its own captain who makes sure that materials are in order and that his or her group members are "with the program." For example, before writing workshop, captains distribute writing folders to all students and make sure that everyone is prepared with a sharpened pencil.

Sometimes the group that is the best prepared to start a new activity, for example, will be allowed to help in dramatization or be the class helpers for that lesson. This provides incentive for team captains to get even the most recalcitrant students to join in with classroom activities.

By organizing the students this way, many of the management tasks are taken on by the students, creating a sense of collective responsibility. Arranging the students in these base groups has the added advantage of freeing up classroom space for dramatizations or classroom meetings where kids sit on the floor.

When students use their decision-making power unwisely, I quickly restrict that power. During reading time, for example, students are often allowed to choose their own groups and books. Most work earnestly, reading cooperatively, and writing regularly in their reading response journals. If a reading group has trouble settling down, I intervene rapidly and give increasingly restrictive options to the students. Other students who work successfully in reading groups model how a reading group should be run: The students not only conduct a discussion in front of the class, but also plan in advance for a student to be inattentive and show how a student discussion leader might respond.

A well-organized class that is respectful and involves the students in some decision-making is a prerequisite for successful learning. Cooperative organization and student involvement alone won't make a class critical or even build a community of learners, but they are essential building blocks in its foundation.

From 'Sit Down!' to Stand-Up:

Laugh Your Classroom Management Problems Away

by Don Rose

My first year teaching, I was the only male on the 7th-grade team. I consistently had "troubled boys" transferred into my room because I was a young male and would be able to better connect to them. It got to the point that I had 22 boys in my PM block and only 9 girls. Needless to say, there was a strong masculine presence during that two-hour period. Mikey had been transferred into my class because he continually cussed out his previous teacher, mainly around diagramming sentences. I can't say I blamed him. When he came to my class,

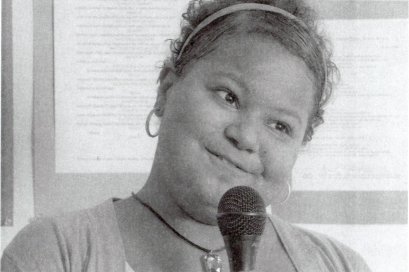

Barbara J. Miner

255

he instantly clicked with the other boys who had landed in my room. Jack and Mikey became class clowns. They had a joke for everything and were actually very gifted with their comedy routine. I couldn't compete.

I tried detention. It didn't work. I tried calling home. It worked for a while but then started up again. Many veteran teachers told me to write them up, meaning a referral, but I wasn't comfortable with this simply because this was a familiar treatment for these boys and hadn't worked in the past. I was stuck with quietly asking them to calm down or to take a break when the clowning got to be too disruptive. Then it came to me.

I had a small white board where I wrote the daily schedule and needed materials. I would usually turn this board around once students were seated so that they could remember what we were covering and when. During silent reading, I pulled Mikey and Jack out into the hallway.

"Look fellas, you two are hilarious. Your peers love you and laugh at almost everything you say. I really can't compete but your jokes typically disrupt class for at least 10 minutes daily. I have an idea."

I offered the boys a 5- to 7-minute time slot at the beginning of each period where they could announce the daily schedule to the class. They could make fun of it but they couldn't be derogatory to any people. They could act out a scene, sing, or dance but after that time they would have to be focused leaders. I also let them know this was not an attempt to quiet them or eliminate them from the fabric of our community but an opportunity to let others voices be heard.

"So, let me get this straight. We get to entertain the class every day doing whatever for five minutes," Mikey asked.

"Yep. Respectfully, of course."

"What if we still goof off?" Jack wondered.

"Well," I said, "that has been going on for a couple of weeks now. I am trying to find a solution, so that your need to be funny and in the spotlight is met but our class's need to learn is met as well. I have thought a lot about this and I really don't know what else to do. Right now, the only alternative I can think of is a referral or time out. I don't think having you leave is the best option, but we need your behavior to be positive."

The boys nodded and started the next day. The first performance was straight out of the Three Stooges. Jack came in and tripped over Mikey's foot. The class broke out in laughter. The board read "Have a pencil, sharpened." Mikey pulled out a plastic knife from one of my drawers and tried to sharpen his pencil. This didn't work so he begin to chew on his pencil. Jack pretended to sprinkle salt on the pencil. The class was a big fan of their first slapstick routine.

The acts continued and the class got its "Mikey and Jack Show" fix. Both of these boys crossed the line during the first weeks, and each time, I lessened the amount of time they had for their performance. The class depended on this performance, and ultimately, Jack and Mikey gave in to the peer pressure. The rest of the year, the boys found a great balance of behavior. They were able to enjoy each other and make their classmates laugh while being positive leaders in the classroom.

Q/A

Do I have to spend my own money on classroom supplies?

Before I ran out to the nearest Office Depot, I always checked with colleagues to see if anything my students needed was already in the building. That helped keep me from spending my own money. In the "supply closet" I sometimes found pencils, rulers, scissors, and standard issue writing paper (a must for the early childhood teacher).

If you go to the teacher supply cupboard and discover it is bare (which has also been my experience at times), don't give up. One year my co-teacher and I drafted a letter introducing ourselves to the parents of our early elementary students. It included a supply checklist for the school year: a 10-pack of No. 2 pencils, a 24-count box of crayons, half a dozen two-pocket folders, glue sticks, two boxes of tissues, a bookbag, etc. We also specified what we didn't want: three-ring binders and the jumbo box of crayons were too bulky; markers were too messy!

We expected our students to all arrive with supplies, but we didn't assume they all would, so I created an emergency stash. First I went through all of the school supplies I'd collected from my own years in school, pulling out my old folders and pencils. Then I asked my sister for crayons and pencils that her children weren't using anymore. Thus I had a small cache of supplies for those children who came to school with nothing.

But that number was extremely low! Even my children whose families really struggled economically arrived that first week with something. Whatever the reason, none of my kids were ashamed, embarrassed, or doing without, and I was not charging boxes of Crayolas on my Visa card.

I also collected everything that we didn't need right away and put it in our community closet. That way it didn't clutter up desks or get used up needlessly or ruined. When a student needed a new homework folder, I knew where to find one.

—Stephanie Walters

Making Rules

by Dale Weiss

I admit it, I was naive. Before I started teaching 1st grade I believed I wouldn't have to make any specific rules for my class. I believed that if I simply treated my students with respect they would naturally respond respectfully, and that would take care of things.

It didn't take long for me to realize I was wrong. In fact I realized it on my very first day.

My first act as a teacher was to corral my students into some semblance of a straight line on the playground and lead them to our classroom, where a big and colorful "Welcome to Room 13" sign adorned the door. One of the kids, Fred, took one look at the sign and said: "Thirteen is an unlucky number. I don't want to be here." I managed a half-smile and ushered the kids, reluctant Fred included, into the room.

I then directed the students to sit in a circle

CLASS RULES
1. Listen when others are talking.
2. Follow directions.
3. Keep hands, feet, and objects to yourself.
4. Work quietly and do not disturb others.
5. Show respect for school and personal property.
6. Work and play in a safe manner.

on the brightly colored rug that lay in front of the semicircle of tiny desks. I had bought this rug a few days before at Goodwill, thrilled as I'd imagined it as the home to hours and hours of wonderful conversations and learning.

Lizzi and Angela started dancing in circles. "No, please sit in a circle," I said, to which Angela responded: "When we stop twirling in our circles we fall down. Then we sit up in the place that we fell down." A few other students sat down at desks. A small group of boys started playing with puzzles. Another group of boys and girls began trying on clothes in the housekeeping area. Six other students were sitting in a corner of the room playing hand-clapping games. Granted, they were sitting in a circle, but not on the rug.

Unbelievable, I thought. How could a direction as straightforward as "please sit in a circle on the rug" be so completely misunderstood, playfully reinvented, or simply ignored?

I was at a loss. And things didn't get better that day. My room was chaos surrounded by four walls and a door.

By the end of the day I was a "born-again rule maker." I felt that although my aspiration to have a rule-free classroom had been a good one, it was nonetheless based more on idealism than on what these 6- and 7-year-old children could handle. I didn't want to be the kind of teacher for whom "well behaved" equals "silent and still." Yet I also wanted my classroom to be less chaotic, though not by totally squelching all the energy and enthusiasm the kids were bringing through my door.

I wanted to create a structure that fostered a safe and well-run classroom community, one that taught students the levels of responsibility that were necessary to experience various levels of freedom, and one in which the voices of students were included as part of the process.

Yes, I would need to make rules after all.

Learning from Chaos

After that first day—much of which I'd spent glaring at nametag after nametag in an effort to separate out those causing trouble from the innocent bystanders—I learned my students' names faster than I have ever memorized anything in my life. On the second day I greeted each student at the door by name.

Then I told each of them to please sit down at his or her desk. I made it clear I was telling them to do it, not asking. I was polite but firm. Perhaps because of this, and because the direction I gave them was more concrete— "there is your chair, please sit on it," as opposed to asking them to work with 20-plus other kids to create a circle— the students quickly complied.

After taking attendance and the lunch count, I told the students that we were going to talk about how our first day of school had gone. Brett started talking about his first day of kindergarten. Aha, I thought. Once again I had forgotten that students, especially young children, need directions to be very, very explicit. So I rephrased my question: "Yesterday was our first day of 1st grade together. Please tell me some things you liked about the day."

"The toasted cheese at lunch was pretty good," said Fred. "I learned to do double Dutch on the playground," responded Lisa. "I'm glad that Lizzi and I are in the same class again," piped in Lindsey. Ah, food and friendship: the cornerstones of 1st grade.

Then I asked if they could think of anything that they did not like about their first day of 1st grade. Hesitation. Finally Angela broke the silence. "It was kind of crazy in here. Like everybody was running around too much." John added: "We could never do that in kindergarten, and if we did, we had to fold our hands together and not even say one word." Lisa chimed in: "And if we did say a word, we had a big time-out in the corner of the room."

Jacob, who the day before had spoken so softly that his words were barely audible, began to cry. "What's wrong, Jacob?" I asked. He started sobbing. His words did not come. I asked if anyone knew why Jacob was crying. John responded: "He used to get in trouble all the time in kindergarten."

I asked the students to tell me if they felt safe in our classroom yesterday. A variety of responses followed:

"Not exactly, because the kids were getting into lots of fights."

"I felt tired because it was too loud in here."

"I was safe because I carried my scissors the right way."

"In kindergarten our teacher told us what to do all the time. You didn't tell us those things so I didn't know if it was OK to do some stuff."

"I liked the housekeeping area but I think there were too many kids in there because we kept fighting about who got to cook the eggs."

"I did some stuff that I did in kindergarten, like throw some Lego blocks. But in kindergarten I got time-outs but yesterday I didn't."

The comments went on and on. I gained many insights. For one, my students had been heavily exposed to rules and consequences during kindergarten. And secondly, the students seemed to be asking for structure.

Drawing Up Rules

I then told my students to once again sit on the rug in a circle. But this time, before anyone left their desks, I explained what a circle was and how they would form one, step by step. Then, as gently as possible, I helped my students place their bodies in a roughly circle-like configuration on the rug. And I sat down in the circle myself and modeled appropriate behaviors for circle time: One person talks at a time; listen with your ears and your whole body when someone else is speaking; don't fidget; be respectful of other people's space, and so on.

Once we were finally in a circle I said: "Who can tell me what you think is needed to make our classroom a safe place to be?" Lots of hands went up.

"We don't hit each other."

"We share."

"Everybody gets invited to the birthday parties."

"At recess we don't trip other kids or laugh if they fall down."

I redirected the conversation a bit, reminding students that for now I only wanted to talk about what we needed to do to make our classroom a safe place. The comments continued.

"We listen if somebody is saying something."

"We don't make fun of other kids."

"If somebody wants to use my crayons I would let them."

"We are respectful."

I wrote all of their responses on a big sheet of butcher paper. The list was long and contained many great ideas. I hung it on the wall and told the kids to look at all their answers and think of one idea that was more important than all the others. They chose: "We are respectful."

After carefully directing the kids back into their seats, I placed three items on each of their desks: sheets of lined paper with space at the top for drawings, a pencil, and a set of large crayons (the kind that is easier for young children to use). I told the students to use the unlined space on their paper to draw a picture of something they would be doing if they were being respectful. Before asking the students to begin drawing, we brainstormed a list of possible examples. I told them that they had great ideas and that their drawings didn't need to look the same—in fact they shouldn't.

Students then brought their pictures back up to our rug space. They were still somewhat clumsy about forming a circle but they managed it this time without step-by-step instruction. They each shared their drawings, explaining what they would do to show they were being respectful. Amanda drew a picture of herself helping another student tie her shoe. Lindsey drew a group of children sitting in a circle reading together. Brett's drawing showed several students taking turns cooking the make-believe eggs in the housekeeping area.

Back at their seats, I wrote under each drawing the words that the student wanted to accompany the picture. While I was going around the room doing this, each student drew borders along the periphery of their page. This kept them occupied while I worked one-on-one with each student.

Then we arranged the pages in quilt form on our classroom wall. We referred to this as our "Acting Appropriately Wall." (I frequently used the word "appropriate" with my students, and made sure they understood its meaning as well as the actions that brought the meaning to life.) The next day Fred said: "I think that wall is like our classroom rules. We only have one rule but the rule has lots of parts to it." Fred was right. From his 1st-grade vantage point, being respectful of others was central to everything else we were doing.

What if Someone Breaks the Rules?

Later that week we began to talk about what should be done if someone in the class chose not to follow our classroom rule of respect. By now I had learned that things needed to be carefully laid out in a clear, concise, step-by-step manner. Again, I told the students to come up to the rug and sit in a circle. (I had purchased tiny carpet squares to use for circle time. Each child took a carpet square and placed it on the rug to mark their sitting spot. This helped to more clearly define the space each student would occupy.) I began by asking what should be done if someone in our class didn't act in a respectful way. To help make the conversation less threatening, I used myself as an example first. "Let's say I choose to not write in my journal during journal time and instead I choose to start playing with the puzzles. What do you think my consequence should be?" Lots of hands went up.

"I think you shouldn't get to play with the puzzles for the rest of the year."

"You should have to write in your journal during recess time."

"You would have to be last in line to recess."

"No recess for a week."

"You could get a warning but if you do it again, you'll get a bigger punishment."

I believe that consequences should be logical and address the misbehavior that has occurred. I also believe that consequences should help to redirect behavior so that students can begin to internalize appropriate behaviors. I do not believe that external consequences—in and of themselves—do much good in any kind of long-lasting way.

I told my students that they'd come up with a great list of consequences, and now I wanted us to decide on one consequence for the inappropriate choice I'd made during journal time. I explained that the consequence needed to help me figure out what I had done wrong and what a more appropriate choice would have been. And if some kind of punishment was appropriate, it needed to make sense for what I had done wrong. Because I was the teacher, I would ultimately decide what the punishment would be (even for myself!). But I made it clear to students that I wanted and valued their input.

After much discussion, the students decided that two things needed to happen. First, I should be reminded that during journal time I was supposed to be writing in my journal, not playing with other toys in the classroom. And second, because I was playing during part of journal time, I should write in my journal during part of free-choice time. I was very pleased. The consequence addressed my misbehavior and was logical.

The students then took turns participating in a role play depicting my misbehavior and the consequence I was given. Afterward, a few students drew a picture of the misbehavior and the appropriate consequence we had decided upon. This picture became the first entry in our "Consequence Wall," which was displayed adjacent to our "Acting Appropriately Wall." This same process was followed when addressing other misbehaviors and consequences.

Now admittedly this was a pretty straightforward example. My "misbehavior" was not all that serious, and there was a way to deal with it within our classroom and within the confines of the same school day.

I realized I would also need to address misbehaviors of a more serious nature with my students. For example, what if one student physically harmed another student? Many of these kinds of infractions were clearly addressed in a handbook on expected student behaviors that was provided by my school. I decided to broaden our discussion on classroom rules to include the concept of school-wide rules and consequences.

What was important to me at this point was that my students were getting exposed to the basic ideas of rules and consequences, and they were getting a chance to practice applying those ideas. It was a first step.

Even with the classroom rules and consequences firmly in place, things did not always run smoothly. My students needed to be reminded constantly what appropriate behaviors looked like and sounded like. We had daily discussions regarding this. During that first year of my career I learned about the incredible amount of time and consistency that is needed to help students learn to internalize appropriate behaviors. Eventually, students became less and less dependent on me for guidance in terms of their behavior, as they learned to rely more both on themselves and each other. Though the ride was bumpy many times, the outcome was well worth it.

Exile Has Its Place

by T. Elijah Hawkes

. . . you can't betray a country you don't have
—James Baldwin

E xile has its place. As an age-old human response to
conflict, its potential value to the healthy matura-
tion of students and the school community should
not be discounted.

Exile or ostracism goes by various names in school.
Students are told: Move your desk. Leave the classroom
and wait in the hall. Go to the office. Go to detention.
You're suspended.

There are those in progressive education circles who
dismiss suspension as a careless traditional response to
a situation better addressed by counseling and alternative, restorative justice methods. Others aptly note that

David McLimans

267

the power to suspend is often abused: used to push out students who might challenge us, thus furthering systemic neglect and mistreatment. If done right, however, suspension, or exile, can be the first step in a restorative process, and a meaningful and fair response to the violation of community values.

Sometimes Kids Just Needed to "Get Out"

At the James Baldwin School in New York City, we've just finished our fourth year. We're under 300 students, mostly transfers from other high schools, majority black and Latino, residing in four city boroughs. It's a vastly heterogeneous population in terms of academic past, scholastic sophistication, and ambition.

Last year I was working with a colleague who was new to the teaching profession and struggling to maintain a respectful climate in the classroom. Wrangling demons and darlings each day, sometimes not sure who was who, he was certain that sometimes kids needed to just "get out." Students kept arriving at my office. So I met with the teacher to discuss what I first wrote him in a note:

Suspending students from class can be an effective strategy, just like suspensions from school, to force certain conversations and reflection, to develop behavior contracts, and to broaden the child's "circle of accountability" to include more people, such as the co-directors, advisor, or parents. However, the classroom environment and community, like our school community, is among our most sacred entities. Excluding people from it (to have them re-enter) should be a strategy of last resort.

We discussed how removal from class, although a last resort, is not an end but the beginning. It initiates a labor-intensive process that includes a re-entry meeting with the student and perhaps the advisor to clarify expectations and establish future consequences, listening well to the child all the while to better understand the root causes of the behavior.

Suspending a Newcomer: Dwayne's Story

As with removal from class, so with suspension from school: It is an ostracism that begins a substantive process of reflection and return. Consider Dwayne. His exile resulted from his assaulting another boy after school. Suspension was a given, for there'd been violence, but we were concerned that it might not be effective because Dwayne was new. He'd been with us so short a time that we hadn't built the requisite sense of belonging. Ostracism should inspire feelings of loss and regret, and these are only likely if some sense of home has been established first.

When Dwayne came to us, he brought colossal mistrust of teachers and some extraordinarily aggressive and lewd habits of interaction. He was thus having trouble establishing relationships with anyone, from peers to his advisor. He didn't feel at home. So, during his suspension, our task was not simply to provide him with assignments, to maintain contact, and prepare the mediation; our work was even more basic. We had to nurture bonds of trust that had barely yet been formed—all the while telling him, and his family, why he was suspended from our community for a time.

The suspension was several days long, and we needed all that time to prepare the re-entry. I spent several hours with him and his parents, hours with him alone, and hours as well with Roland, the other boy involved. Other staff also spent time with the boys; it became clear that some classic seeds of conflict were at root: attraction, disrespect, betrayal, sexuality, and turfs both interpersonal and material.

Dwayne acknowledged feeling threatened by things Roland was saying and texting. He admitted feeling disliked and hurt, especially because Roland was spreading comments from kids who'd known Dwayne at his old school. They said he just wasn't worth liking. He felt unfairly followed by a reputation and helpless to shed it. He was angry and still defensive, but after a few days he was able to verbalize some positive qualities in Roland, that he's "generous to his friends" and would "go the distance for them." I kept notes and gave them to his advisor and to the counselor who facilitated the mediation. That was about six months ago. We'll see how things unfold, but so far, since his return and the mediation, while there have been other issues, he hasn't been in a violent conflict.

The extensive time preparing Dwayne's return was well invested: We listened to him, asked questions, got to know him better. We showed we had high expectations for him, asserted that we were willing to forgive—and that he could, too.

Senior Drama: A Fight Between Two Cliques

In a world of different circumstance, consider Monica, a student we'd known not three months but three years, and her story of exile and return. It was two springs ago, and emotions were running full and high. Monica and friends were one group, and Sara and friends were counterpoised. Over the course of months there were constant ups and downs, some minor mendings, then fresh affronts: a text message of disrespect, a shoulder bump in the hall, a name on the bathroom wall. There were times when one girl would make a threat and everyone expected a fight after school. Classrooms were disrupted. We're a small school, so we felt each reverberation of even the smallest incident. It was more than a situation or incident, it was a subculture of ire and cutting eyes.

Each girl had her motives and needs. I think that at the heart of it for Monica were two compelling circumstances. One was that on the periphery of Sara's group was Janelle, who'd once dated Monica's boyfriend—thus, a rival. The other circumstance was that the previous year, in another context, Monica had been beaten very unexpectedly, publicly, and painfully by an emotionally disturbed older girl. This new conflict plucked at thick cords of meaning inside

Monica: She couldn't let herself again be a victim or feel inferior.

The staff had strong bonds with Monica and many of the other girls and their families. We were intent to guide them to peace. But our efforts—individual counseling, mediations, family meetings, warnings that college recommendations and participation in the graduation ceremony were at stake, even a half-day retreat for the factions hosted by our counselor and social worker—all seemed to have little lasting impact. We consoled ourselves, however, that there had never been a physical fight.

Until the Fight

Monica and two friends jumped Sara and two of the others. Allies piled on, some trying to de-escalate, others making it worse. A phone was lost in the scuffle on the sidewalk. And the police happened to be on the block, so it was quickly removed from my authority. Tears, fear, and screaming, and some of the girls were suddenly in the heavy hands of the cops, who quickly shaped the missing phone into larceny. Then there were handcuffs, more humiliation, and police custody all night for four girls.

On the broad scale of pain that any day can trouble the children of New York City and their schools, this was minor: no one hospitalized, no one killed, and the charges against the girls eventually dropped. But it felt deeply painful still. As staff, we felt like failures. It was June and we were exhausted. But for us and for the girls, it was just the beginning of several stories of suspension and return.

Exile and Return

Some families decided to keep their daughters out of school for the remainder of the year, beyond any exile we imposed. There were just two weeks left, and the families of three seniors decided that they'd simply do their course work from home and then graduate. But none of us was comfortable—even the students and families, I think—with the idea that their exile, self-chosen or school-imposed, wouldn't include some restitution and closure. Nor were any staff—despite some strong differences of perspective on these events—willing that seniors on either side of the conflict participate in our graduation ceremony without some repair.

We decided that in order for any of them to march at graduation, they had to engage in a public accounting before staff and younger students, to confront the past and the legacy of their actions.

Just as suspension is kin to age-old stories of exile, so too our forum for repair was cousin to something ages old. I was reminded of Gacaca, a practice for communal restitution in Rwanda. Similar structures exist among the First Nations of North America and in other cultures in other times. It happened in a circle. It was intergenerational. It was a public reckoning.

There were 13 students, one from each advisory group, and as many staff as could attend. The younger students were first asked to reflect on why their advisors had chosen them for the meeting. Some needed coaxing but eventually each spoke of some good quality that their advisor might have seen in them. These proclamations of their own moral strength both served to validate why they'd been selected and helped the students set high expectations for the meeting and for themselves. The adults did no talking at this point. I then asked the students to imagine what it would feel like to be one of the seniors right now. Some responded judgmentally with what they thought the seniors should be feeling. I interrupted and again asked them to simply imagine what the girls were actually feeling. Students said the girls might feel nervous, embarrassed, angry at themselves, regretful, and some noted that it would take bravery to do this.

Each senior, one at a time, came in accompanied by her advisor, who sat beside her, with me at her other side. I wanted each girl to feel supported, not simply confronted face to face. I first told her that her peers thought it took courage to come before us. Then I asked the senior to reflect on the lessons she'd learned, what made her proud and what she regretted. After she spoke, the younger students were asked to paraphrase what they'd heard and to do this with "I" statements, such as, "Monica, what I heard you saying was . . ." After hearing the younger students' paraphrasing, the senior was asked if there was anything else she wished to add or comment. We heard her thoughts and then we all turned to a conversation about how to make the school stronger next year.

We did this four times, with four girls, a two-hour process. Each senior admitted something she would have done differently. Some of the most meaningful comments came from Monica and Sara, who made simple unsolicited statements of being sorry for choices they'd made and for how it unsettled the community. They'd not been told that an apology was required. Each time this happened, I stopped the conversation. I asked the group if anyone was willing to accept the apology. Various students spoke to say yes.

The apologies and the future-focused conclusion of the meeting gave us some closure and hope. The thoughts from the students on how to strengthen the community were good ones: peer resources for conflict resolution, more guidance groups, and after-school classes to allow students to know each other in extracurricular settings and to help decrease the likelihood of cliques. Each senior who participated was allowed to take her place at our commencement ceremony, a most important rite.

No Return Without Restitution

There was one senior, Angela, whose family hadn't allowed her to come to the meeting with the younger students. In the end, she couldn't have marched in commencement anyway, because she was two credits short of graduating. But she was still a member of the class, had been with us for two years, and she fervently wished to attend the ceremony. It was difficult, but we refused to let her come.

This spring, Angela called. She had completed her coursework over the summer and graduated without ceremony last August. Now she wanted to wear a cap and gown this June. We explained she would need to participate in a process of restitution. She was willing. We gathered students and staff and took a few days to prepare. A year had passed but we recognized that this story of exile and return still had the potential to heal—both her and us.

"I played a big part in the feud, fueling it," she said to start. "It was a learning experience. . . . I got locked up. . . . I realized I don't want that for myself." We asked her to explain why she wanted to participate in this ceremony. "Because graduating from high school is really big. . . . This year I was in college but I still felt like I was in high school. I didn't have that closure." After other questions and reflections, including an apology to the eldest student in the room, she was asked to leave so we could deliberate. Should her request be granted? The students spoke first. "Yes, she should be allowed," the eldest said. "She's a new person. She made a change." And the youngest thought Angela had "really re-evaluated herself . . . and made a big step in apologizing here in person." A third student said, "If I was in her shoes, I'd feel the same. Being in college without the graduation ceremony from high school, something's missing." The teachers then reacted to the students' observations. We agreed, in the words of one teacher, that "she should participate in our graduation ceremony because she and society and our school will be better for it."

We continue to reflect and continue to learn from these stories of exile, return, and repair. There's often a lot to be learned from excluding and being excluded. It's an essential aspect of knowledge development and identity formation: belonging and not belonging, category and classification, comparison, juxtaposition, groupings. And many stories tell us that there are few more powerful punishments than exclusion from a group to which you feel you belong. School leaders should levy this punishment with discretion and clarity, as wise elders have through the ages—for if our schools feel like communities, then exile can have its place, provided time and love are invested in the return.

Helping Students Deal with Anger

by Kelley Dawson Salas

"**L**et me go! LET ME GO!!!" Michael's screams fill the entire second floor hallway. I imagine the noise bolting like lightning down the stairway, forcing its way through the double doors at the bottom and arriving abruptly in the principal's office.

Arms flail and one of Michael's fists connects with my teaching partner's ribs. I speak in what I hope is a soothing voice, although I know it is tinged with tension: "Michael, it's gonna be OK. We just need you to settle down a little bit first, Michael. As soon as you settle down we can let you go."

Scott Bakal

Michael was normally an outgoing, upbeat kid who was well liked by his classmates and teachers. But from time to time he would just "drop out" of what the class was doing. Sometimes he would simply put his head down and withdraw. Sometimes he would start pushing and shoving his classmates. And sometimes he would escalate to a full-blown tantrum, which would grind the entire classroom to a halt. This was one of those times.

By the time Michael was allowed to bring his hoarse voice and his 3rd-grade body back into our classroom the next morning, I had decided that I needed to teach my young students some strategies on dealing with anger.

I was in my first year of teaching, trying to get my bearings. I was learning what kids were all about for the very first time. I was under the added pressure of going to school twice a week to meet the requirements of my alternative certification program. I simply didn't feel I had the time or the experience to help Michael respond to his emotions more appropriately.

Earlier in the year, after Michael's first few outbursts, I had pursued a different strategy and sought help for Michael from people outside of our classroom. I referred Michael for Collaborative Support Team action. "What can we do to find out what is behind Michael's angry behaviors?" I asked my principal and the members of the support team. "Is there some kind of anger management program he can participate in outside of the classroom? Can he receive counseling from the social worker or psychologist?" Michael did see the psychologist a few times after that. Both the social worker and I made calls to the family.

But the flare-ups continued. In the classroom, nothing really changed. And of course I was not the only person in the classroom noticing Michael's behavior. The students also were keen observers. They saw how Michael put his head down on his desk and covered it up with his coat from time to time. They took a step backward as he pushed a chair out of his way and into theirs, or hit another student on the playground and called it an accident. And several times, in situations when Michael exhibited angry behaviors, they had seen me give him a choice of "cooling down" and getting back to work or being asked to leave the classroom. More than once, they had witnessed him fly into a tantrum.

Other staff also were aware of Michael. During one episode, when there was a lull in Michael's screaming, I overheard the comments of a specialist who had stepped in to supervise my students: "We have to be real careful of Michael when he comes back to the classroom. We don't know what he'll do, do we?"

I didn't like the sound of that. As Michael's classroom teacher, I had observed that he sometimes had a difficult time handling his emotions and dealing with what I perceived as anger. I did not think about him as an angry person, and I was determined not to allow his peers or other staff members to categorize him as such. I felt this was especially important in a classroom where I, the teacher, was Anglo, almost all of the students were Latino, and Michael was one of three African American boys. I did not want our classroom to be a place where students or staff were allowed to reinforce stereotypes that link anger with boys and men, especially African American boys and men.

But the emotionally charged interactions that took place fairly regularly in our classroom indicated that something needed to change.

As I tried to help Michael through a long process of learning how to identify his feelings and emotions and respond constructively, I also went through an important learning process.

Lessons on Anger

I had to consider all the factors that contributed to our classroom dynamic. I had to examine my own beliefs, attitudes, and responses to Michael's behaviors. I had to consider how my actions as a white teacher of students of color affected Michael's emotions and responses. I had to try different approaches. These responsibilities weighed on me as I planned my course of action, and I continue to consider them as I reflect on what I did and what I might do differently next time.

For example, at the time I characterized Michael's outbursts as anger. Whether that is the appropriate emotional term, I am not sure; perhaps he was expressing frustration, or loneliness, or pain. I realize, in retrospect, that I used the term "anger" to describe strong emotional outbursts that may have had their origin in any number of emotions.

Teaching about anger immediately after a conflict with Michael didn't make sense. All eyes were on him. If I taught about anger during these moments, I would only be singling Michael out and escalating the problem. The rest of the students would pick up on my cue and would probably label him as an angry person. I might send an incorrect message that the only people who feel angry are those who act out the way Michael did.

Instead, I tried to plan a few simple lessons that would help all students consider what anger is, what other emotions or experiences anger is linked to, and how we can respond. I drew upon my own personal experiences with anger and tantrums to put the lessons together.

The resources I used were minimal: I am sure there are much more extensive curricula on this topic. The important thing for me and my students was that these lessons helped us create a common framework for thinking about anger. Later I would refer to this framework in crisis moments or in interventions with Michael.

Safe Responses to Anger

I wanted my students to be able to identify the experiences and emotions that lead to what might be described as angry behaviors. I wanted them to recognize different responses to anger that they and others use. Most importantly, I wanted students to consider the choices we have for responding to strong emotions such as anger. I wanted them to recognize that when we are upset, we can either choose a course of action that is unsafe or unhealthy for ourselves and others, or we can choose a course of action that is safe and healthy.

I hoped this discussion would lead students not only to see that it is unacceptable to allow anger and strong emotions to explode in outbursts, but also to identify and practice safe responses when they feel angry.

I led three discussions with my students. First, we made a list of "things that make us angry." Students cited a great many sources of anger, from the trivial to the unjust. Some of their responses: "I get mad when I can't find the remote"; "when people treat me like I'm stupid"; "when we lose part of our recess"; and "when my mom hits me."

Second, we made a list of "things people do when they're mad." I encouraged the students to share examples of things they personally do when they're mad, and allowed them to share things they'd seen other people do. Many student responses were negative, hurtful, or unsafe, such as: "I punch the nearest person"; "I hurt myself"; "I bang my own head against the wall"; "I kick or slam a door as hard as I can"; and "I yell at the person who's making me mad."

A couple of students offered up what I would categorize as "safe" responses to anger: "I go for a bike ride to blow off steam"; "I go in my room and read until I'm not mad anymore"; "I talk to my mom about what's making me mad." I asked the students: "Can you think of any other things like that, things that would help you to cool down or solve the problem?"

Other Sources of Anger

Our discussions around anger focused mostly on interpersonal relationships, and sought to understand what an individual can do when he/she feels angry. Looking back at this focus on individual interactions, I see that I missed an opportunity to guide students in an inquiry into other types of anger. I think it is important to help students understand that anger exists not only on an individual level, but can be related to societal issues of oppression and injustice.

This in turn could lead to a discussion of the role anger can play in the fight for social justice. As an activist for social justice, I use my anger at injustice to guide my own actions on a daily basis. Students can and should be aware that emotions often described as anger are not categorically "bad." Just as anger on an individual level can compel us to address a problem or make a change, the anger we feel when we witness injustice on a societal level should guide us toward changing unjust and oppressive systems. Rosa Parks comes quickly to mind as an example any 3rd grader can understand.

They suggested a few more: "You could talk to an adult you trust"; "go for a walk or go outside and play"; "tell the person who's making you mad how you feel."

Finally, we made a large poster to hang in the classroom that showed different responses to anger. The students each made their own copy of the poster for their own use. In the center, the question "What can you do when you feel angry?" prompted kids to remember the responses we had brainstormed in the previous activity. The top half of the poster was reserved for writing in safe or healthy responses to anger, while the bottom half was labeled "unsafe/scary." While completing this activity, we had a chance to discuss the idea that each person must make a choice when angry about what course of action to take. I again reminded the students that some responses to anger are safe and some are not.

By helping students see the connection between their responses to anger and adults' responses, I tried to encourage them to understand that each of us has a lifelong responsibility to resolve anger appropriately and safely.

Rather than just telling students to respond "safely" to a situation that makes them mad, they need to be taught to consider the source of their anger and to develop a response that is not only safe but also effective. Routine bickering with a sibling might be effectively solved by some time apart, for example, although a series of name-calling incidents or physical bullying by a classmate will not be resolved just by walking away one more time. Students should be encouraged to see the difference between a response that simply helps them blow off steam, and one that actively seeks to address the cause of their anger and solve the problem.

Michael Joins In

Several complexities surfaced in our discussions. Michael, who in addition to his tantrums had also been known to crumple his papers in frustration, asked about how to classify these kinds of actions. "Is it safe to crumple up your paper? You're not hurting anyone if you do that."

"Well, let's think about that one," I responded. "It might not be physically dangerous to anyone, but is it hurting you in any way? Does it hurt you when you put your head down for hours and decide not to learn or do your work?" My hope was that Michael would slowly come to realize that he was hurting himself with some of his behaviors.

Michael participated during these sessions just as any other student. I did not single him out or use him as an example. In fact, I tried hard not to allow myself or the other students to refer to his behavior in our discussions. I did keep a close eye on him, and noticed that he participated actively. His brainstorming worksheets also gave me an idea of some of the things that made him angry, and some of his usual responses to anger at school and at home. This was important to my work with Michael because it allowed me to think about possible causes of his behaviors without having to do it in a moment of crisis, and without making him feel like he was being singled out.

'Why Do Adults Do It?'

I should make clear that I did not assume or suspect that Michael was dealing with anger or violence in his own family. Rather, I planned this lesson in order to address the students' concerns, and to give students a clear message that adults are responsible for making safe choices when faced with anger.

During our talks about anger, students' questions provided a springboard to an additional discussion that could have turned into a whole unit of its own. As we looked together at the abundance of unsafe or violent responses to anger, a few students began to ask: "If we're not supposed to throw tantrums, why do so many adults do it?"

They're right, I thought. How can I tell them that they should choose safe responses to anger when so many adults choose verbal outbursts or even physical violence? How and when can we hold adults responsible for their angry behaviors? I allowed my teaching to take a brief detour in pursuit of an answer to these important questions.

I designed a lesson in which I talked about my own experiences with adults and anger, and shared a poem about a parent's angry outbursts. Together we discussed a few key concepts about adult anger and tantrums. We discussed the fact that adults, just like kids, must make choices about how to act when they are angry. Some adults make poor choices, I said.

I also wanted to make sure that my students didn't internalize feelings of guilt over an adult's anger, as if they were somehow to blame for the outburst. I pointed out that it is not a child's fault if an adult they know responds to anger in a way that hurts others. I referred back to a previous unit we had done on human rights and asserted that as human beings, we have a right to live free from the threat of angry outbursts and violence. We agreed that it is important for us to talk with someone we trust if someone is threatening that right. Adults can change their behaviors, and may need help to do so.

These affirmations provided a very basic introduction that could have easily turned into a much more profound examination of anger and violence in families—our discussion only scratched the surface.

Some Changes, Some Progress

The school year went on. Michael did not miraculously change overnight, but he did make some changes, and so did I. In situations where he resorted to angry behaviors, we had a language in which to talk about his feelings and his choices for responding to them. I also had developed more sensible and effective strategies for helping Michael through tough times. Many times, I said to him: "It's clear to me that you're feeling frustrated or angry. Are you choosing to deal with your feelings in a safe way?"

Later in the year when Michael was angry, he was no longer as likely to say to me: "Look what you made me do." He knew I would respond by saying, "You choose what you do."

Things got easier. The cooling-down periods got shorter. He seemed to be taking more responsibility for his actions and developing some strategies for what to do when he felt frustrate d or angry.

For my part, I tried to become more flexible and to stop trying to force Michael to respond exactly as I wanted him to when he felt angry. I always tried to get to what triggered his discontent and to acknowledge his feelings.

Perhaps most importantly, I learned not to touch Michael while he was angry, or to try to move him physically. I had seen that that simply did not work.

I was relieved that we had found a somewhat workable solution to Michael's behavior in our classroom. Part of me continued to wonder whether there were circumstances in Michael's life that were causing anger and frustration to build up. I kept working with his family and advocating with school support staff for additional help for him. I talked with him often about his feelings and tried to be alert to signs of a more serious problem without making unfounded assumptions.

Michael and I worked together for a year and I think each one of us made some progress. As I struggled to become an effective teacher in my first year on the job, I was willing to learn from anyone who wanted to teach. Michael proved to have a lot of lessons in store for me. How little I would have learned had I simply written him off.

For his part, Michael could have just as easily turned his back on me. I am thankful to him for giving me a chance to be his teacher and to learn from him.

Chapter 5

Making Change in the World Beyond the Classroom

Why We Need to Go Beyond the Classroom

by Stan Karp

School power comes in many pieces.

As teachers, we understandably focus on our own classrooms, where we have daily opportunities to project a vision of democracy and equality. Whether it's developing curriculum that includes the real lives of our students, encouraging young people to examine issues of race, class, and gender as they build academic competence, or organizing activities that promote cooperative skills and spirit, classroom teachers can often find ways to promote social justice despite the institutional agendas and bureaucratic practices imposed upon us.

Barbara J. Miner

But what if we stop at the classroom door? What if critical teachers see their role only in terms of classroom practice? Is our job solely to create "safe spaces" inside an often ineffective and oppressive educational system? Can we sustain ourselves for years as committed professionals by focusing solely on the 30, 60, or 150 students for whom we assume direct responsibility each September? What about the other arenas of educational activity beyond our classrooms: schoolwide change, community and district education politics, teacher unionism, and state and national education reform policy? What do these have to do with next week's lesson plans?

One unavoidable answer is that teachers will never really succeed at their jobs until conditions of teaching and learning improve dramatically. We need more resources, better preparation and support, smaller classes, more effective partnerships with the communities we serve, and, especially in poorer areas, a vision of social change that can replace poverty and despair with progress and hope. We need effective responses to violence, racism, drug abuse, family crisis and the many other problems that surface daily in our classrooms. Teachers have to address these problems in the course of their professional lives as surely as our students have to study and do their homework to achieve individual academic goals.

Grassroots Voices Are Essential

Adding "extracurricular" activism to a classroom teacher's workload may seem overwhelming. But it is a necessity that's been forced upon us. Whether the issue is vouchers, funding, multiculturalism, testing, or tracking, schools have become public battlegrounds for competing social and political agendas. Yet many "reform" proposals would only make matters worse. If education reform is going to make schools more effective, more equitable, and more democratic institutions, the voices of grassroots teachers, parents, and students are essential. If we don't help to change our schools from the bottom up, we will have them changed for us from the top down.

Education activism is also crucial to finding the allies we need. It is naive to believe that we can transform our schools and our students' lives by ourselves. Although we can admire and strive to emulate teachers who through hard work and commitment manage to perform classroom "magic," the real hope for educational transformation does not lie in the development of isolated "superteachers" but in the reconstruction of school life. We need better, more collaborative relations with our colleagues and the space to nurture those possibilities. We need better, more cooperative relations with parents and communities, particularly where cultural and racial differences exist. And we need more democratic practices in our schools, our unions, and our districts, which can only come with contacts and activism beyond classroom boundaries.

How to Get Involved

Before deciding how to get involved beyond our classrooms, we need to do some hard thinking about where to invest our time and energies. Site-based school councils, teacher unions, and teacher activist groups are three types of organizations that have the potential to move our classrooms and communities closer to more just and more democratic arrangements. As you consider the existing organizations in the community where you teach, it can help to measure your choices against the possibilities each organization offers.

School Site Councils

At their best, site-based councils can make school governance more representative and democratic. Where site councils have real power, parents, teachers, and others in a school community can make significant decisions about resources, curricula, and school policies in ways that can nourish community/school/teacher collaboration. Site councils can become places where members of a school community work to reconcile different perspectives and priorities, and learn to build trust and respect over the long term.

At its worst, however, site-based reform can become simply another bureaucratic layer in a system that doesn't work. It can consume valuable time and energy in a seemingly endless cycle of unproductive meetings designed to give a veneer of legitimacy to bureaucratic agendas. Instead of representative bodies, site councils can be empty shells dominated by administrative appointees, or bodies that marginalize parents (or classroom teachers) in ways that promote old antagonisms rather than new alliances.

Whether or not a particular site-based project is worth a teacher's investment of time and energy probably depends on the answers to a variety of questions: Has the council been created in response to a top-down directive or is it the product of grassroots, union, or community action? Does the site council have direct control over resources or policies that can have substantial impact on the school? Is the site council a place where teachers and parents really have a chance to engage in dialogue and form alliances? Is the process characterized by an increase in communication, access to information, and debate by key constituencies? Is site-based reform accompanied by a tangible investment in the time and training needed to make it work? Is there buildingwide or districtwide discussion of how such reform will change the roles of all concerned, or is it being grafted on to existing structures?

Even where the answers to such questions are mixed, asking them will help measure the potential of a given site-based project and prepare teachers for critical participation in the process.

Teacher Unions

Teacher unions offer another mix of opportunities and obstacles for teachers looking to effect change. Like public schools themselves, teacher unions are both deeply flawed institutions, and, at the same time, indispensable to hopes for educational democracy and justice. Labor unions in general, and teacher unions in particular, have won historic rights and better conditions for those they represent. In most school systems, unions serve as some check on the arbitrary power of the politicized bureaucracies that manage school districts. More significantly, they are an important reservoir of collective strength and resources for reform that need to be protected from a variety of antilabor crusades in education today, including privatization, voucher schemes, and legal restrictions on organizing and the right to strike.

Unfortunately, in too many cases, teacher unions have become bureaucratic partners in the management of failing school systems. And sometimes they focus too narrowly on salary and contract concerns at the expense of a broader vision of educational justice and change. As a result, they can pit the short-term interests of their members against the long-term interests of schools and the communities they serve. Ultimately, this weakens public support for both unions and schools.

But teacher unions are our organizations, and our involvement can help to enlist them in creative campaigns for better schools. A teacher looking for connections with other colleagues and potential allies should definitely consider becoming a building delegate, reviving a dormant instructional committee, organizing a classroom discussion caucus, or proposing a union-sponsored community forum on some hot educational issue. Even if a year or two of union work leads you to conclude that the space for change in your union local is limited, you're likely to have made valuable contacts and positioned yourself and others for a broader challenge to the union status quo as the education crisis deepens and more unions find business-as-usual strategies unequal to the tasks before them.

Teacher Activism and Study Groups

Another major reason for critical teachers to look beyond the classroom is to break out of the confining isolation they often face. Most school cultures are not very supportive of critical thought, change, or even collaboration among staff. Starting a teachers' study group can be a way of finding allies to sustain committed teaching over the long haul. A teacher group might begin as an informal after-school social hour where teachers trade stories, resources, and ideas. To encourage discussion beyond the "gripe session" stage (a chronic tendency that infects many faculty rooms) it's often helpful to pick a specific topic like tracking, assessment, or discipline, read a background article, and then talk about the issue's impact on your own school and classrooms. Once a group establishes some cohesion and continuity, it can address more difficult issues such as multicultural relations among teachers and students, or differing parent-teacher perspectives. It's often useful to invite outside participants for frank conversations about sensitive issues often avoided in typical "inservice" programs.

Discussion or study groups have a variety of attractions for teachers looking to move beyond the classroom. They're flexible, and can set their own agendas and pace without interference. If the interest in one school is insufficient to sustain a group, teachers from several schools can begin coalescing a local network of progressive educators. They can draw on a variety of national resources and networks for ideas and support (see "Action Education: Teacher Organizers Take Quality into Their Own Hands," page 343) and can develop into a safe space for critical reflection and mutual support not readily available elsewhere. Eventually, discussion and study can lead to action, public discussion, and local campaigns to improve schools. With public attention increasingly focused on education, a local teacher group has the potential to evolve into an important local, grassroots institution. One person posting a sign on the faculty bulletin board or approaching a few colleagues can initiate a low-risk strategy that can pay big dividends.

Local, State, and National Education Activism

The opportunities discussed above can each provide ways to promote social justice in education and at the same time sustain individual teachers in their daily efforts in the classroom. There are many key educational issues that will be determined not primarily inside local schools and classrooms, but in the larger context of community, state, and national politics. These include voucher plans, school privatization, funding inequities, and the imposition of state and national testing standards. Teachers need to be informed about these issues and, where possible, help to resolve them in positive ways.

But in the end, what's important is not that classroom teachers assume an impossible burden of individual responsibility for solving all the social and educational problems that affect their classrooms. What matters is that they see and understand the connections between those classrooms and the society around them, and realize that efforts to apply critical teaching are tied to broader efforts to promote democracy and equality in society. If teachers can find ways to link the two, they will strengthen both.

Q/A

Should I leave the school I'm in?

You have to make an assessment of whether or not you can survive at the school you've landed in. Is there a fundamental mismatch with your values in terms of pedagogical approach? And if there is, can you struggle to change things within your school? Are there enough allies to do that? Or do you have to find a new school? Maybe you can find a new setting and move in and be comfortable because it's already established, or you can do what some of us did and create a whole new public school like when we started La Escuela Fratney in Milwaukee. However, I would not underestimate how hard it is to create your own school.

—Bob Peterson

So What Is a Teacher Union Anyway?

by Stephanie Walters

Many of us who come to teaching arrive at our first jobs without really knowing what a union is or what purpose it serves. It's not something covered in most teacher education programs. I was lucky. My mother was a telephone operator, so as I grew up there was talk in our house about contracts and negotiations, strikes and picket lines. But many of my colleagues just don't have that experience to draw upon.

So here's a down-and-dirty overview of teacher unions and what they do for us teachers. And the more we all get involved in our unions, the more they will reflect our values and what we stand for as educators.

The Nuts and Bolts of Union Membership

A union is an organization that advocates for better wages, benefits, and working conditions for its members. It's thanks to workers' struggles to establish unions that we enjoy the five-day workweek.

There are two national teacher unions: the National Education Association (NEA) and the American Federation of Teachers (AFT). Each has local affiliates in school districts across the country; the NEA also has large state associations. Membership in either of these organizations helps protect you from the arbitrary whims of administrators, false accusations of parents or students, and even unfair layoff or termination from your position.

Depending on where you teach, the protections and benefits offered by your union can vary greatly. In states like Wisconsin, New York, and Ohio, you become a union member by virtue of signing your contract. Once you enter the classroom, you are afforded the protections the collective bargaining agreement (or contract) provides. Membership also provides you the opportunity immediately to participate in the life and direction of your union.

There are also states like Florida, Texas, and North Carolina where laws are much less hospitable toward unions and actually prohibit public sector employees (like you) from bargaining for fair wages, hours, and working conditions. These are often referred to as "right to work" states. If you live and work in these locales, unions are much weaker. You have to sign up to become a member of your union, and you are not automatically afforded the rights and protection enjoyed by your counterparts in other states. Sadly, you are often at the mercy of administrators to do the right thing—something that in my experience they do not always do.

To check out what your union has to offer, go to its website: www.aft.org or www.nea.org. Or ask a veteran teacher when the next union meeting is, so that you can attend. You will discover that in addition to representing you, unions provide great benefits that you might never have imagined.

(Need some life insurance? NEA can provide it. How about a low-interest credit card? AFT has one for you.)

The most important thing to know now is that teacher unions are built on democratic principles. They're not always perfect, but they usually strive to serve their members as these principles dictate. Members elect presidents, vice presidents, and building leaders to represent them. Like any democracy, their strength is derived from the active involvement of their members. They need you—the member—to be involved. And there are many ways for you to become involved! Some local unions focus their efforts on wages, hours, and working conditions—or what you might hear referred to as bread-and-butter issues. But teacher unions also sponsor forums on important educational issues, hold curriculum exchanges, participate in community social justice coalitions, and organize book group study circles. Teacher unions are our organizations. What they become depends largely on what we make them. And we can help our unions reflect our passions and priorities if we get involved. Our unions can and will speak for us if we want them to.

Read Your Contract!

I know, I know. As a new teacher you want to make a good impression. You don't want to look like a slacker to your colleagues or your principal. You want to make sure that everyone knows you're willing to go the extra mile for the kids, and take one for the team if need be.

So when the principal comes to you and asks you to volunteer to cover lunch duty one afternoon, you enthusiastically say yes. You want to show her how dedicated you are to the school and that you're willing to help out.

Then she asks you again and again, every day for a whole week. You start to wonder: Is this OK? Well, the answer is . . . it depends, and it is very important for you to find out, because you may be getting hosed.

As teachers we usually have rights that are negotiated through our contracts. If you do not have a copy of this very important document, you should obtain one ASAP.

Your contract outlines all the things you're entitled to as an employee of a school district. There is no standard contract: They vary from district to district.

For example, in the Milwaukee Public Schools, teachers are entitled to a duty-free lunch period of 45 minutes. If an administrator is going to assign you to do duty during that period, it can only be for 15 minutes, and you must be paid for that time. There's no way around it: Principals have tried to skirt this rule and they have failed. That's the rule and administrators can't just ignore it. There are consequences if they try.

I know what you're thinking, because at one time I thought it myself: What's a lousy 15 minutes? I'm a professional. I'm dedicated. I don't mind giving a little extra.

Yes, it is true, we are professionals. But your individual choice to work without pay for those extra 15 minutes harms other teachers both now and in the future because it sets the precedent for other infringements on our rights as teachers. If you were an accountant or software engineer, perhaps you'd be able to leave a little early or come in a little later. Not so for teachers. Who would watch the kids? Likewise, taking a longer lunch is definitely out of the question for you. You're a teacher. Can't happen. Your situation is unique.

So there really is a rhyme and a reason for why teachers are in unions, why we have contracts, and why they should be followed.

OK, you're saying, but honestly, you expect me to ask to be paid for a measly 15 minutes? Well, let's do some arithmetic. In my school district, a teacher currently earns $24.94 an hour for doing lunch duty. So if you did 15 minutes of lunch duty every day for two weeks that would total $62.35. Now multiply that by 20 weeks. That's $1,247. See what I mean?

Or, let's look at this duty-free time (your time) from a different angle. Let's say that in 15 minutes you can comment on four student papers. Over those same 20 weeks you missed a chance to comment on 160 papers. I'm not saying you should spend your duty-free lunch responding to student papers. The point is that duty free is just that: duty free. And what you do during that time cannot be mandated by administrators. It's a contractually protected right that we all need to honor and defend.

The Union Just Protects Bad Teachers, Doesn't It?

I am sad to say that this is a refrain you will hear often from opponents of teacher unions. You might even hear it from colleagues in the hallways and workrooms in your buildings. It is a perception that is based on incomplete data. It is true that collective bargaining agreements afford all teachers due process, so that if allegations are made against you, you are afforded the right to a representative to speak on your behalf. You also have the right to a fair and thorough investigation. Not every allegation of misconduct, incompetence, or inappropriate behavior is true. In fact, many of the cases I have had to deal with in my current job as a union staff representative have turned out to be false. Without the protections of the contract, those teachers would have been suspended or even worse. On the other hand, there are times when teachers will need to be disciplined. When this happens my job is to make sure that discipline is for just cause, and to make sure that it is issued in a fair and consistent manner.

Moreover, our unions are deeply concerned about the growth and development of new teachers. In many cities, unions have worked in conjunction with administrations to create mentoring programs to assist teachers during their first years in the classroom. Still other local unions have been able to effectively address the issues like peer review and how to provide assistance to veteran teachers who do need assistance in the classroom. In the not too distant past, these were topics that were "off-limits," but increasingly unions saw the need for teachers to assist fellow teachers. The reasons are really simple: teachers assisting teachers helps the new teacher (or the struggling veteran) and it improves the practice of the mentor teacher. The profession is strengthened by our collective efforts.

Getting a Copy of Your Contract

If you don't have a copy of your district's contract, you should get one, and now! I know that having my contract handy and being able to reference it when I had a question was one of the most important components of my professional development, so much so that I had two copies, one for home and one for school.

In most buildings there is an elected teacher (or teachers) who volunteers to deal with union issues at the building level. Usually this person is called the building representative or chapter chair. Ask your representative for a copy of your contract. If she doesn't have a copy, she may direct you to your union's website where you can access the contract, or the local union office, which will be happy to send a hard copy to you. (When I became the representative at my school, I was gladder than ever that I had copies of my contract at home and at work.)

Once you get your contract, read it like a letter from home: Study every word. Remember, knowledge is power. The more you know about your rights, the more confident you'll be when you need to take a stand. All the answers might not be in there, but the majority of them will be. If you're unsure about anything you read, ask one of your representatives first. These folks are teachers and union activists who want to make sure that you succeed in your career. They have received training in how to answer your concerns and get you the answer you need. If for some reason there is no person like that in your school, you may need to contact your local union office and speak to a staff person. (Depending on how large or small your district is, there may be only one staff person, and you may have to wait for an answer.)

Contracts typically are in effect for two years, and then expire. However, everything in the expired contract, including salary, remains the same until teachers in your district ratify a new contract. So if you get a copy of your contract from the union or read it online and it says it expired last year, relax, it's still good.

There will be times that you will encounter an administrator who says, "Do it or else!" Unless it's something that endangers your life or the lives of others, go ahead and do it, then take the matter up with your representative and union officials.

And although some of our work is done to protect teachers from unfair and arbitrary treatment, the work of the union extends far beyond the words of the contract. Much of my work revolves around working with veteran teachers to help new teachers work through their licensure process. I also work with teachers to track changes in curriculum in our district. The union needs to know what the new curricula will be and how teachers are or will be involved in assessing the success of new programs implemented. At the national and state levels, NEA and its affiliates are working with members to proactively address professional issues like National Board Certification, licensure, student assessment, teacher evaluation and alternative compensation models. This work is critical to the vitality of our associations. They are issues that are important to teachers and teachers need a collective, cohesive voice to speak out on our behalf—that voice is our unions. Advancing the dialogue on some of the more thorny issues, like alternative compensation, isn't always neat and pretty, but if NEA and AFT don't engage in the conversations, our silence could result in damaging consequences to the profession.

Over the years, some teacher union locals have joined coalitions with parent and neighborhood groups to address issues of jobs, economic development and other issues of social justice that affect the communities in which we live and teach.

Last tip: The best way to learn about and have influence on the direction of the union is to get involved. There are many entry points. Whether your concerns are curricular, social, or somewhere in between, there is a place for your voice. Our unions will only be as strong as the members—especially new members—who work to make it that way.

For more information on progressive teacher unionism:

The Role of Teacher Unions—A complication of articles from Rethinking Schools. http://www.rethinkingschools.org/special_reports/union/unhome.shtml

Teacher Union Reform Network—A nationwide network of more than 50 union locals promoting progressive reforms in education and in teacher unions—to improve student achievement, increase teacher connectivity, and elevate teachers' voices in the reform debate. http://www.turnexchange.net/blog.html

Transforming Teacher Unions—A Rethinking Schools book that presents a vision of "social justice teacher unionism" that challenges teachers and unions to help improve schools and conditions in the broader communities they serve.

More On Teacher Unions

Teachers first organized themselves into unions in the early and mid-1900s to defend their rights against administrators and school boards. During the past two decades teacher unions have also been instrumental in helping to pass legislation to improve the educational landscape of the country. They have been on the cutting edge of reform of our profession, providing professional development, peer coaching for veterans, and mentoring to new teachers.

This hasn't always been a smooth process, mind you. In 1997 Bob Chase, who was then president of the National Education Association (NEA), angered many union officials when he called for the NEA to "broaden our focus" and "devote as much attention to the quality of the product we produce as we do to our members' wages, benefits, working conditions, and security." Some NEA members worried that Chase was setting up union members to lose hard-won wages and benefits. But Chase remained adamant that teacher unions "cannot afford to continue standing along the sidelines of the education reform debate."

Today many of those tensions remain. But unions have clearly made strides in helping their members become better teachers, while continuing to protect them from unfair treatment on the job.

—Stephanie Walters

Teachable Moments Not Just for Kids

by Susan Naimark

"Teachable moments around racism" was the topic of an editorial in the summer 2008 issue of *Rethinking Schools*. Although relevant curriculum is critical, we don't need to wait for new social studies textbooks to be adopted to identify such teachable moments. A simple look around our schools is an equally compelling starting point.

I recently began writing about my experiences as a white middle-class parent whose white children went through the Boston public schools. Fifteen years ago, in my sons'

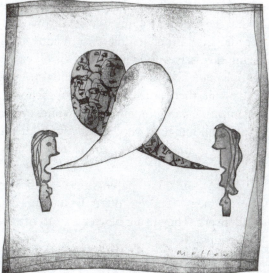

elementary school, the parent organization was more than half white—in a school where 85 percent of the students were children of color. This imbalanced parent involvement was too often interpreted as "those other parents just don't care about their kids' education." As I got to know some of the parents who did not come to our meetings, I heard a different story. And as I met parents from other schools through my citywide parent organizing work, I found these stories to be recurring themes—stories about working two and three jobs, not having reliable transportation, and not speaking English adequately to feel comfortable communicating with school staff. Although these barriers to participation are not unique to parents of color, many parents of color also have their own hostile childhood schooling experiences holding them back, I learned. When I talked with parents who faced these obstacles, they expressed as much concern about their children's education as the parents who came to our parent meetings. The confluence of racism and poverty created a host of obstacles to their involvement in our school.

As I began to share my writing about these experiences, I learned that little has changed in the past 15 years. If anything, this racial disconnect between parent involvement and student enrollment has become more acute since racial quotas in student assignment were thrown out over the past decade. In Boston, middle-class, white families are organizing themselves to identify and enroll en masse in public schools they believe have the potential to meet their needs. As a result, there are now many more schools whose parent organizations are predominantly white, even as the student population remains overwhelmingly children of color.

If we value parent involvement, what's wrong with this?

Many of these parents are advocates for school improvement. They're often well connected and savvy fundraisers. They bring new energy to often dormant parent groups.

But there's an unsettling side effect to this involvement. And herein lie the teachable moments.

One such school became the target of a group of white, middle-class families a few years ago. Although the school still predominantly serves students of color, the white student population has slowly and steadily increased. Two years ago, the parent organization, comprised mostly of white parents, held a fundraising event that raised $10,000 for the school. By all accounts of those present, it was a lovely event. The parents and principals of other schools began to compare notes, and this generated peer pressure to see who could raise the most money through such parent-run fundraisers.

The problem was that the cost of a ticket to this particular event was much more than most parents in the school could afford. Was it a success? The answer is still being debated.

The dispute emerged when a low-income parent of color spoke up at a parent meeting. She reported that the event was too costly for her and not something she would feel comfortable bringing friends to. And this was not the first time a parent-run event had felt exclusionary. The ensuing debate opened up a Pandora's box. Several of the white parents who organized the event felt unappreciated for all the hard work they put in. A few of the original organizers dug in their heels, threatening to hold the event without the support of school leadership. Others advocated to transform it into a different kind of event, welcoming to the entire school community. Some volunteers simply dropped out, tired of the arguing that dragged on through the better part of a school year. Meanwhile, the impasse resulted in the cancellation of that year's big fundraiser.

If the adults in this school community could stay with the conflict, it could be transformed into a teachable moment. A racially mixed group of parents began working with the principal to do just this. They asked the parent organization to step back and talk about shared values and goals. They are cautiously hopeful that these conversations have laid the foundation for making decisions about fundraisers and other activities, and provided a moral compass for evaluating their efforts. They also began to facilitate conversations about diversity, which they hope will illuminate some of the dynamics of race and privilege.

"Enough process," several of the white parents responded to these efforts. "We have work to do."

But isn't this the work?

Our public schools are among the few places where we have the opportunity to engage people of different races, ethnicities, economic circumstances, and life experiences. These schools are rich learning environments, not just for children, but also for parents, teachers, and other adults who make up the school community. By avoiding such discussions, we model for our children how not to talk about race and racism.

I've heard many people of color say that racism is not what it used to be. A Jamaican parent organizer once showed me how it works. As we sat in a meeting one day, she said, "It's like this." She covered her red and silver Coke can on the table in front of her with a white paper napkin.

"All covered up nice and pretty, so we don't have to see it or talk about it."

The white parents who put in long hours to organize school fundraisers would hardly consider their actions racist. They have created wonderful new events and raised sorely needed funds for their children's schools. But the problem with their efforts has nothing to do with personal prejudice. It's about how their actions perpetuate a system that advantages them at the expense of others. If you remove the covering, what's underneath? One set of actions among many that alienate other parents from feeling that the school is theirs, too. In a school system where black and Latino students fail at twice the rate of white and Asian students, such parents' sense of ownership is not a luxury. It is critical to student achievement.

When my kids were in elementary school, we took some baby steps toward educating ourselves through conflicts such as this and changing school practices. When I became co-chair of the parent organization, I had long conversations with the black co-chair about the racial dynamics of the school. By this time, I had become fed up with silent complicity in what appeared to be a highly inequitable situation. Such selective activities as the school chorus, student newspaper, and student council were comprised of predominantly white kids, year after year. The "best" teachers had high percentages of white students in their classes whereas the less popular teachers had all children of color. We wanted to know why.

We brought up our observations at parent meetings. At first, conversations were awkward and halting. Nobody knew what to say. We gradually learned that we could name the inequities out loud and the sky didn't fall in on us. The parent organization decided to launch its own research on how school privileges were distributed to students. A few parents, white and black, agreed to survey teachers about how they selected children for volunteer school activities. The teachers interviewed insisted that they used "objective" criteria or "fair" practices based on good behavior, grades, and an active interest. A few got defensive that we were even questioning them. One day during our research, the black co-chair of the parent organization found a sticky note on the teachers' room wall stating that the parents were taking over the school. These were predominantly black teachers, and they didn't want to talk about race any more than many of the parents.

Despite the resistance, a pattern emerged. Many of the white parents were comfortable aggressively advocating for their children. Their children, in turn, internalized a set of expectations concerning what they deserved. And we all carry our own image of what potential in a child looks like, acts like, and dresses like. Such potential is elusive in the quiet girl dressed in hand-me-downs who stays up too late at night watching her baby brother while her mother is at work, or in the rowdy boy who imitates his big brother gangbanger.

The extracurricular activities in question were a strong selling point of the school. In most cases, they happened only because of the volunteer time and commitment of the teachers involved. The principal dragged her feet when we suggested she challenge their practices, unwilling to risk losing their goodwill. She had a strong team of teachers to support and keep happy, and we had run into a dead end.

We then turned our attention to classroom assignments. Every year, a few parents of my sons' white friends called me in June.

"Whose class is Ben going to be in next year?" they wanted to know.

My husband and I had selected for our sons a loosely organized Spanish-language program that moved up through the grades. Its teachers were not the most sought-after in the school, but we found them warm and caring. This decision allowed us to circumvent the annual scramble for popular teachers, whose classrooms were consistently majority white.

When the parent organization started to investigate, we discovered that some parents routinely lobbied the principal in June for their preferred teacher for the following school year. Many of the white parents wanted their children to be in classrooms with their friends, who were more often than not the other white kids. This resulted in a large group of white students moving from year to year through the school in a herd, so to speak.

We invited the principal to a parent meeting to discuss how students were assigned to classrooms. The discussion that unfolded exposed the practice of advocating for favored teachers, widespread among white parents. Almost every parent of color in the room dropped their jaw or shook their head when they heard it explained; they had no idea that lobbying for specific teachers was an option. I was stunned at the complete racial divide this exposed.

By putting this practice on the table, we arrived at a new way of assigning students to classrooms. The new procedure encouraged parents to send a note to the principal at the end of the school year describing the type of teacher and learning environment they believed would be best for their children. The school staff then made assignments to ensure the best possible matches for all students. This put pressure on the active parents and the parent organization to be sure all teachers were of a quality we would want for our own children. Parents could no longer guarantee what teachers their children would get.

One white parent threatened to transfer her children out of the school if she could no longer handpick teachers every year. She didn't follow through on the threat, but I appreciated her honesty. There were undoubtedly other parents who had every intention of continuing to lobby the principal but weren't willing to say it out loud.

This experience was one of my first lessons in the "entitlement gap"—the vast difference in understanding about what we are entitled to in our interactions with the school system. When we white, middle-class parents understand how our sense of entitlement excludes others, we begin to find our own teachable moments about racism. We then can speak up, find allies, and take specific actions to "spread the wealth."

Q/A — What should I do if I suspect a student is a victim of abuse?

It's very important that you know the procedure for your school or district. In most cases the answer is very clear: You are required by law to report suspicion of sexual or physical abuse.

Having said that, it's critical that these situations are handled sensitively and safely. Get some advice from the support staff (social workers, psychologists, counselors) or community resource people who work with your students.

If you make a report, ask for assurances you will not be identified as the reporter to the suspected abuser.

—Rita Tenorio

'We Must Act as if All the Children Are Ours'

An Interview with Parent Activist Lola Glover

Lola Glover is director of the parent- and community-based Coalition for Quality Education in Toledo, Ohio. Glover is also a past co-chair of the National Coalition of Education Activists and has served as a co-director of the National Coalition of Advocates for Students. She was interviewed by Barbara Miner.

How did you get involved in education?

I'm the mother of nine children and I started the way most parents do. And that's the PTA, Mothers' Club, room mother, chaperone, chairperson for the bake sales, that kind of thing. This was 30 to 35 years ago.

Barbara J. Miner

Because I was at school a lot, I began to notice things that I felt were not conducive to the educational or emotional well-being of students. I began to realize there was a pattern to certain things, instead of something I observed for one day. I began to question those actions, or the lack thereof, and to talk more to my own children about school. It was then that I started to get involved in my children's actual schooling and in academic issues.

I always made sure, however, that I was active in such a way that all the students in that particular classroom or school would benefit, not just my child. When I advocated only for my child, not a lot changed. The teachers and administrators would just make sure that when I was on the scene, or when they dealt with my child, they would do things differently.

I don't believe that we will ever get all of the parents involved in the ways that we would hope. I believe that those of us who have made a commitment to get involved must act as if all the children are our children.

Do you sense that some teachers are reluctant to have parents involved in more than homework or bake sales, that there is a fear that parents are treading on the teachers' turf if they do so?

Absolutely. And I don't think much of that has changed over the years.

Let's say I'm a teacher, and I come in and do whatever I do in my own way, in my own time, and nobody holds me accountable in any way for providing a classroom environment conducive to learning, or for student achievement. I get pretty set in my ways—and defensive with people who might question what I do.

I've found the teachers who are reluctant to have parents involved are those who know they aren't doing the best they can for their students.

Then there are some teachers whose degrees gave them a "new attitude" and who question these folks who didn't graduate from high school, and surely didn't go to college.

Such teachers question what these parents are doing in their classrooms. It doesn't matter that they are the parents of their students.

I also have found some really great teachers in our district. They don't have any reservations or problems about parents getting involved in their classrooms or schools. In fact, they welcome and encourage parent involvement.

How can teachers and principals make parents feel more welcome?

One of the biggest mistakes that teachers make is not being in touch with parents until there's a problem. And most parents don't want to hear the problem. They would like to think that little Johnny or Mary is doing fine all the time, and if not, they don't want to hear you putting their kid down. If you start off that way with a parent, it will take some real doing to get on the right foot with them again.

It's not going to be easy to build an alliance with 30 parents, so start with one or two. Get those parents to be your liaisons. Let them know how much you care and what you are trying to accomplish in the classroom. Give them the names and addresses of parents of the kids in your classroom, and ask, "Would you help me contact these parents and explain to them that I would really like to talk to all of them personally." Find out when will be a good time for everyone to meet, and set a date.

Why is it so important to foster mutual respect between parents and teachers?

I am convinced that if students begin to see parents and people in their community and their schools working together, a lot of things would change. First of all, the kids' attitudes would change. Right now, kids' attitudes have not changed about school because they don't see any connection between home and school. They do not see any real efforts being made by either side to come together for the purpose of improving their schools or educational outcomes.

I don't think any of us have the answers to solve these problems. But I do believe that if we come together out of mutual respect and concern, we will make a difference in what happens in our schools and our communities. I know we'll never find the answer if we keep this division between us. For the sake of our children, public education, and our future, we can ill afford not to work together. Make the first move.

What should I do about the parent who keeps showing up in our classroom unannounced, or a parent who's upset and wants to meet with me during the school day?

Q/A

Even though you may have made it clear to parents at the beginning of the year that "our classroom door is always open and you are always welcome," that doesn't mean a parent visit is always convenient. With luck, parents will be willing volunteers who can help you improve teaching and learning in your classroom. But sometimes parents arrive at a time that is inconvenient for the teacher and students, demanding immediate action.

First of all, find out why the parent is there. Does she have a concern about her child's behavior or the way other children are treating her child? Does he want to talk to you about the way that you or another adult in the building disciplined his child? Is she upset with her child's report card? Does he have some extra time and want to help out?

Ask to set up a time outside of the school day to talk with the parent. State things in terms of what you can do, not what you can't. For example, instead of saying, "This is a bad time because I'm in the middle of teaching," say: "I'd like to talk with you when I can give this my full attention. I can meet with you at 4 p.m. on Wednesday or 8 a.m. on Friday. Would one of the those times work for you?"

When you talk with the parent, ask questions, listen, and get as much information as you can. Restate and validate the parent's feelings and concerns. As you discuss potential solutions, try to direct things in a way that address the parent's concern, but also work for you and your students. Tell the parent what steps you will take to address the concern, and write these steps down for yourself to make sure you follow through. Taking notes on the entire conversation is a good idea; save them, since you may need to reference them later.

It can also help to inform the administrator as soon as possible about the situation, explaining what you are doing to address it. Having a record of all your contacts with the parent is helpful, since it allows you to show what you have been doing all along to work on the problem.

If a parent or guardian seems particularly difficult, it may be worth talking with the child's teachers from previous years. They may be able to provide insight on the parent and give you information about what worked and what didn't with that family. The union representative in your building may also have ideas for how to work with a difficult parent.

—Kelley Dawson Salas

Unwrapping the Holidays

Reflections on a Difficult First Year

by Dale Weiss

My teaching career began on the picket line. After I was hired to teach 1st grade in a small town outside of Seattle, I spent my first month in front of the school instead of in the classroom.

After 30 days, our union settled the strike and won smaller class sizes for 1st and 2nd grade, better health benefits, and a slight raise in salary. And on a personal level, I felt that I had really bonded with my colleagues. Most of the teachers who worked at this school had been born and raised in that small town and they showed extraordinary kindness to me during the strike. My father was having

major surgery and I was extremely sad and worried. Each day, teachers inquired about his health. Other teachers showed concern about my lack of income and brought me bags of food. One teacher, Joseph, even brought me several bags of plums from his tree.

But through the course of the year, many of the bonds we formed on the picket line dissolved as I became involved in a controversy over holiday curricula.

Before I became a teacher, I had spent years as a political activist. I saw my work as a teacher as important political work and wanted to create a classroom where students would learn to challenge biases and injustice and take action against unfair situations. Since this way of viewing the world seemed normal to me, I naively assumed my colleagues—with whom I experienced solidarity on the picket line—shared the same worldview. I could not have been more wrong.

Holiday Decorations

Before Thanksgiving, two 6th-grade girls approached me to ask if my 1st graders could make ornaments for the Christmas tree that had been put up in the library.

I replied, "We have been learning about four different winter celebrations: Kwanzaa, Hanukkah, Christmas in Mexico, and Winter Solstice, and we are in the process of making a book about each celebration. We could put our books in the library for other children and teachers to read as our contribution." The 6th-grade girls were persistent and still wanted to know if I would have my students make ornaments.

"I don't think so," I said, and then returned to my classroom.

I remember wondering if I would be depriving my students of something by my decision, but in my heart I felt I was doing the right thing. I was teaching them that not everyone celebrates Christmas, that there are many celebratory practices in the month of December, and that each celebration is richly marked with unique customs and beliefs. Not making Christmas ornaments would not rob my students of anything—except the belief that only Christmas occurred in December.

Thinking back to the Christmas tree in the library and feeling that holiday decorations should reflect diversity, I decided to speak with my principal, Oscar. Referring to the decorations in the library, I emphasized that I thought public areas in the school should reflect as much diversity as possible. Oscar was very supportive and agreed to discuss the issue the following day at our staff meeting. He cautioned me that many staff members might not agree with my opinions and that he found the staff to be very conservative, particularly about change.

At our staff meeting, I expressed my concern about the public Christmas displays and also mentioned the four different December celebrations we were studying in my classroom. And I shared an experience that had recently occurred in my classroom with Lindsey, a child who was a Jehovah's Witness. Her mother had expressed concern about the class study on Christmas in Mexico. After I explained that our study emphasized the cultural and not religious aspects of the celebration, the parent was relieved. I shared that as a Jew, I also did not celebrate Christmas. The next morning Lindsey ran up to me, gave me a big hug, and said: "My mom told me you don't celebrate Christmas either. Now I'm not the only one." I shared my student's reaction as an example of the pain children can experience when they don't fit in. I also felt responsibility as an educator to minimize that pain in whatever ways I could.

As the staff meeting ended, two staff members thanked me for opening their eyes to new ways of looking at things. But mostly there was silence. Later in the day I heard secondhand that Robert, the librarian, was upset about what I had said during the staff meeting.

I approached him and asked if we could talk. He responded that he usually does not decorate the library with so many Christmas items but did so this year because a few 6th-grade girls kept "hounding him." He also shared that this was the first year there had ever been a Christmas tree in the library. What bothered him most was that he felt blamed for the library decorations, despite the fact it was the 6th graders who had put up the decorations. I told him that I was not blaming him; I was merely concerned about decorations in common areas within the school.

As the day progressed, I began to notice other teachers distancing themselves from me. I visited one teacher, Linda, during our lunch hour to ask if I had inadvertently offended her. When I got there, she was speaking to another teacher and did not see me come into the room. Linda—with very large motions—was ripping the "Merry Christmas" banner off her wall, saying, "We used to be able to do anything we wanted to at Christmastime, but apparently not anymore."

I asked if she was referring to what I said at the staff meeting, and she replied: "Well, yes. Plus, I don't teach about Hanukkah because I just don't know how to pronounce all those words. Besides, I just don't feel comfortable teaching about something I don't know much about." I shared that my viewpoints were not only based in my being Jewish—though this is a part of who I am—but because I believe it is important for children to have exposure to all different kinds of people, customs, and belief systems. I also shared that I, too, have a hard time teaching something new and that one way I learn is to read books written for children. Alexis then responded: "We're used to doing the same things every year. When December rolls around, we always take out our December boxes and put on the walls whatever is in those boxes. And we really don't think about it. We prefer it that way." Just then the bell rang and our conversation ended.

As the days went on, I noticed lots of Christmas decorations coming off the walls. The library was almost barren. And, where the library Christmas tree once stood, a book was placed on Hanukkah. Though I had stated my hope that decorations should be more inclusive and had not requested all Christmas decorations to be removed—and certainly not that a book about Hanukkah take their place—what people heard was something quite different.

The following day, Friday, Oscar shared with me that my comments at the staff meeting had really stirred things up and that people had been speaking with him about the meeting all week. He said he wanted to put the issue on the agenda of the upcoming faculty committee meeting, a group that met periodically to discuss teacher concerns and was made up of representatives from each grade level. I was the representative for the 1st-grade unit.

On Monday morning, as I arrived at school, I was greeted with an anonymous letter in my mailbox. The message said, "Rights for homosexuals next?" I felt incredibly upset and scared. After showing the letter to Oscar, he said he would share the contents of the letter with the faculty committee at our meeting on the following day.

When the meeting began, one teacher suggested we start the meeting with my re-explaining what I had said and meant at the previous staff meeting. Before I could begin, she stated she felt it was important for me to understand that teachers have done things a certain way for many years at the school and that the holiday curriculum was not offensive because it was well within the district's student learning objectives. I then repeated what I had stated at the staff meeting and said that it had not been my intent to hurt or offend anyone and if I had, I was truly sorry. Another teacher piped up that she had taught for 20 years—in comparison to my two-and-a-half months—and she felt no need at all to have to explain her curriculum to me. She ended by reminding me "to check things out before jumping to conclusions about the way things are done at our school."

I thought a lot about what she said. I always had seen myself as a person with a commitment to understanding other people's views and who takes the time to talk things through. I have never been comfortable with people coming in from the outside and trying to change things immediately. I wondered if I had become that kind of person. When I first noticed the Christmas tree in the library and had thoughts that holiday decorations should reflect diversity, I shared this with Oscar prior to saying anything at the staff meeting. Should I have checked things out with other teachers as well?

A few other teachers said they wished I had brought up my concerns in October, before the holiday decorations went up. I replied that, as a new teacher, I wanted to wait and see what happened, rather than assume how things would end up. I thought I was sitting back, waiting and watching—but others saw me as a newcomer barging in, but somehow barging in too late.

Joseph (the same man who had kindly brought me plums on the picket line) then stated, "You know, several of the staff of Germanic background are extremely upset by the fact that the Christmas tree in the library was removed and in its place put a book on Hanukkah." I felt shocked by his comment. I said that I had no idea who removed the Christmas tree and whoever had, did so at their own discretion. I also did not know who put the book on Hanukkah in its place.

Oscar then shared the contents of the anonymous letter I had received, commenting that this was an example of how far things had gone and how ugly they had gotten. People were shocked and could not believe that "someone from a staff as kind as ours could have done something like this."

As the meeting came to a close, Oscar reiterated the importance of openly speaking with one another when differences occur and that talking behind one another's backs would only serve to divide the staff further. He said he hoped the staff could heal and move forward with understanding.

Oscar checked on me several times during the day, letting me know how offensive he found Joseph's comment about "staff of Germanic heritage." I appreciated his support since Joseph's comment really shook me up. I kept thinking it would have been one thing if Joseph had simply said "several staff," but adding "of Germanic heritage" meant something very different. It felt like a brief look into the hatred of the Nazis toward the Jews.

Misunderstandings

Prior to the faculty committee meeting, I had not realized the extent of misunderstanding and anger that existed. I felt scared and continued to search my mind for who might have put the anonymous letter in my mailbox. Up until the prior week I had looked forward to each day of teaching with great eagerness and pleasure. I now dreaded coming to school.

I felt trapped, wondering if the only way out was to join the opinion of the majority. Realizing I could not trade my beliefs for a few moments of "relief," what instead seemed to pull me through was a feeling of strong empathy for all who struggle for something that is right.

I thought about people throughout history who took the first step—and sometimes alone—to bring awareness to an injustice. I thought about people who risk so much while working to bring about a more just world, who stand on the shoulders of those who came before them and know they must keep trying. It was an empathy that forced me to keep trying as well.

In the days that followed, a few staff members offered their support, for which I was immensely appreciative. I thought back on the first days of picket duty, when relations with my co-workers seemed so promising. I was glad for these memories. They helped soften the present wounds.

At the same time, I had to acknowledge that while the strike served to unify the staff and was a way for me to become acquainted with my colleagues, sharp differences also existed. They were differences that went beyond whether or not someone was nice.

I had popped open a huge can of worms, too big to shut. My original intention was not to change others but to see more diversity reflected in the library and other common areas within the school. But what in my mind was a simple request upset the teaching foundations of many teachers, caused resistance and upheaval, and resulted in alienation among many staff members and myself.

It was a long year, that first year of teaching. I tried my best to remain cordial with my colleagues, something that was often difficult—yet important—to do. In January of that year, Oscar shared with me he would be leaving for the remainder of the school year due to poor health. He left in February and his replacement, Jeanne, offered me incredible support—both as a new teacher and as someone attempting to teach from a social justice perspective. This definitely helped me finish out the rest of the school year. Before the school year ended, Oscar died. It is to his memory and his support of, and belief in, me that first year that I have always dedicated my life as a teacher.

I remained at that school one more year, at which point I transferred to a school in Seattle.

Lessons Learned

What I have come to refer to as the "December incident" provided many valuable lessons for me. Where I believe I fell short was on several fronts.

First, I had not sufficiently assessed the staff regarding their potential reactions to being asked to be more inclusive in the school's December celebrations. I assumed I "knew" the staff because we had walked the picket line for 30 straight days. I naively equated solidarity around union issues with pedagogical agreement. In addition, I was the first new teacher to be hired at this school in many years, and I was viewed as an outsider.

Second, I did not take into consideration that many teachers held negative attitudes toward the administration because of the strike that began our school year; although the strike was over, the administration was still viewed by many as the "enemy." In addition, my positive rapport with Oscar was viewed by some teachers as aligning with the administration and too frequently entering "enemy territory."

Finally, what I am now able to recognize years later is that for the staff of my school, the celebration of Christmas represented much more than merely honoring a holiday that falls in December. It represented an entire belief system and something they valued and wanted to pass on to their students.

If I could turn back the wheels of time, I would definitely do things differently. I would sit through a "Christmas season" first, modeling my own beliefs within my classroom, but not pushing for change within the entire school. By allowing Christmas to happen first "as it always has," I would better be able to assess people's attachments to doing things in a particular way. I would then bring up the "Christmas issue" in the spring when the issue might not be so emotionally charged.

If I could do it again, I would start by assessing people's viewpoints and beliefs instead of assuming they would understand or desire to do anything differently. For example, my co-workers prided themselves on being nice. They heard my request for diversity as meaning they had not been nice to people who do not celebrate Christmas. Although I believe that my co-workers misinterpreted my original intent, I also think that I was partially responsible for this.

I went about things in a way that did not first acknowledge the values held by most of the staff. Perhaps by first acknowledging how important the Christmas season was to the vast majority of the staff, they might have been more open to adding a bit of diversity to what to them was the "normal" way of celebrating December. Since I didn't start by acknowledging their values, people's defenses were up and they did not hear what I was trying to say. As a result, people clung more tightly to their own belief systems and my efforts essentially moved things backward.

Introducing change into a school environment—especially one that has been firmly established for many years—is a complex process, one that I vastly underestimated. Although I don't condone the reactions of many of my colleagues, I do feel I understand what precipitated their response.

I also did not fully consider that people's reactions to me might be based on the fact I was a first-year teacher.

I can now see that not all veteran teachers—particularly those who have shaped the school culture and prefer things to stay a particular way—welcome new teachers with open arms.

I assumed my passionate devotion to my values could enhance the curriculum that already was in existence. I spent most of my first year of teaching trying to meld the world of my political activism with the new world I was entering as a teacher. I still believe that our best teaching occurs when we live first as authentic human beings, so I would never advocate leaving one's values at the classroom doorstep. I would, however, suggest a balance of caution and wisdom when embarking on this delicate journey.

What should I do if I am asked to take on extra-curricular duties or coaching responsibilities as a new teacher?

The fact that I could coach swimming was the deciding factor in landing my first teaching job in a large city high school. If didn't accept the swim coaching position, I wouldn't have the teaching position. Coaching cross-country at an American Indian boarding school in New Mexico offered me opportunities to get to know my students and their families that I will never forget. Working on a curriculum planning team for a new small high school and then making the school a reality was one of the most professionally rewarding experiences I've had in my career. And now, in my current high school teaching position at an all-boys school (after a more than 10-year detour to university classrooms), decorating the gym for a dance, planning a "trash for pizza" campus cleanup day, or pushing through legislation with the student government give me a window into the lives and concerns of the boys I teach.

Yet, if I was beginning my teaching career today, I'd give extracurricular options much closer scrutiny before jumping in and saying "yes."

First of all, if the extracurricular responsibility seems like the central reason for the job offer (as it was in my case in my first teaching job), make sure it is something that you really want to do. Fresh from my summer lifeguard job, I was happy to take on the challenge of a swim team, and I had a pretty good knowledge base from which to develop training programs and organize meets. And my school's swim program wasn't at an elite level, so pretty much whatever I did was going to be fine with the athletic director. Yet, if the offer is either a huge stretch for your background or seems like it will be too much for your current level of expertise, you may engender more respect and a more manageable first year of teaching by declining the opportunity.

Next, gather information about the exact duties that the position entails, including realistic time commitments, availability of help and mentors, and any special assignments that come along with the territory. When I agreed to coach cross-country in New Mexico, I never considered the extra responsibilities I'd have as a coach. Most of our meets were quite a distance away and some required overnight stays in the homes of families in pueblos across the state. I was also responsible for driving the team to the meets in a van, washing the uniforms, and organizing and finding staffing for a major invitational meet. With two-a-day practices, three preps, and science labs to prepare, I was stretched way too thin. The only saving grace to my schedule was the fact that the season ended by Thanksgiving! Also consider whether the time spent will be worth the compensation offered. Although my stint as a cross-country coach filled a need for my school and provided me with priceless experiences, at $500 for the season, I might've made about 13 cents per hour. If I had it to do over again, I would've supported the team by attending a few meets and helping with the home invitational and passed on the actual coaching position.

Beyond student activities, teachers are asked to serve on schoolwide or districtwide committees. When faced with these offers, it is best to seek advice from a mentor. If you don't have an "official" mentor assigned to you, seek out a trusted colleague or two in order to gain some background about the context, history, time commitment, and compensation. If you have an interest in the purpose of the group, agreeing to participate can be a great way to meet new people and gain a larger view of your school and its issues. Some of my closest "teacher friends" are those I worked with on a small school in the nineties. If I need advice about an educational issue, my colleagues from that era are tops in my go-to inner circle and I wouldn't trade this experience in creative school reform for anything.

Before you commit to an extracurricular, find out how many new teacher meetings will also be on your calendar so you can determine if you'd even have time for the extra work involved. Last year, I was a first-year high school teacher again. I was surprised at how quickly my calendar filled up.

Finally, as you ponder possibilities for extra assignments in your school, remember the central role you have as a classroom teacher is to teach. It will take longer than you think to prepare for each new day. You will need all of your energy for the daily unpredictable human encounters in your classroom as the personalities and the content mix it up in unique combinations each day. With exposure to rooms full of new germs, you might also find yourself sick a few times during the year, especially if you don't get enough rest.

So, search your heart, get some advice, and consider extracurricular duties carefully. They can make you or break you as a new teacher.

—Terry Burant

Getting Students
Off the Track

by Jessica Singer Early

"Just make it through the year," said the teacher sitting next to me at one of the first English department meetings of the school year. "Wait to think
about what worked and what didn't until it's all over."

And though my colleague was trying to be supportive,
his words served as a reminder that many teachers—both
new and seasoned—think that a new teacher's major goal
is to survive the school year.

I was feeling overwhelmed. I had just been hired as
an English teacher at Cleveland High School in Portland,
Ore. I was teaching two freshmen honors classes, two

Barbara J. Miner

331

sophomore "regular" classes, and one senior honors class. But I didn't want to put my head down and plow through the year, only to look up in June as my students walked away. I wanted to think about what was happening in my classes and in my school.

I decided to approach my year from a place of inquiry—and this grew into an effort to dismantle the tracking system that was in place in our school.

I bought an artist's sketch book and used it to jot down thoughts about individual classes, students, department meetings, and my school as a whole. I found time between classes, during meetings, and with students to take note of my teaching life. This journal provided a place for me to record thoughts that I would have otherwise allowed to float away without notice. I used my journal to ask questions: Where can I find poems that speak to these students? Why does Kyle always sit in the back and never take off his backpack? Where is the heart of this school?

Cleveland is a predominantly white (77 percent) urban school serving 1,300 students in the heart of southeast Portland. One of the first things I noticed was the way students were divided into two groups: honors and regular. Honors is the name assigned to all classes where students earn honors credit by taking the class, and regular classes are the classes that are considered less challenging and move at a slower pace. The content in these classes is not parallel. Although I had taught for one year in a public high school in Eugene, Ore., I had never taught in a tracked system and I was naive about the divisions, assumptions, and learning cultures created and perpetuated through tracking.

I participated in the Portland Area Rethinking Schools Steering Committee, a group of new and experienced teachers, parents, and community members. Our conversations and work together reminded me to trust my voice and instincts. That year, our group's focus was on creating an alternative to the state's system of evaluating schools through standardized testing. We created an Alternative Report Card. I kept thinking about one of the questions from the report card: "Who is represented and honored in the school? Consider hallways, library, and overall school environment." New questions began to form as well: How are students separated by social class, gender, and/or race? How does the language we use as educators mask or perpetuate divisions among students? In what ways does my school provide places for students to feel connected and seen as members of the same community? Are all students given equal opportunities to succeed?

Gathering Data

As I walked to my classroom each morning, I looked at the school with the eyes of an anthropologist gathering data. And I began to notice that my regular students were not given a place in my school. Their faces were not photographed as members of student government, their names were not in the entryway's honor roll, they were not members of the yearbook staff or the newspaper. Many of them worked half time and some even full time at after-school jobs. Many students had responsibilities caring for younger siblings or ailing grandparents.

One issue of the school newspaper printed an article with an enlarged photo of a lineup of Honda Accords and seniors standing in front of each car. The article said the Honda is the most desired and owned car at Cleveland High School. One of my sophomores walked into class that day and said: "Who does this paper think it's talking to? I wish I had a car—don't they get that some of us have to use the city bus?"

I noticed that the daily lineup in front of the discipline vice principal's office was often made up of regular students and—more often than not—students of color. I noticed how some counselors visited only honors classes to hand out college and scholarship information. I went to the counseling office to ask a counselor about this policy. She said: "Well, this saves me time. I mean, it's clear that the other kids aren't going on to study. If they were, they would be in honors classes."

It became obvious that the choice to be in honors does not happen from year to year—or at all—in high school. My second period senior honors class was made up of 32 students, most of whom had been together since first grade. They often shared stories from 5th grade and then laughed together like a family that had built a collection of shared stories through the passing of time. These students not only shared a history, they also shared a culture. Here they were in high school, in my classroom, together again for one last year of English. School authorities had designated these students as honors students from the day they entered elementary school.

The makeup of my regular classes was more diverse: They came from the poorer and less respected middle and elementary schools. Many students were recent transplants to Oregon. Some had transferred school districts or bused across town, hoping to get away from a rough start somewhere in the past.

As I observed the differences in my classes, I wanted to know more. I talked to my curriculum vice principal about my concerns, and together we looked up the zip codes of students in honors and regular classes and found that more than 90 percent of honors students came from the affluent neighborhood that fed into our school.

I carried my curiosity about my students and school into my teaching practice. I approached student papers, conversations, notes, and absences as data that could inform me more about my teaching and school culture. This approach to my teaching changed my outlook as an educator. The blur of bells, phone calls, attendance notices, overflowing classes, daily plans, piles of papers, meetings, and new curriculum became less overwhelming as I began to see it all from the eyes of a teacher-researcher. When things went well, I asked myself what worked so I could use a successful strategy again. When I came across road bumps in my teaching or with colleagues, I formed questions in my mind or in my teaching journal to collect answers on how to work toward change. My questions made teaching feel like a process instead of a race.

My students became my teachers about what a system of exclusion can do to hinder learning and achievement. Heather, one of my sophomore regular students, started crying when I introduced a unit on college preparation and essay writing. "My counselor told me my freshmen year that I was not college material," she said, "She said I am a regular student and I should just hope to get through the next four years. Why are you making me write a college essay when I am not headed there?"

I was not alone in my inquiry. My neighbor and ally in the east wing was another new English teacher, Deanna Alexich. Her teaching assignment consisted of all regular classes. Deanna's concern was that conversations about curriculum and books did not fit the needs of many of the kids she worked with. At one point she told me: "I feel like I am tracked in our department because I am not an honors teacher. I'm seen as just a regular teacher and my kids don't matter." Through our discussions, we decided to raise the question of tracking with the English department. As new teachers raising a difficult question, it helped to raise it together.

VOICES
FROM THE CLASSROOM

"Observe master teachers and take notes on everything they say and do. Figure out what you can emulate. Make the school your home. Put down roots in the school community—go to students' games or performances; sit next to your kids' parents. Learn all you can about the community your school serves. Call parents; make them your allies. Especially call them to praise their kids and to learn more about them."

—Dale Weiss

Deanna and I talked for a few weeks before we decided to bring our thoughts to the department. I was nervous. It is ideas that feel outside the realm of common conversation. Through my conversations with Deanna, we decided that the most effective way to share ideas was through questions. We wanted to invite a dialogue, to hear our colleagues' perspectives, and to see where our conversations led. Now, looking back, I believe that this approach is one of the main reasons that change became possible. It created a safe venue to share ideas.

Who Is Honored?

I started a department meeting asking one of the questions that had been sitting with me for the past weeks: Who is honored here? As soon as this question was asked, the room became uncomfortable. We all knew who was honored at Cleveland, but the question forced us to actually talk about it. This topic was not on my department's agenda, but by asking the question it had to be. I began to share some of my research. As a new teacher, I had an advantage. I felt I had a kind of permission to share my observations as a naive and new agent.

I began to share the data I had collected throughout the previous months. One of my colleagues, Jim, who is a fellow teacher in the English department, nodded. He said, "As a teacher who has been in this field 25 years, I miss teaching diverse classes with a true mix of kids." As our department began to answer the question of who we honor at our school, we could not avoid the topic of tracking. We all started in different places in the way we talked about our students and teaching. One teacher said: "My regular students are lazy and hard to deal with. I hate having regular classes at the end of the day. They aren't here to learn and they don't care." I added my perspective as a new teacher in the department. "I keep searching for the heart of this school. I can't help feeling uneasy in that the department and system I am a part of are perpetuating divisions among the haves and have-nots." Deanna asked:

"What does it say about us as educators if we are only feeling successful with an already successful group of kids? Aren't we failing a huge section of our population?"

That day we all began to ask questions about our teaching and the setup of our department and school. We began what would become a two-year dialogue and mission to change the way we talk, think, and work with students. This dialogue was not easy. It began from a place of questioning, which led to conversation, and then, more questioning. Our conversations were, and often still are, quite heated. When things get too uncomfortable, we often stop ourselves and restate ideas in the form of questions. This may sound corny, but it works. We have chosen to work toward becoming a department that truly communicates together in order to work toward change. Having true conversations as educators about difficult and important topics means pushing aside smaller differences to focus on a larger vision of equity and justice in our school.

Our department's conversations led us to untrack our 9th grade. We decided that all students should begin their time at Cleveland High School with an opportunity to be seen equally—without preassigned labels. As a result of this work, freshmen classes now represent the true population of our school with equal numbers of boys and girls, students from different neighborhoods, and diverse backgrounds. A colleague in my department who was initially resistant to the idea of untracking, walked into my classroom and said: "I love teaching my freshmen classes. In all my years of teaching this age group these classes are more engaged and more fun to teach than any I have taught before." The freshmen team has a common meeting time during fourth period each day to work on 9th-grade curriculum and to discuss teaching strategies, behavioral issues, and successes. This team has presented at districtwide workshops to share our work on untracking. As a result, a neighboring public high school untracked their 9th-grade English classes. At Cleveland, freshmen who struggle significantly with their literacy are offered a second English course called Freshmen Success to work with teachers and tutors on writing development, reading fluency, and homework. A few of the freshmen teachers in the English department are collaborating with teachers in other departments to create Freshmen Academies, where groups of students study multiple subjects together, integrating the curriculum.

As a new teacher, I realized that to see past my own experience meant looking deeply into it. My inquiry process helped to demystify my students, school, and teaching. I learned how to collect data, ask questions, share ideas with a network of support, and instigate change to help create the kind of school I wanted to be a part of over time.

I'm grateful that I did not take my colleague's advice. I didn't wait to think about what worked and what didn't until the end of the year. Inquiry through journal writing, working with other like-minded teachers, and listening to the concerns of other teachers and students can effect positive change in schools.

Moving Beyond Tired

by S. J. Childs

"We who believe in freedom cannot rest."
—Sweet Honey in the Rock

I was tired. But I had heard that these Rethinking Schools people were hot, really hot. I just had to go and see. I walked up the steps of a typical old-style Portland home. I heard voices coming from inside. Would I be welcome? What was the point? Wouldn't a plate of spicy chili noodles and a bad video be a better way to spend a Friday night? It was my first year of teaching, and I was exhausted.

I knocked and pushed the door open. I placed the token bottle of apple juice on the dining room table, next to three other bottles of juice, a plate of brownies, a bowl of popcorn, and some chips. I kept thinking about those hot chili noodles.

Someone I vaguely knew started speaking to me. I nodded and smiled and pretended I understood everything and was energized and interested. I still wanted to be on my couch, comatose and regenerating from teaching five classes in four different subjects: two classes of law for freshmen, including several who couldn't read; an English class for freshmen, including several who wouldn't read; and two global studies classes that included many students who didn't care.

How would coming to this scraggly group of inspired, committed teachers do me any good?

Fighting the Isolation

The meeting was held by the Portland Area Rethinking Schools group (PARS), a network of teachers who meet around issues of equity and education quality. The group holds a "Thank Goodness It's Friday" potluck about every six weeks, and over the years the group's teachers have played an important role in education politics within the district, the city, and throughout the state.

My first PARS meeting focused on the effect of a property tax cut on education and how we could stop the budget-cutting madness. There was talk of publishing articles, signing petitions, lobbying legislators. There were plans for parent meetings and phone trees. It all sounded great. But I was too tired to do more than listen.

That was years ago. I would like to say that listening to that energetic and committed group immediately got me out of my isolation and exhaustion. But it didn't. Not because it couldn't, but because I wouldn't let it. Instead, I stayed in my classroom by myself, working day and night to create curricula about social justice.

I didn't go back to another meeting for years. What kept me away is probably what has kept other teachers in the city from coming, has kept other teachers in other states from creating similar groups. It wasn't that their causes weren't my causes or their goals not my goals. It definitely wasn't the people.

But I just couldn't figure out where they got the energy and the time to have all those meetings. My students always came first. I love teaching, and I put all I could into creative and critical lessons. There wasn't much left over for meeting and organizing and fighting back.

The standards and testing movement convinced me I needed to start going to the PARS meetings. I needed to fight back. I realized that if I didn't start participating, everything I loved about teaching might be lost. If I didn't become one of those "hot" people who always have meetings, my classroom could be reduced to a tedious nonsensical world of rote memorization and multiple-choice testing. And the thought of that made me sick to my stomach.

But I have come to realize that it was also more than that. It's also about community, and hope, and inspiration. PARS member Jackie Ellenz described it well: "Meetings are our churches," she said.

PARS members are devoted and dizzy with the possibilities of change. They come back again and again because the meetings are a promise, a way to keep hope alive, a way to help teachers find each other. Through their connections and experiences in PARS, members know they can speak up and not be alone. They have learned how to organize and how to stay strong. They respect and admire one another. Over and over again, members have told me that although it's the political issues that create the need to join, it's the people in the organization that keep them coming back.

The Conclusion of My Tired Story

When I think about it, that is why I am going to those meetings. I go because the meetings give me a sense of connection and community. I can listen to the critical reflection of my peers and know that I am in good company. They make me feel good about teaching when usually there is no one else but my students to cheer me on. My colleagues are no longer people with whom I sit in a lunchroom and groan about the students or the administration. These are people whose thoughts and actions keep me excited.

The meetings help create community—not just because they allow for focused collective conversation, but because they provide the human contact that is so vital to the profession yet might not otherwise happen. Now I am not only going to the meetings, I speak on panels and lead subcommittees.

Today, when my 8-year-old daughter is playing and I could be reading student papers, I am more likely to be baking banana bread for this afternoon's TGIF. I think about what Linda Christensen told me, about her daughters who are now in their 20s.

"My kids have grown up as activists," she said. "I see it in them now. I have given them a model for how to respond when things are unfair."

What greater gift can we give to our students and our children than the inspiration that comes from seeing us struggling for social justice?

Action Education

Teacher Organizers Take Quality into Their Own Hands

*by Stephanie Schneider and
Melissa Bollow Tempel*

Ll across the country, educators, parents, students, and community members are uniting to create social change—and improve teacher quality. The proliferation of these groups demonstrates the power of teachers working together to improve lives for students and teachers, both inside and outside the classroom.

Though not a comprehensive survey, this essay describes some of the many ways these groups are making things happen, through workshops, curriculum fairs, teach-ins, discussion groups, and protests.

NYCORE protest / Bree Picower

The New York Collective of Radical Educators (NYCoRE)

The New York Collective of Radical Educators (NYCoRE) is an organization of public school teachers in New York City whose mission states, "The struggle for justice does not end when the school bell rings." NYCoRE follows this mission by working both inside the classroom through developing curriculum, and outside of the classroom by mobilizing teachers to action and to work with community and parent organizations.

NYCoRE organizes itself around nine points of unity that lay out its commitment to addressing and challenging multiple forms of oppression. NYCoRE also holds monthly meetings that include some kind of political education event as well as the meeting of working groups to focus on specific issues. NYCORE organizes an annual conference, publishes a social justice plan book along with the Education for Liberation Network, facilitates book clubs, and sponsors an educators of color group.

A way to get involved is to participate in one of NYCoRE's "inquiry-to-action groups" (iTAGs) that meet on a regular basis throughout the school year. These are less action oriented than working groups, but offer educators the opportunity to reflect on their own classroom practices. The iTAGs usually end with some cumulative result, such as a curriculum developed by the participants focusing on a particular social justice issue. The NYCoRE website is www.nycore.org.

Teachers 4 Social Justice (T4SJ)

Teachers 4 Social Justice (T4SJ) is a grassroots, nonprofit teacher support and development organization in the San Francisco Bay Area. According to its mission, T4SJ provides "opportunities for self-transformation, leadership, and community building to educators in order to effect meaningful change in the classroom, school, community, and society." Every fall, T4SJ hosts a free one-day conference bringing together social justice educators from around the country. The group also puts on an awards ceremony to honor local teachers titled "Thank a Teacher for Social Justice."

In addition, T4SJ offers a number of ways to get involved, including study groups, salons and bookclubs. The study groups meet for several sessions and are facilitated by teachers. The curriculum is built around the investigation of specific topics through research and personal experience. Some previous topics of study have included critical pedagogy, support for beginning teachers, a Haiti study circle and an examination of race in schools and teaching practice. T4SJ's salons are one-night discussion groups, based on a scholarly or timely article. T4SJ has regular general meetings and is governed by an advisory board of educators. The T4SJ website is www. t4sj.org.

Teachers for Social Justice (TSJ)

In Chicago, Teachers for Social Justice (TSJ) organizes to bring about change through hosting a curriculum fair, developing curriculum, and working on organizing campaigns in coalition with other community groups. Made up of teachers, administrators, preservice teachers, and other educators working in Chicago-area schools, TSJ organizes and acts on the principle that schools should empower students to be socially conscious citizens guided by ideas of equity and social justice.

TSJ has tackled issues like school militarization, privatization of schools, and the gentrification of Chicago's poor communities. TSJ's Social Justice Curriculum Fair takes place annually in the fall, growing each year in size and scope. Teachers lead workshops and present curriculum they have developed and used in their classrooms. Students often attend the fair, so they can present their work and discuss education with their teachers. TSJ is online at www.teachersforjustice.org.

TAG Boston

Teacher Activist Group (TAG) Boston is an educator activist group in the greater Boston area that believes "education is essential to human liberation." TAG Boston organizes an annual social justice education conference as well as works on a variety of issues in coalition with youth and other community members. In addition, TAG Boston organizes numerous political education events such as film screenings and invited speakers. It organizes social events, gatherings for educators of color, and inquiry-to-action study groups. More on TAG Boston can be found on its website: www.tagboston.org.

MAPS Atlanta

Metro Atlantans for Public Schools (MAPS) is a network of educators, parents and community allies that believe public education should be "democratic, well-funded, and community-supported." MAPS takes a strong stance against privatization and believes schools should be community controlled and accessible and welcoming to all students. MAPS organizes book studies, film screenings, and social events, and runs inquiry-to-action groups as well. More information on MAPS can be found here: https://sites.google.com/site/metroatlantansforpublicschools/.

The People's Education Movement

The People's Education Movement (PEM) is a teacher activist group in Los Angeles. This collective of educators believes in the creation of liberatory spaces both inside and outside of the classroom and maintains that, "In an effort to rebuild our communities, we engage in collective inquiry for knowledge of self. In doing so, we will reclaim indigenous wisdom to restore our humanity and envision another world."

PEM strives toward this vision through a variety of activities, including a curriculum fair and hosting inquiry-to-action groups and screenings, as well as various social and wellness events. PEM's website is www. peoplesed.org.

Educators' Network for Social Justice (ENSJ)

The Educators' Network for Social Justice (ENSJ) is a network of educators from Milwaukee-area schools that includes preservice teachers, classroom teachers, and postsecondary educators. Committed to promoting pro-justice curricula and policies so that all students in the Milwaukee area are better served, ENSJ holds general meetings that focus on a timely topic in education. In addition, ENSJ organizes political education events such as film screenings and various speakers. ENSJ also holds an annual Anti-Racist Anti-Bias Conference. ENSJ's website is ensj.weebly.com.

Teacher Action Group (TAG)

In Philadelphia, Teacher Action Group (TAG) is an all-volunteer organization that "partners teachers with parents, students, and community groups to foster school transformation, environments where students and teachers can thrive, and ensure community ownership and influence in Philadelphia public schools." TAGPhilly hosts an annual curriculum fair and conducts inquiry-to-action study groups that cover a wide variety of topics related to education and social justice. TAGPhilly has a number of ongoing projects, ranging from planning political education events, mobilizing teachers to action, and promoting the voice of teachers in the media, helping to change the narrative around teachers and school reform. TAGPhilly is online at www.tagphilly.org.

Portland Area Rethinking Schools (PARS)

Portland Area Rethinking Schools (PARS) began as a small study group in 1985. Today it is a regional network of teachers, teacher educators, student teachers, and others concerned about creating just schools and society. Throughout its history, PARS has worked around a diverse array of issues, including tracking, standardized testing, No Child Left Behind (NCLB), budget cuts, school food, and the wars in Iraq and Afghanistan. PARS has sponsored teacher workgroups that included topics such as global justice curriculum development, new teacher support, critical elementary teaching, and research on the effects of NCLB.

PARS sponsors "TGIFs with a Point"—gatherings that bring together educators of conscience to share resources, discuss burning issues, hear local and national speakers, and engage in exemplary curricula—as well as occasional teach-ins on current issues. Along with Puget Sound Rethinking Schools, Social Equality Educators, Oregon Save Our Schools, and the Oregon Writing Project at Lewis & Clark College, PARS hosts the annual Northwest Conference on Teaching for Social Justice: www.nwtsj.org. The PARS website is www.portlandrethinkingschools.org.

Puget Sound Rethinking Schools (PSRS)

Puget Sound Rethinking Schools (PSRS) is a group of educators and parents/guardians in the Seattle area. The group discusses the impact of standardized testing, the importance of multicultural and anti-racist education, union issues, global and international education, and local education issues.

Teacher involvement plays a key role in the group's activities. Teachers keep up with events, share resources, and dialogue through email, postings, and a Yahoo group. Small groups of members also hold monthly meetings and attend special events together. The group also hosts educational forums, such as the forum on the impact of the Washington Assessment of Student Learning (WASL), a NCLB response group, and more. PSRS can be reached at shmcfar@earthlink.net.

Association of Raza Educators (ARE)

Based in California, the Association of Raza Educators (ARE) arose as a response to the continued stereotyping and violation of the civic and human rights of the Raza community. ARE believes that "education is essential to the preservation of civil and human rights. It provides the foundation for all political and economic progress and it must be a basic right of all people." Two representatives from each of the chapters in cities throughout California make up the Statewide Leadership Concilio. Together these chapters publish a quarterly newsletter, *Regeneración*, and host an annual conference. ARE chapters meet monthly to uphold the rights and liberties of the Raza community by uniting teachers, students, families, and community members to fight for rights including higher education opportunities and against school closings, and teacher layoffs. ARE's website is www.razaeducators.org.

TAG (Teacher Activist Groups)

Many of these groups are part of a larger national network known as TAG (Teacher Activist Groups). These groups, along with Rethinking Schools and the Education for Liberation Network, participate in monthly conference calls and share resources, ideas, and support. TAG members collaborate to strengthen each individual organization's efforts and coordinate work in various cities. TAG's current projects include web-based solidarity campaigns such as No History Is Illegal, which supported the fight to save ethnic studies in Tucson, Arizona. TAG has also authored a national education platform, which serves as an organizing tool to unite teacher groups around a positive vision for schools. For more information, visit www.teacheractivistgroups.org.

CORE, the Caucus of Rank and File Educators

The Caucus of Rank and File Educators (CORE) strives to make the Chicago Teachers Union a member-driven union and to ensure a publicly funded public education system. CORE members have organized around many issues—including school closings and reconstitutions, high-stakes testing, and discriminatory hiring practices—and ran a successful slate of candidates who were elected in 2010 and again in 2013. The CORE website is www.coreteachers.com.

MORE, the Movement of Rank and File Educators

In New York City, the Movement of Rank and File Educators (MORE) is a progressive caucus in the United Federation of Teachers (UFT) that organizes to create a more democratic union by educating and activating the rank-and-file membership. MORE fights not only for a strong contract but also for quality curricula that includes a firm stance against high-stakes testing. In addition, MORE includes in its mission an opposition to the corporate takeover of public schools and insists on popular control of the school system. MORE's website is www.morecaucusnyc.org.

Social Equality Educators (SEE)

Social Equality Educators is a progressive caucus of the Seattle Education Association that believes in a member-driven union that organizes for full, equitable funding, a fair contract and culturally relevant teaching as it pushes back against corporate school reform. SEE organizes protests and direct actions, teach-ins, and forums and works in coalition with parent and community groups. SEE was an unconditional and key supporter of the MAP test boycott by the Garfield High teachers. More information can be found online at www.socialequalityeducators.org.

The Education for Liberation Network

The Education for Liberation Network is a national network of educators, youth, parents, and community activists who "believe a good education should teach people—particularly low-income youth and youth of color—how to understand and challenge injustices their communities face." The Education for Liberation Network hosts the "Free Minds, Free People" national gathering every two years. They also offer an online "laboratory" that facilitates the sharing of curriculum. It works with NYCoRE in publishing *Planning to Change the World*, a social justice plan book. More information on the network can be found at www.edliberation.org.

Media Connections

The media organizations mentioned below are part of an ever-expanding movement that offers vital resources and support for social justice education work around the country.

Teaching for Change

Teaching for Change is an essential distributor of curriculum resources for teachers, parents, and education activists. It sees its mission as providing tools to transform schools into socially equitable centers of learning. The online catalog, www.teachingforchange.org, is easily accessible. Its book *Putting the Movement Back into Civil Rights Teaching* has been adopted as the core curriculum for the Smithsonian Institution Traveling Exhibition Service for *381 Days: The Montgomery Bus Boycott Story*.

Teaching Tolerance

Teaching Tolerance provides free educational materials that promote respect for differences and appreciation of diversity in the classroom and beyond. Teaching Tolerance publishes a free quarterly magazine and offers curriculum kits that have been widely acclaimed. The organization also provides web resources, materials for student-led activism, classroom activities, examples of grants for anti-bias educational projects, and a monthly e-newsletter. Teaching Tolerance can be found online at www.tolerance.org.

The Zinn Education Project

The Zinn Education Project—coordinated by Rethinking Schools and Teaching for Change—promotes and supports the use of Howard Zinn's book *A People's History of the United States* and other materials for teaching a people's history in middle and high school classrooms across the country. Its goal is to introduce students to a more accurate, complex, and engaging understanding of U.S. history than is found in traditional textbooks and curricula. The website offers free downloadable lessons and articles organized by theme, time period, and reading level. The project's website is www.zinnedproject.org.

The New England Literacy Resource Center

Based in Boston, the New England Literacy Resource Center publishes *The Change Agent* to support educators bringing social justice issues into the classroom, with a focus on adult education. This publication uses media to mobilize teachers to advocate for educational issues. The center's website is www.nelrc.org.

Rethinking Schools

And of course, Rethinking Schools publishes a national quarterly magazine, books, and classroom resources. At www.rethinkingschools.org, teachers can access lessons and articles from the magazine's back issues. Rethinking Schools links activist educators around the country to current events while providing curricula, resources, and a classroom perspective on national policy debates. Rethinking Schools' award-winning books are the best resources for social justice teaching. Some of the most popular titles include *Rethinking Columbus*; *Rethinking Mathematics: Teaching Social Justice by the Numbers*; *Reading, Writing, and Rising Up*; *Rethinking Elementary Education*; *Rethinking Globalization: Teaching for Justice in an Unjust World*, and *Rethinking Multicultural Education*. We encourage readers of *The New Teacher Book* to subscribe to *Rethinking Schools* magazine and to rely on its important teaching resources.

Chapter 6

Resources

Other Resources from Rethinking Schools

Much of the advice in *The New Teacher Book* centers on the importance of finding and building community as we attempt to become the kind of teachers we want to be. Through the quarterly *Rethinking Schools* magazine and our books, you can join together with other educators around the country who are linking values of social and environmental justice with their work in schools.

Founded by classroom teachers and community activists in 1986, Rethinking Schools provides a forum for teachers to share exemplary teaching practices, compare notes on the obstacles to good teaching—and how they are working to overcome those obstacles. Rethinking Schools publications also analyze trends in education and features inspiring stories about educational activism. For more information on these publications—including tables of contents, sample articles, and information about ordering online—visit our website at www.rethinkingschools.org. And while you're there, check out everything the website has to offer: articles from past issues of the magazine, excerpts from our books, and special collections on important education topics.

Rethinking Schools—the Magazine

This independent quarterly is written by teachers, parents, and education activists—people who understand the day-to-day realities of today's schools. Every issue is filled with innovative teaching ideas, analyses of important policy issues, and listings of valuable resources.

Rethinking Schools—Special Editions

Some past issues of *Rethinking Schools* magazine have focused on special topics. The Summer 2009 issue, *Teaching for Environmental Justice*, is a collection of articles that connects the classroom to environmental crises, especially global warming. The Winter 2011-12 issue, *Stop the School-to-Prison Pipeline*, focuses on the relationship between increasing incarceration rates, especially among black youth, and campaigns to improve public schools. Includes thought-provoking analysis and teaching ideas for the classroom. For information on these and other special issues, see <u>www.rethinkingschools.org</u>.

Reading, Writing, and Rising Up: Teaching About Social Justice and the Power of the Written Word
by Linda Christensen

"My students walk out the school door into a social emergency," Linda Christensen writes. "I believe that writing is a basic skill that will help them both understand that emergency and work to change it." This practical, inspirational book offers essays, lesson plans, and a remarkable collection of student writing, all rooted in an unwavering focus on language arts teaching for justice.

Teaching for Joy and Justice: Re-Imagining the Language Arts Classroom
by Linda Christensen

In *Teaching for Joy and Justice*, Linda Christensen's sequel to *Reading, Writing, and Rising Up*, she demonstrates how she draws on students' lives and the world to teach poetry, essays, narratives, and critical literacy skills. Part autobiography, part curriculum guide, part critique of today's numbing standardized mandates, this book sings with hope—born of her more than 30 years as a classroom teacher, language arts specialist, and teacher educator.

Rethinking Our Classrooms, Volume 1: Teaching for Equity and Justice

Since the first edition was published in 1994, *Rethinking Our Classrooms* has sold more than 200,000 copies. A revised and expanded edition includes new essays on science and environmental education, immigration and language, military recruitment, teaching about the world through mathematics, early childhood education, and gay and lesbian issues. Creative teaching ideas, compelling classroom narratives, and hands-on examples show how teachers can promote values of community, justice, and equality while building academic skills. Nowhere is the connection between critical teaching and effective classroom practice clearer or more accessible.

Rethinking Our Classrooms, Volume 2: Teaching for Equity and Justice

This companion volume to *Rethinking Our Classrooms, Volume 1,* presents a rich collection of from-the-classroom articles, curriculum ideas, lesson plans, poetry, and resources—all grounded in the realities of school life.

Rethinking Early Childhood Education

edited by Ann Pelo

Early childhood is when we develop our core dispositions—the habits of thinking that shape how we live. This book shows how educators can nurture empathy, an ecological consciousness, curiosity, collaboration, and activism in young children. This anthology is alive with the conviction that teaching young children involves values and vision.

Rethinking Columbus: The Next 500 Years

edited by Bill Bigelow and Bob Peterson

Why rethink Christopher Columbus? Because the Columbus myth is a foundation of children's beliefs about society. Columbus is often a child's first lesson about encounters between different cultures and races. The murky legend of a brave adventurer tells children whose version of history to accept, and whose to ignore. It says nothing about the brutality of the European invasion of North America. *Rethinking Columbus* has more than 80 essays, poems, interviews, historical vignettes, and lesson plans packed with useful teaching ideas for kindergarten through college.

Rethinking Mathematics: Teaching Social Justice by the Numbers
edited by Eric Gutstein and Bob Peterson
In this expanded second edition, more than 50 articles show how to weave social justice issues throughout the mathematics curriculum, as well as how to integrate mathematics into other curricular areas. *Rethinking Mathematics* offers teaching ideas, lesson plans, and reflections by practitioners and mathematicians. This is real-world math—math that helps students analyze problems as they gain essential academic skills.

Rethinking Globalization: Teaching for Justice in an Unjust World
edited by Bill Bigelow and Bob Peterson
This comprehensive 400-page book helps teachers raise critical issues with students in 4th through 12th grades about the increasing globalization of the world's economies and infrastructures, and the many different impacts this trend has on our planet and those who live here. *Rethinking Globalization* offers an extensive collection of readings and source material on critical global issues, plus teaching ideas, lesson plans, and resources for classroom teachers.

Rethinking Multicultural Education: Teaching for Racial and Cultural Justice
edited by Wayne Au
Rethinking Multicultural Education collects the best articles dealing with race and culture in the classroom that have appeared in *Rethinking Schools* magazine over the years. Moving beyond a simplistic focus on heroes and holidays, and foods and festivals, it demonstrates a powerful vision of anti-racist, social justice education.

Open Minds to Equality: A Sourcebook of Learning Activities to Affirm Diversity and Promote Equity
by Nancy Schniedewind and Ellen Davidson
An educator's sourcebook of activities to help students understand and change inequalities based on race, gender, class, age, language, sexual orientation, physical/mental ability, and religion. The activities also promote respect for diversity and interpersonal equality among students, fostering a classroom that is participatory, cooperative, and democratic.

A People's History for the Classroom
by Bill Bigelow
This collection of lively teaching articles and lesson plans emphasizes the role of working people, women, people of color, and organized social movements in shaping history. The teaching activities included raise important questions about patterns of wealth and power throughout U.S. history. Through improvisations, role plays, imaginative writing, and critical reading activities, students learn a more accurate and engaging history.

The Line Between Us: Teaching About the Border and Mexican Immigration
by Bill Bigelow
The Line Between Us explores the history of U.S.-Mexican relations and the roots of Mexican immigration, all in the context of the global economy. And it shows how teachers can help students understand the immigrant experience and the drama of border life. Using role plays, stories, poetry, improvisations, simulations, and video, veteran teacher Bill Bigelow demonstrates how to combine lively teaching with critical analysis.

Rethinking Popular Culture and Media
edited by Elizabeth Marshall and Özlem Sensoy
Rethinking Popular Culture and Media begins with the idea that the "popular" in classrooms and in the everyday lives of teachers and students is fundamentally political. This anthology includes outstanding articles by elementary and

secondary public school teachers, scholars, and activists who examine how and what popular toys, books, films, music, and other media "teach." These thoughtful essays offer strong critiques and practical teaching strategies for educators at every level.

Rethinking Elementary Education
edited by Linda Christensen, Mark Hansen, Bob Peterson, Elizabeth Schlessman, and Dyan Watson
Collects the finest writing about elementary school life and learning from 25 years of *Rethinking Schools* magazine. The articles in this volume offer practical insights about how to integrate the teaching of content with a social justice lens, seek wisdom from students and their families, and navigate stifling tests and mandates. Teachers will find both inspiration and hope in these pages.

Pencils Down: Rethinking High-Stakes Testing and Accountability in Public Schools
edited by Wayne Au and Melissa Bollow Tempel
This powerful collection takes high-stakes standardized tests to task. Through articles that provide thoughtful and emotional critiques from the frontlines of education, *Pencils Down* deconstructs the damage that standardized tests wreak on our education system and the human beings that populate it. Better yet, it offers visionary forms of assessment that are not only more authentic, but also more democratic, fair, and accurate.

Unlearning 'Indian' Stereotypes DVD
Narrated by Native American children, the DVD *Unlearning "Indian" Stereotypes* teaches about racial stereotypes and provides an introduction to Native American history through the eyes of children. The DVD includes teaching ideas, lessons, and resources.

Contributors

Bill Bigelow (bill@rethinkingschools.org) is the curriculum editor of *Rethinking Schools* and author or co-editor of numerous Rethinking Schools books, including *Rethinking Columbus* and *A People's History for the Classroom*. He is a former high school social studies teacher.

Terry Burant (tburant@uwyo.edu) taught high school biology, environmental science, chemistry, and English for nine years. She currently teaches in the Department of Educational Studies at the University of Wyoming in Laramie, Wyo.

S. J. Childs (sjchilds@spiritone.com), formerly a high school teacher, is now a media specialist/teacher-librarian at Jackson Middle School in Portland, Ore. She is still involved in the Portland Area Rethinking Schools group.

Linda Christensen (lchrist@aol.com) is currently director of the Oregon Writing Project at Lewis & Clark College in Portland, Ore. She taught high school language arts for 30 years. She is a *Rethinking Schools* editor and is the author of *Reading, Writing, and Rising Up: Teaching About Social Justice and the Power of the Written Word* and *Teaching for Joy and Justice: Re-imagining the Language Arts Classroom* (Rethinking Schools, 2009).

Mary Cowhey (mcowhey@hotmail.com) has been teaching 1st and/or 2nd grade at Jackson Street School in Northampton, Mass., since 1997. She is the author of *Black Ants and Buddhists: Thinking Critically and Teaching Differently in the Primary Grades* (Stenhouse Publishers, 2006).

Jessica Singer Early (jessica.early@asu.edu) taught English at Cleveland High School in Portland, Ore., and is now an assistant professor of English education and a director of the Central Arizona Writing Project at Arizona State University in Tempe.

Lola Glover (cqetoledo@buckeye-express.com) is director of the Coalition for Quality Education, a grassroots community organization in Toledo, Ohio, and is a past co-chair of the National Coalition of Education Activists.

T. Elijah Hawkes (tehawkes@yahoo.com) is principal of the James Baldwin School in New York City and has contributed articles to *Rethinking Schools* magazine.

Sudie Hofmann (shofmann@stcloudstate.edu) teaches at St. Cloud State University in Minnesota and has contributed articles to *Rethinking Schools* magazine.

Annie Johnston (anniej@igc.org) coordinates Community Partnerships Academy, a small school at Berkeley High School. She teaches history at Berkeley High and is a doctoral student at the University of California, Berkeley in the Leadership for Equity in Education Program.

Stan Karp (stan.karp@gmail.com) taught English and journalism to high school students in Paterson, N.J., for 30 years. He is currently director of the Secondary Reform Project for New Jersey's Education Law Center and is an editor of *Rethinking Schools* magazine.

Herbert Kohl (hkhkohl@aol.com) is an educator and writer who lives in Point Arena, Calif. He is author of more than 35 books on education, including *The Herb Kohl Reader: Awakening the Heart of Teaching* (New Press, 2009).

Enid Lee (enidlee@aol.com) is an internationally known educator, author, and consultant whose work focuses on anti-racism and promoting multiculturalism.

Tom McKenna (mckenna0307@comcast.net) teaches at Portland YouthBuilders in Portland, Ore., and has contributed to *Rethinking Schools* magazine.

Kelly McMahon (kellymcmhn2@aol.com) teaches 5-year-old kindergarten for Milwaukee Public Schools. She served as co-chair of the Milwaukee Teachers' Education Association Early Childhood Committee.

Gregory Michie (gmichie38@gmail.com) is a Chicago-based teacher and teacher educator. He is the author of *See You When We Get There: Teaching for Change in Urban Schools* (Teachers College Press, 2004).

Larry Miller (millerlf1@gmail.com) is an elected member of the Board of Education in Milwaukee and a *Rethinking Schools* editor.

Susan Naimark (sbnaimark@comcast.net) was active in School Parent Councils in her children's schools for nearly two decades. She was a founding member of the Boston Parents Organizing Network and served two four-year terms on the Boston School Committee, the school board for the city of Boston.

Bob Peterson (repmilw@aol.com) teaches 5th grade at La Escuela Fratney in Milwaukee and is a founding editor of *Rethinking Schools*. He edited, with Bill Bigelow, the Rethinking Schools books *Rethinking Globalization: Teaching for Justice in an Unjust World* and *Rethinking Columbus: The Next 500 Years*.

Melanie Quinn (melanie.quinn@evergreenps.org) is an in structional coach at Crestline Elementary in Evergreen School District, Vancouver, Wash.

Don Rose (drose@pps.k12.or.us) is a middle school teacher in Portland Public Schools and is an Oregon Writing Project coach for the district.

Kelley Dawson Salas (kdsalas@sbcglobal.net) is a communications and publications specialist at the Milwaukee Teachers' Education Association, and a former bilingual elementary school teacher in the Milwaukee Public Schools.

Stephanie Schneider (stephanie.schneider@gmail.com) teaches 3- to 6-year-olds at a public Montessori school in Milwaukee and is an active member of the Educators' Network for Social Justice.

Melissa Bollow Tempel (meljoytempel@gmail.com) teaches bilingual 1st grade at La Escuela Fratney in Milwaukee. She is the mother of two girls and an active member of the Educators' Network for Social Justice.

Rita Tenorio (tenorirm@milwaukee.k12.wi.us) is principal of La Escuela Fratney in Milwaukee and is a founding editor of *Rethinking Schools* magazine.

Floralba Vivas (fvivasd@aol.com) was born in Venezuela and teaches 5th grade at La Escuela Fratney in Milwaukee. She has done several translations for Rethinking Schools.

Tracy Wagner (tjwagner@uwalumni.com) teaches 9th-grade English at Charlestown High School, a public school in Boston.

Stephanie Walters (stephwalters69@wi.rr.com) is an organizer for the Wisconsin Education Association Council, an affiliate of the National Education Association. She taught in Milwaukee Public Schools for nine years and is an editor of *Rethinking Schools*.

Dale Weiss (miskamarie@gmail.com) teaches 3rd grade at La Escuela Fratney in Milwaukee.

Kathy Williams (kat-ran@sbcglobal.net) is former director of the Division of Teaching and Learning for the Milwaukee Public Schools (MPS). She was an elementary-level classroom teacher for more than 20 years and served as co-chair of the steering committee of the MPS Multicultural Curriculum Council. She is an editorial associate of *Rethinking Schools* magazine.

Index

Note: Page numbers in italics indicate illustrations.

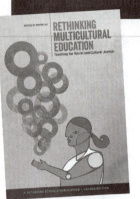
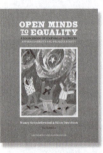
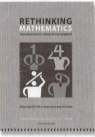
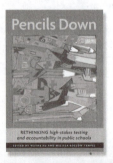

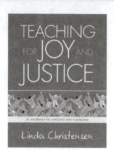

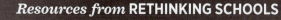
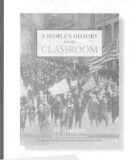

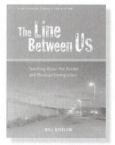